ᴄ∕ꝺ María Amparo Ruiz de Burton ᴄ∕ꝺ

María Amparo Ruiz de Burton

Critical and Pedagogical Perspectives

❧ ⚜ ❧

EDITED BY

Amelia María de la Luz Montes
& Anne Elizabeth Goldman

University of Nebraska Press
Lincoln and London

Publication of this book was assisted
by a grant from the Jane Robertson
Layman Fund.

"Beasts in the Jungle: Regional 'Aliens'
and Boston Natives" by Anne E.
Goldman previously appeared in
Continental Divides: Revisioning American Literature (New York: Palgrave/
St. Martin's Press, 2000). Copyright
© Anne Goldman. Reprinted with
permission of Palgrave Macmillan.

Library of Congress Cataloging-
in-Publication Data
María Amparo Ruiz de Burton : critical
and pedagogical perspectives / edited
by Amelia María de la Luz Montes and
Anne Elizabeth Goldman.
p. cm.—(Postwestern horizons)
Includes bibliographical references
and index.
ISBN 0-8032-3234-9 (cl. : alk paper)
1. Ruiz de Burton, María Amparo, 1832–
1895—Criticism and interpretation.
2. Ruiz de Burton, María Amparo, 1832–
1895—Study and teaching.   3. Women
and literature—California—History—19th
century.   4. Hispanic Americans—California—History.   5. Hispanic Americans
in literature.   6. California—In literature.
I. Montes, Amelia María de la Luz, 1958–.
II. Goldman, Anne E., 1960–.   III. Series.
PS2736.R53Z74 2004   813'.4—dc22
2003061289

Contents

Acknowledgments

Producing an anthology is a *testimonio* created with the *ayuda* of a thousand spirits. As editors on this journey, we witness a series of collaborations — some new, others of long standing. Therefore, we would like to thank our contributors and each other for the countless long-distance phone calls, the many meetings at conferences over the last several years, the revisions of paragraphs, arguments, and essay drafts, which, taken together, have rewarded and helped to sustain our intellectual life, providing a counterpoint to the more solitary work we do as scholars.

The editors and writers in this book have been supported by the time, advice, and expertise of colleagues, friends, and family who have from the outset encouraged our efforts. We would like to thank the scholars who have mentored this book: Tey Diana Rebolledo, who first led us to the Huntington collection of Ruiz de Burton letters; María Herrera-Sobek, model editor, who shared with us advice drawn from her longtime experience; Lisbeth Haas, whose insights as a historian have provided a valued complement to our literary perspectives, and Genaro Padilla, first literary scholar to work on the Californio narratives, who brought to our attention several of the writers featured in this anthology and who has generously provided critical commentary on the book as a whole. Kris Gandara's meticulous compiling of the book's bibliography and her assistance with research, as well as Sandy Byrd's photocopying, helped us to meet more than one deadline. We also thank June Levine for her valuable editorial comments on the introduction.

Our thanks go as well to those institutions and curators who have enabled us to reprint archival materials: the Bancroft Library at the University of California at Berkeley, the Huntington Library in Los Angeles, and the Santa Barbara Mission Archive Library in Santa Barbara. We are grateful for the valuable assistance we received from the Huntington Library curators, Bill Frank and Peter Blodgett, and from Dr. Virgilio Biasiol, director of the Santa Barbara Mission Archive Library. We also recognize the University of Nebraska–Lincoln Research Council, whose generous grant supported our work.

We would like to thank our parents for always expressing their support for our work: Amelia's parents, Joseph and Emma Montes, and Anne's parents, Barbara and Michael Goldman. Their encouragement, a gift of faith, expects no compensation. Finally, to those who have listened patiently to us at home, who have shared our enthusiasm over our work despite the fact that it has often taken us away from them, we wish to dedicate this book: Amelia's partner, Emily Levine, and Anne's daughter, Zoë Pollak.

María Amparo Ruiz de Burton

Introduction

AMELIA MARÍA DE LA LUZ MONTES
and ANNE ELIZABETH GOLDMAN

Mine shall be the mission to redress. Onward! ♣ (*Don Quixote de la Mancha: A Comedy in Five Acts*, ACT I, SC. I)

Since the 1992 republication of *The Squatter and the Don* (1885), María Amparo Ruiz de Burton has become a key figure in the recovery of nineteenth-century Mexican American literature specifically and the reconfiguration of nineteenth-century American literary culture more generally. No one who reads her two novels can fail to raise an eyebrow at the sharpness of her political judgments, the frankness with which she acknowledges feminine desire, and the deftness of her emancipation from sentimentalism. She assesses corporate capitalism in *Who Would Have Thought It?* (1872) ("in this free country we are the subjects of railroad kings and other princes of monopolies; we obey their wishes, and pay our money") with no less asperity than any contemporary editorial that excoriates the latest scandal in business. And while she satirizes the lovesick "silliness" of this novel's middle-aged Boston bourgeois, her candid avowal of feminine erotic longing remains distinctive. How many recent films or television comedies devote any screen time to the romantic trials of women over forty? As for narrative convention: She makes use of sentiment, to be sure, but undermines its daydreams with an efficiency that foils audience expectations about "lady" writers. "Really, our romance is spoiled," Mercedes's sister teases her in *The Squatter and the Don*. "It would have been so fine — like a dime novel."

Given this strikingly current quality, it is not surprising that Ruiz de Burton's novels have increasingly been invoked across a variety of fields, including American literature, Chicana and Chicano literature, cultural studies, ethnic studies, American studies, history, gender studies, and women's studies. Her fictions transgress with impunity our critical assumptions about race and region, making her a particularly compelling writer in the context of cultural studies. A Californiana who championed the rights of Mexicanos following the conclusion of the U.S.–Mexican War, Ruiz de Burton lived for a decade on the East Coast, where in 1872 she published *Who Would Have Thought It?* a critique of Boston mores and American politics during the Civil War. She called attention to the illegal appropriation of Mexican land as forthrightly in fictions such as *The Squatter and the Don*, written in English, as well as in the scores of letters she exchanged in Spanish with longtime friend and prominent Californio Mariano Guadalupe Vallejo. As a descendent of one of the oldest and most respected families in Mexican California, she identified with an aristocratic political tradition. Nonetheless, she campaigned successfully at the White House to obtain an audience with President Lincoln to request a raise in her husband's pension (Aranda, *When We Arrive* 93). An intimate of Lincoln's wife, Mary, she also maintained a friendship with Verena Davis, the wife of Confederate president Jefferson Davis (Aranda, "Contradictory Impulses" 561–62).

Her novels likewise develop links across American sectional and ethnic divides, questioning in the process the boundary lines of conventional literary history. Her reappraisal of the Civil War in light of the long shadow cast by the war with Mexico, for instance, juxtaposes virtually contemporaneous conflicts that remain segregated in American studies. With their convoluted sentimental plotting and rapier-sharp satire, their lampooning of feminine vapors and masculinist political institutions, her fictions also establish points of intersection between genres typically framed as distinct: the novel of social protest and the novel of sentiment, muckraking journalism and feminist critique, plantation fiction and historical romance. Ruiz de Burton's rhetoric resists the cult of mourning's tendency to memorialize. Unlike contemporaries Lydia Maria Child and Helen Hunt Jackson, who tend toward the baroque in sentimental writing, her crisp commentary, at its best, recalls the astringent economic pragmatism of Jane Austen and the clear-eyed appraisal of class relations characteristic of Rebecca Harding Davis's prose.

Today most readers know Ruiz de Burton as a novelist, thanks to the republication of her two fictions, but in the nineteenth century she was equally well established as a playwright. Recent scholarly evidence locates her squarely within the theater. Ruiz de Burton lived with her husband and family at Mission San Diego de Alcala between 1853 and 1857; it was here, in 1855, that the Mission Theatre (built on church grounds) opened its doors. Irene Phillips believes that Ruiz de Burton wrote Mission Theatre's most successful plays, and Frederick Oden supports her assertions. Phillips's theory is not substantiated. However, Oden argues that her "speculation seems all the more likely in light of Mrs. Burton's later publications" (27).[1]

Ruiz de Burton resided for much of the late 1850s as well as the closing years of the 1870s in San Francisco. According to theater historians Felicia Londré and Daniel Watermeier, "Between 1849 and 1869, San Francisco would become California's theatrical capital" (133). That the city's theaters catered to Spanish-speaking Californios as frequently as to recently arrived English speakers is clear from a reading of theater playbills. *La Cabaña de Tom*, for instance, an adaptation of *Uncle Tom's Cabin* translated by Ramón Saavedra, opened on July 19, 1874, at the Maguire Opera House (Kanellos 4, 204). Just two years later, Ruiz de Burton's own dramatic reenvisioning of *Don Quixote* would be published a few blocks away at the Washington Street publishing house of John Carmany.

This volume of essays offers, for the first time, commentary on both the 1876 play and Ruiz de Burton's work for the stage. It is designed both to introduce readers to the literary pleasures of a writer who so easily bridges a century's divide, and to engage her work as a means of thinking through and across the critical schisms we conventionally impose upon nineteenth-century literary cultures in America. The scholars featured in this critical anthology are animated by a complex sense of the cross-connections that Ruiz de Burton's novels establish between nineteenth-century Mexican American literature and the contemporary Chicana and Chicano canons.

Julie Ruiz, for instance, links the rhetorical strategies that nineteenth-century Mexican American women writers like Ruiz de Burton exploit with revisionist figurations that twentieth-century Chicana authors develop in their own work. The nineteenth-century Mexican American women writers assert their authority as citizens in part, Ruiz argues, by abrogating native origins and asserting, instead, claims to Spanish descent. On the other hand, contemporary writers like Sandra Cisneros, Lucha Corpi, and Cherríe Moraga assert Mexican femininity by representing denigrated female archetypes such as La Malinche and La Llorona as subjects. Across a century, then, both groups of women writers claim (gendered) authority by figuring their locations as U.S. subjects in relation to indigenous America.

José Aranda encourages us to consider relationships between Mexican and Mexican American literatures over time by analyzing how wars figure as metanarrative. Far from distancing women from history, he argues, a consideration of both sets of texts from the Mexican American War (1846–48) through the Mexican Revolution (1910–18), to World War II (1941–45) suggests that "as disjunctures in time, space, and culture . . . military conflict . . . provided women with unique if compromised opportunities to enter the history of the nation" (Aranda, "María Amparo Ruiz de Burton" 311). Vincent Pérez asks how Californios and contemporary Chicanos narrate their respective pasts, using Ruiz de Burton's work as the point of departure from which to link colonialist and neocolonialist projects as fashioned in the literary imagination.

The essays featured here also encourage students to read Ruiz de Burton's work over and against a number of intersecting late-nineteenth-century political movements and literary traditions: from the California populism of Frank Norris and Josiah Royce to the Californiana testimonios of Eulalia Pérez and Angustias Ord, from Henry James's experiments with the novel of manners in *The Bostonians* to Mariano Guadalupe Vallejo's experiments with personal narrative in his five-volume 1874 autobiography, *Recuerdos históricos y personales tocante a la alta California*, from Helen Hunt Jackson's sentimentalized portrait of indigenous California in *Ramona* to native writer John Rollin Ridge's novel *The Life and Adventures of Joaquín Murieta*. These essays point to relationships between Ruiz de Burton's writing and the work of Anglo American and African American women writers recovered through, respectively, the American Women Writers series (Rutgers) and the Schomburg Library of Nineteenth-Century Black Women Writers series (Oxford). And they encourage students to connect her representations of indigenous America with Native American written and oral narratives of the period.

At once richly historicized and critically nuanced, these essays appraise a politically complex Mexican American writer alternately celebrated as marginalized and censured as a snob. The collection documents the distinctiveness of Ruiz de Burton's work, which, as Vincent Pérez argues of *The Squatter and the Don*, stands alone among nineteenth-century American fictions for its intervention in the politics of land entitlement in the Southwest. The scholars featured here also examine the racial inflections of Ruiz de Burton's fictions, contributing in the process to contemporary theorizing about whiteness. They read her critique of New England social institutions in light of expansionism in order to offer more nuanced accounts of the relation between domestic policy and empire. They consider her satirical rendering of the middle-class American home during the Gilded Age to formulate theories of class and culture that explain women's roles as consumers, and they locate her novels within a complex discursive context that includes testimonials and the memoir, scientific writing and Darwinian theory, promotional travel writing and regionalism, narratives about health, medicine, and neurasthenia, and histories of California and the West.

Working within and between genres, literary traditions, historical and critical rubrics, these essays honor the richness of María Amparo Ruiz de Burton's canon and articulate the contradictions of colonial identity in California. By asking us to put aside the standard critical zonings of literary territory, they encourage readers to work toward new definitions of literary and political relationships, not only for the nineteenth-century nation, but also for our own.

The volume is designed to speak both to scholars working within specific disciplines in American studies and to student readers — college and secondary school level — in courses ranging from the Chicana and Chicano literary canon to nineteenth-century U.S. history, American material culture, and the American novel. By situating an American writer within and across multiple contexts we hope to model for students an understanding of U.S. cultures in their broadest sense, as well as to encourage them to understand that any close study — whether it be of a literary figure, a political event, or a cultural movement — is enriched when undertaken with attention to the crosscurrents and dialogues animating it. At the same time, this book is offered in the spirit of furthering curricula that will more adequately represent the United States' Mexican past and present. However impassioned and persuasive, scholarly critique alone will not change the content of the curriculum beyond the postsecondary level.

Accordingly, this collection of critical writings on Ruiz de Burton is also the first of its kind to connect critical theories about narrative with pedagogical discussions for teachers. Selections from interviews with the contributors, all of whom have extensive experience teaching Ruiz de Burton, offer instructors a variety of approaches for use in the classroom. Along with this discussion, the scholar-instructors featured here have generously shared with readers their methods of teaching, course assignments, and questions for discussion. The essayists discuss the range of texts they have taught alongside *Who Would Have Thought It?* and *The Squatter and the Don* to enable students to locate these novels within nineteenth-century literary discourse. Beth Fisher, for example, offers one such approach to this kind of contextualization: "Reading [*The Squatter and the Don*] alongside contemporaneous Californio testimonios as well as Anglo American accounts of westward expansion — including diaries as well as earlier fictions such as Caroline Kirkland's *A New Home, Who'll Follow* (1839) — highlights the contradictory terms through which the family figures as a trope for the nation in the nineteenth century, a contradiction that Ruiz de Burton refers to explicitly in the story of the confrontation between the Darrells and the Alamares" (correspondence with editors, March 3, 2002).

The writers also discuss the ways in which teachers can enrich understandings of Ruiz de Burton's work by supplementing lectures and discussion with excerpts from appropriate historical, cultural, and political materials. Andrea Tinnemeyer, for instance, "finds both historical and literary contexts . . . helpful for framing [her] novels. . . . These works provide [students] with necessary historical information about California life after the Mexican War (Indian Removal, Land Acts, Treaty of Guadalupe Hidalgo, Gold Rush, etc.) and allow them to recognize Ruiz de Burton's politics (her revision of the historical romance, for example)." In addition, she "provide[s] a brief lecture on the Mexican American War, the Treaty of Guadalupe Hidalgo, legal statutes such as the Land Commission of 1851, and racial and feminist issues during the period the novels treat" (correspondence with editors, March 3, 2002).

Excerpts from *The Treaty of Guadalupe Hidalgo* and facsimiles of the writer's protracted legal struggles to maintain title to her land provide students and first-time readers with additional discursive and historical contexts within which to situate her fictions. To foster comparative work, a chronology identifies important dates in the author's life and work alongside historical events in California, in Mexico, and in the eastern United States. Finally, an annotated bibliography provides students and researchers with a broad, interdisciplinary range of sources, including archival documents and critical studies in history, gender studies, economic theory, the history of science, and literature. Our objective, then, is to create an anthology that becomes a working guide for students, teachers, scholars, and professors.

Note

1. See Phillips, *Women of Distinction*, 14; also quoted in Oden. See also Sánchez and Pita, *Conflicts of Interest*, where they concur with what Oden and Phillips believe: "The mission, with a repaired roof and a second story added, was used as barracks until about 1859, and it was there that [Ruiz de Burton] first staged her play *Don Quixote*, with soldiers playing the parts" (91).

❧ I ❧

Locating Ruiz de Burton in
the Nineteenth Century

Returning California to the People:
Vigilantism in *The Squatter and the Don*

JOSÉ F. ARANDA JR.

It seems now that unless the people of California take the law in their own hands, and seize the property of those men, and confiscate it, to re-imburse the money due the people, the arrogant corporation will never pay. They are so accustomed to appropriate to themselves what rightfully belongs to others, and have so long stood before the world in defiant attitude, that they have become utterly insensible to those sentiments of fairness animating law-abiding men of probity and sense of justice. ❧ María Amparo Ruiz de Burton, *The Squatter and the Don* (366)

As the epigraph above suggests, this essay understands María Amparo Ruiz de Burton's second novel, *The Squatter and the Don* (1885), as directly responding to the role that vigilantism played in post–Civil War politics and social debates in southern California. Crucial to this argument is Ruiz de Burton's siding with the vigilante unrest that grew out of an agrarian conflict known regionally as the Battle of Mussel Slough (1880). Most Chicano/a critics view the novel's critique of the status quo as indicative of Mexicans' widespread disenchantment with and resentment of Anglo American colonization of California after 1848. While the novel clearly champions the civil rights of Californios on the issue of illegal land dispossession, most Chicano/a critics have been reluctant to acknowledge the many paradoxical instances where Ruiz de Burton's political and literary strategies ally her with Anglo American constituencies much like William Darrell, the "squatter" of the novel. Her novel's reference to the Anglo farmers who struggled against the Southern Pacific Railroad in the San Joaquin Valley is a case in point.

By 1880, Mussel Slough had become a rallying cry for vigilantes who dared to challenge the unbridled political and economic power of the railroad monopolists. This well-publicized event was also responsible for consolidating growing interest in populist, anti-monopoly literature. In the wake of this incident, Ruiz de Burton wrote purposefully toward a new literary audience that had been born in a social and political environment that understood vigilantism as a fundamental right of popular sovereignty (Henderson, introduction). In short, she wrote a novel that detailed the unjust downfall of the Californio and crafted a social architecture that would rescue elite native Californios from economic and political ruin and cultural anonymity. For her, the Battle of Mussel Slough raised the possibility of organizing the masses toward collective ends that were populist and nostalgic at the same time. Given her social background, this combination of social forces underwrote the novel's plea to reclaim a lost golden age of California.

I

In 1998, I argued in *American Literature* against the subaltern thesis that had critically reintroduced María Amparo Ruiz de Burton to a late-twentieth-century audience. In particular, I dismissed the possibility of viewing her as either a classic subaltern figure or a more sophisticated "subaltern mediator" (573). Neither position could adequately deal with the contradictory nature of Ruiz de Burton's writings with regard to class, race, gender, and nationalist loyalties, nor could these two positions reasonably reconcile the disjuncture between elite Californios and Californios of lower class, mestizo, or native origins. While I was satisfied that my argument had made its case vis-à-vis *Who Would Have Thought It?* (1872), and in general terms with *The Squatter and the Don* (1885), the text of the latter had frustrated my efforts to find a reading that would not simply repeat my original argument. I wanted to find some angle that would push my contention that she and her writings reflect competing colonialisms at work in California after 1848. Yet the main form of competition in the novel was overtly economic: agrarian capitalism with feudal labor practices versus monopoly capitalism with mechanized labor practices. In this regard, I felt Rosaura Sánchez and Beatrice Pita, the novel's recoverers, had accounted for these economic tensions by employing Antonio Gramsci's "semiotic rectangle" and Fredric Jameson's "symbolic resolution to a concrete historic situation." The more I taught the novel, though, the less persuaded I became by what they identified in their 1992 introduction as the "concrete historic situation." Despite the best efforts of Sánchez and Pita, I concluded, the novel eluded the specificity of their analysis.

By contrast, José David Saldívar's idea of Ruiz de Burton as a mediator (*Border Matters* 170) has been, I must admit, tantalizing, but if she was not a subaltern mediator, then what kind of mediator was she, and why? And could seeing her as a mediator help to understand the multitude of anomalies in the text that make it a difficult novel to teach, much less historicize? Why, for instance, does the title favor squatter Darrell spatially over Don Mariano Alamar? Don Mariano's death is more or less reasonable given the text's realist attempt to document the decline of the Californio. By contrast, squatter Darrell survives, albeit wiser and sadder. Why does the narrator condition the reader to see squatter Darrell as more educated and reasonable than his lower-class white associates? For that matter, why is Mercedes Alamar so conclusively "white," with blonde hair and blue eyes, and so fluent in French and Newport etiquette, that she must act the role of New England coquette out East but simultaneously must be obsessively devoted to Clarence Darrell out West? Whatever happened to the model of Mexican American citizenry that one found in Lola Medina of *Who Would Have Thought It?* Related to the "whitening" of her Californio characters, how do we understand when non-Californios suffer tragic fates more typically associated with Californios? Is this another symbolic resolution? And most beguiling of all, how do we make sense of a romance narrative that finds no closure in the marriage plot but instead evolves into a didactic form that self-consciously recruits a mass collective response to the political and economic machinations of actual, historic monopolists? What kind of novel is this text, which ranges from individual tragedy to mass insurrection? And who are "the people" this novel was written to champion?

Since the novel's republication in 1992, there has been considerable effort to historicize the populist trends in the text. In essence, attempts have been made to understand who is hailed as the people by the novel. Sánchez and Pita framed the "people" here within a working-class Chicana/o studies framework that resonates with "la raza." Further, they established the current dominant reading of this text in their introduction as a "narrative space for the counter-history of the sub-altern, the conquered Californio population" (5). Locating Ruiz de Burton within the field of subaltern studies, Sánchez and Pita see *The Squatter and the Don* as a defiant set of discursive, resistant strategies that critique the colonialization — political, economic, social — of Alta California by Anglo America. They interpret the novel's final call to arms as the ultimate form of resistance available to contest late-nineteenth-century capitalism and imperialism. Though they acknowledge that the novel offers no immediate better life for the socially demoted and economically constrained Californio, Sánchez and Pita link up Ruiz de Burton's subaltern critique to a historic tradition of resistance within the Mexican American community: "Yet despite the pauperization and proletarianization of Californios and the subjugation of all Californians by powerful monopolies, there is an implicit challenge in the novel, an interpellation of today's reader, as citizens, or as descendants of Californios, to resist oppression, to slay the monster who has not ceased to be victorious" (51). Interestingly, Sánchez and Pita's gesture toward present-day ethnic politics invokes a populist

Mexican American tradition of contesting big business that includes Cesár Chavez, Dolores Huerta, and the United Farm Workers Union, but this gesture with Ruiz de Burton as a figurehead is terribly misplaced and misleading.

Although their rhetorical language of slaying the monster is borrowed from the novel's characterization of the railroad monopolies, Sánchez and Pita do not locate this metaphor of resistance within the widespread Californian populism that was contemporaneous with events depicted in the novel. Specifically, they do not view the final chapter of the novel within the various vigilante movements that were prominent from 1849 to 1900 in California, nor do they consider the deep significance of Ruiz de Burton's racial characterization of the true victims of the monopolies as "the white slaves of California" (372).[1] Although Sánchez and Pita are careful to establish *The Squatter and the Don* as a precursor to more prominent antimonopoly novels like Josiah Royce's *Feud of Oakfield Creek* (1887) and Frank Norris's *Octopus* (1901) and how the Battle of Mussel Slough figures prominently in these later novels, they underestimate the alliances the novel forges between elite Californios and civic-minded Anglo American settlers. Instead, Sánchez and Pita call attention to the fact that Ruiz de Burton voices "the bitter resentment of the subaltern" (8), while simultaneously reckoning with her aristocratic and elitist sensibilities. There is undoubtedly bitterness in *The Squatter and the Don*; the text is antimonopoly, after all, but Ruiz de Burton's antimonopolist stance in the novel should not be viewed as her attempt to shape a narrow socialist, antiracist politic. The novel does not support such a claim. Instead, what the novel does support is a political future where the civic ethos of an evolving, educated Californian citizenry takes as its founding mythos a nostalgic embrace of Californio ranch culture.[2]

What was Mussel Slough about then? In large measure, the seven deaths that constitute the Battle of Mussel Slough on 11 May 1880 came as the result of the local marshal's attempt to evict farmers from lands deemed by the courts to be property of the Southern

Pacific Railroad. William Conlogue writes, "The Mussel Slough tragedy became one of the most important and noticed events in California history, symbolizing as it did for many people then and now the epic struggle between the common people and large corporations that seemed to characterize the late-nineteenth-century state and nation" (41). Apart from its folkloric status, Conlogue is particularly interested in the propaganda literature that followed in the wake of Mussel Slough. He cites *The Struggle of the Mussel Slough Settlers for Their Homes! An Appeal to the People, History of the Land Troubles in Tulare and Fresno Counties: The Grasping Greed of the Railroad Monopoly*, a pamphlet published in 1880 by the local Settlers' Committee, as instructive of the political moment, but also equally important for rhetorically setting the stage for later writers like Royce, Norris, and now forgotten contemporaries like William Chambers Morrow, who wrote *Blood Money* (1882). If Conlogue's assertion about the circulation of this event in California is correct, it is highly probable given Ruiz de Burton's political contacts and voracious reading habits that she too knew this pamphlet well. The penultimate paragraph of the novel specifically mentions this event in connection to the demise of the Texas Pacific Railroad: "The line of this road was changed without authority. [Mr. Huntington talks in his letters about convincing people to make this change.] Thus the Mussel Slough farmers got taken in, into Huntington's lines — as was stated by the public press" (372). We do know that only two months after the deaths in Mussel Slough she wrote to a friend to say that she had started a new novel.[3] This novel would become *The Squatter and the Don.*

Present-day notions that nineteenth-century vigilantism was a form of Robin Hood justice would suggest that Ruiz de Burton held or believed in some kind of proto-socialism. The opposite is more the case for Ruiz de Burton, and it is worth noting here that vigilantism, even the kind of vigilantism that fueled the Battle of Mussel Slough, has historically been conservative and reactionary rather than liberal and progressive (R. Brown 91–94). The brand of vigilantism expressed in this novel has more in common with the ideology of displaced white Southerners in California for whom an antigovernment, antimonopoly populism had become a political strategy during Reconstruction.[4] That Ruiz de Burton would side with this kind of populism, which was also nativist, is representative of the difficulties her writings pose to Chicano/a critics looking for a positive "usable past" in the nineteenth century. On the other hand, because her writings so clearly appraise the political, social, and racial character of her contemporary moment, it is imperative to make use of them to better measure the historical moment. In this context, Ruiz de Burton's literary battle for the reestablishment of Californio social prominence coincides with the post–Civil War struggles over land and resources that emerged out in the West between Mexican Americans, Native Americans, and Anglo settlers and the consolidation of big business interests like the railroad.

II

Doña Josefa evidently did not believe that because "misery there must always be in the world, no matter who causes it," that she was called upon to stoically submit to unmerited infliction. In a mild and dignified way, her mind rebelled. She regarded the acts of the men who caused her husband's ruin and death with genuine abhorrence. . . . "No doubt those people think they have a right to rejoice and feast with the money extorted in crushing so many people — the killing of my darling. Doubtless they say that they earned the money in BUSINESS, and that allegation is all sufficient; that one word justifies in the pursuit of riches everything mean, dishonest, rapacious, unfair, treacherous, unjust, and fraudulent. After a man makes his money no one cares how he made it, and so those people dance while I mourn for my beloved." (363)

Doña Josefa's soliloquy quoted above comes in the penultimate chapter of the novel. It stands out in my mind both for its vehement condemnation of the newly enriched monopolists who constitute the powerful of San Francisco, and hence California, and for the seemingly sudden emergence of Doña Josefa's voice as the moral and political center of the novel. The symbolic content of this soliloquy is linked and expanded in crystal clarity, I argue, in the final pages of the novel. In the conclusion, the narrator breaks completely from a Dickensian coordination of romance, satire, social history, sentimentality, and continental utilitarian philosophy to launch a partisan call to arms against the railroad monopolists featured in the novel. Because the novel's Big Four — Leland Stanford, Collis P. Huntington, Charles Crocker, and Mark Hopkins — were historic figures, the novel's conclusion dissolves any pretense that the text is solely fiction. Nor does the text ultimately perform the kind of cultural work usually associated with a novel like Harriet Beecher Stowe's *Uncle Tom's Cabin* (1852). By contrast, *The Squatter and the Don* aims to incite direct political action. The narrator employs an altogether alternative form of narrative persuasion that is aggressive, impatient, and vigilante.

In the conclusion, the narrator has absorbed the individual moral outrage of Doña Josefa's soliloquy and resituated it into the broader populist politics of the novel. Doña Josefa's big "BUSINESS" has been recalibrated to reflect the title of the final chapter: "Out with the Invader." While "invader" resonates within the global experience of the Mexican American War, Ruiz de Burton means to expand this notion to include the defeated American South, a region whose reconstruction/rehabilitation of its Southerners is every bit as difficult in the West, if not more so. When the narrator connects the defeat of Colonel Scott's Texas Pacific Railroad to the gunfight at Mussel Slough, she does so to parallel the racial politics of the South with those found in Southern California. As noted throughout the novel, the monopolistic efforts to control the California economy have resulted in the corruption of government, from local courts to the Supreme Court, from the state legislature to Congress itself. The narrator argues that intervention into this widespread corruption is imperative: "Our representatives in Congress, and in the State Legislature, knowing full well the will of the people, ought to legislate accordingly. If they do not, then we shall — as Channing said 'kiss the foot that tramples us!' and 'in anguish of spirit' must wait and pray for a Redeemer who will emancipate the white slaves of California" (372). Just exactly who this Redeemer is, or what it is, is not clear. What is clear is that the novel's liberation strategy would "emancipate the white slaves of California." Between Mussel Slough and the racial and economic utopia imagined in the narrator's vigilante war lies Doña Josefa's soliloquy.

Doña Josefa's "mild and dignified" rebellion of mind is hardly unreasonable. She reminds herself what she has suffered at the hands of the cruel monopolists: dead husband, dead in-law, impoverished sons, a lost way of life. Doña Josefa's rebellion here and her insistence at the very end of the novel that she will speak the truth, no matter how uncomfortable it makes the nouveau riche or the risks to her social standing, is nevertheless startling to apprehend. When she first appears in the novel, she embodies the quintessential characteristics of a doña: elegance, propriety, exquisite timing, and devotion to the domestic sphere. She is neither docile nor mindlessly submissive, but intimately aware of the political climate of southern California as made evident in her responses to Don Mariano and George Mechlin in chapter 2. Yet for the most part the novel represents her thoughts within the context of maternal sensibilities and limited personal agency. She sighs, holding onto the Don's arm when she asks: "Is it possible that there is no law to protect us; to protect our property; what does your lawyer say about obtaining redress or protection; is there no hope?" (65). A little later the narrator notes Doña Josefa's feelings when she offers the following political assessment: "Mexico did not pay much attention to the future welfare of the children she left to their fates in the hands of a nation which had no sympathies for us" (66). Although the novel clearly represents men as embodying a range of passionate emotions, their emotions have public outlets and consequences; it is clear that any action to resolve their family problems will come from Don Mariano, his male lawyer, sons-in-law, and male neighbors. By the novel's end, though, all these traditional male interventions have come to an impasse. With this impasse, there comes the impassioned choice Doña Josefa has made, even if it transgresses proper female decorum in the public sphere: "Oh, very well, let it be so. Let the guilty rejoice and go unpunished, and the innocent suffer ruin and desolation. I slander no one, but shall speak the truth" (364).

How has Doña Josefa come to this conviction? Only now does she feel compelled, as opposed to when the "troubles" began in 1846, to tell the truth. And only now does she mean to tell a "truth" that refuses to observe the social niceties and protocols of the upper class, especially its allegiance to wealth for wealth's sake? In a novel so marked by loss and moral indignation, it is noteworthy that it reserves its most subtle but significant political transformation for Doña Josefa. Indeed, Doña Josefa's metamorphosis is especially important because she voices the final sentiments of the elder generation of Alamares who came of age during the Mexican period in Alta California. Their traditional economic order has yielded unwillingly to an advanced and aggressive capitalism, to be sure. This tension is clearly at work when Don Mariano offers to help the squatters become cattle ranchers:

Yes, I may say, I feel sure, it is a mistake to try to make San Diego County a grain-producing county. It is not so, and I feel certain it never will be, to any great extent. This county is, and has been and will be always, a good grazing county — one of the best counties for cattle-raising on this coast, and the very best for fruit-raising on the face of the earth. God intended it should be. Why, then, not devote your time, your labor and your money to raising vineyards, fruits and cattle, instead of trusting to the uncertain rains to give you grain crops? (91)

On the whole, the Alamares perceive this new economic order as less refined, definitely more mechanized, stock-driven, greedier, ruthless in the creation and manipulation of cheap labor, and — most threatening to them — less dependent on landed gentry. The oligarchy of the past with its faith in sacred providential history has met its demise at the hands of the oligarchy of the future and its faith in stock markets and technology. In this context, Doña Josefa, like both the narrator and the author, is unable to see the historic irony in the new economic order.

This irony is perhaps telling, but not as telling as the novel's desire to return California to a previous golden age of ranchos, fruit orchards, and vineyards, all of which grew out of the repressive and coercive mission system that colonized native lands and native people into feudal labor. This economic and social nostalgia is the novel's "siglo de oro," but so lost by 1885, the year of the novel's publication, that there are no effective "hidalgos" for the role of Don Quixote, though plenty of Sancho Panzas are to be found. Also included in this nostalgia are sympathetic newcomers like James Mechlin and Alfred Holman. In their audience with Gov. Leland Stanford toward the end of the novel, it is Alfred Holman who reproduces this nostalgia like a native Californio: "If our county does not take the lead as wheat growing, it certainly can take it as fruit growing. We have no capital to make large plantations of vineyards or trees, but what has been done proves, conclusively, that for grapes, olives, figs, and in fact all semi-tropical fruits, there is no better country in the world" (314). The failure of Don Mariano, James Mechlin, and Alfred Holman to end Stanford's opposition to a railroad through San Diego County signals the death knell for an elite Californio way of life. In fact, Mechlin sounds it deeply and accurately when he says, "I feel a prophetic warning that neither you nor I will ever see light in this world. These men — this deadly, soulless corporation, which like a black cloud, has shut out the light from San Diego's horizon — will be our funeral pall" (320). Like Don Mariano, Mechlin will come to suffer a Californio fate. Mechlin's demise has scores of historical counterparts in European Americans like John A. Sutter of Sutter's Mill fame, who also suffered at the hands of uncultured squatters, unscrupulous lawyers, and corrupt courts. By the novel's conclusion, the narrative has carefully identified those European Americans who came to California before and after 1846 not to invade it but to be adopted by it. There were dozens of individuals who married into a Spanish/Mexican colonial past and experience. Over time, where family connections, prosperity, and adherence to Old World values dominated, these immigrants acculturated into and were accorded the honorific of don or doña. Locally, John Sutter was more familiarly known as Don Juan. His was not the only case.

It is the displacement of the older economic order, not just the illegal dispossession of Californios from their lands, which fuels the narrative of this novel. This novel is precisely about economics and its resistance to the new world order that grows out of the Civil War. In this context, the true competitors for California are the state's Big Four monopolists versus a consortium made up of landed, elite Californios, Jeffersonian agrarians, patrician Whig professionals, and Southern sympathizers. Given the content of the final chapter, and especially its vigilante call to arms, it is difficult to reduce Ruiz de Burton's intended audience to any one faction. The Californio elite is undoubtedly at the center of this novel, but so too are others. Instead, it would be more accurate to say that the novel is defending an economic order that originated among nineteenth-century Californios of Spanish/Mexican descent. This defense included other European Americans and, equally significant, new ways of accumulating capital that required little or no change in the social and gender hierarchy of pre-1848 Alta California.

By locating Ruiz de Burton's cultural politics with vigilantism and Mussel Slough, the textual anomalies of the novel suddenly make more sense, especially in lieu of Ruiz de Burton's use of time. Ruiz de Burton very carefully notes the start of the novel as 1872. Doña Josefa's soliloquy that ends the romance narrative of the text occurs in 1876. By contrast, the narrator's abrupt intrusion brings the text up to 1880 at the mere mention of Mussel Slough. In terms of historic time, then, the reader is forced to make sense of these two end points. Intertextually, 1872 represents the year of Ruiz de Burton's first published novel, *Who Would Have Thought It?* Curiously, Don Alamar's death in 1876 coincides with the publication of her play translation of Miguel de Cervantes's *Don Quixote de la Mancha: A Comedy in Five Acts.* Biographically, 1848 marks both her marriage to a West Point officer, Henry S. Burton, and the signing of the Treaty of Guadalupe Hidalgo. Ruiz de Burton's resettlement in California that year is mirrored by her character William Darrell, who crosses the continent in 1848 to settle in California with his wife, three children, and the teamsters Gasbang, Miller, and Mathews. In 1859, Henry Burton's military duties force the family to live out East for the next ten years. He dies in 1869 while commandant of Fort Adams, Newport, Rhode Island. This connection to Rhode Island explains Ruiz de Burton's facility with narrating Mercedes Alamar's acceptance by Newport high society. In 1870, Ruiz de Burton and her children return to Rancho Jamul in San Diego. When she arrives, she is appalled to find that the ranch is heavily in debt, squatters are living on the land, and she has no financial resources. Her husband had been widely known as a spendthrift and a holder of many ious. Henry Burton, like many in the county, had speculated with the coming of the railroad as early as the 1850s; he was even a board member of the local landowners' association, set up to maximize the eventual sale of private lands. But as chronicled in the novel, 1876 is the year that the Big Four successfully blocked Colonel Scott's effort to build a southern railroad route through San Diego County. Ruiz de Burton's return to California and Rancho Jamul turns out to be one economic and legal crisis after another until her death in 1895.

Her second novel is her chance to address all these personal matters but on a much larger scale, and it is also her attempt to fund her family's life and land litigation. It is therefore interesting to contemplate Ruiz de Burton's use of time as her way of claiming the significance of the Battle of Mussel Slough for her own political project. The enemies of the Mussel Slough farmers were the same individuals who undermined and "killed" the Texas Pacific Railroad. The Big Four struck first in 1876, only to strike again in 1880. In this context, Doña Josefa's soliloquy can also be taken as prophesy. If only the truth had been told in 1876, and told widely, maybe the power of the monopolists could have been curbed, their victims compensated, and the Battle of Mussel Slough avoided altogether. Achieving this prophetic quality is important given how Ruiz de Burton maintains the unified status of the Big Four throughout the novel. Mark Hopkins's death in 1878 reduced the Big Four to the Big Three. This information never gets translated into the novel, either literally or otherwise.

Symbolically, the geographic removal of the Alamar family from San Diego to San Francisco signals an important concession on the part of Ruiz de Burton. Doña Josefa moves to no ordinary city in California. She takes up residence in the de facto headquarters of vigilantism in California since 1850. It is here in this city that vigilantism and populism combine to contest the accumulation of wealth and power in the hands of a few in the years immediately after the Gold Rush. By 1885, the lessons learned over the intervening thirty-five years have established a well-oiled muckraking press, populist groups, and state-roaming agitators. This is the site Ruiz de Burton chooses for Doña Josefa's political transformation and the center of a discursive community she hoped would transform her economic future. The squatter precedes the don in the title of her novel precisely because she believes that if

squatters like William Darrell are educated to see the truth behind the efforts of the Big Four, they will more likely side with
vigilante efforts to contest the corruption and economic power of
monopolies. Ultimately Ruiz de Burton rests her fate in the hands
of individuals like the repentant William Darrell at the end of the
novel and, of course, the true son of California's future, Clarence
Darrell.

Doña Josefa's concluding remarks declare a "vote of no confidence" in the nineteenth-century practice of exercising "moral
persuasion" to effect political and social change in the nation. In
terms of genre, the novel declares the domestic politics of sentimentality void. *Uncle Tom's Cabin* may have solicited Abraham Lincoln's
appraisal of Stowe as "the little lady who started a war," but in the
post–Civil War era, sentimental literature is quickly giving way to
experimental trends that would come to be associated with natural-
ism, realism, and muckraking journalism. Doña Josefa will speak
the truth plainly. She will not follow Emily Dickinson's example —
"Tell All the Truth but Tell It Slant" — nor will she tell the truth
on behalf of the powerless, speechless other as in Helen Hunt
Jackson's *Ramona*. Firsthand witness to the Mexican American
War (1846–48), the California constitutional convention (1849),
the consequences of the Gold Rush (1848–50) and the Civil War
(1861–65), and finally the loss of her own beloved Rancho Jamul to
debt, squatters, and costly litigation, Ruiz de Burton resorts in the
end to a most American political tradition: "fighting words." As a
cornerstone of vigilante practices, the political ideology of "fighting
words" has its origins — and this might seem ironic to some — in
such documents as the Declaration of Independence and the U.S.
Constitution and especially in the Bill of Rights, which guarantees
the freedom of speech, assembly, and significantly the right to bear
arms. By 1885, Ruiz de Burton understood well that to tell all the
truth in the United States could be a deadly business for a single
family or for the hundreds of families who constituted for her the
people of California.

José F. Aranda Jr.

Notes

My eternal gratitude to Amelia María de la Luz Montes and Anne E. Goldman for their support of my work and the inclusion of this essay in their collection.

1. For more on the role that "whiteness" plays in this novel, see González.

2. For more on Californio ranch culture, see Pérez, "Teaching the Hacienda."

3. See "Letter to Professor Davidson, July 15, 1880," Sánchez and Pita, introduction, 11–12.

4. For more on the novel's Southern sympathies, see Pérez, "South by Southwest."

Remembering the Hacienda: Land and Community in Californio Narratives

VINCENT PÉREZ

The 1849 of California, of America, of the world! It was the pivot on which the framework of human progress turned a fresh side to the sun, a side breeding maggots hitherto, but now a new and nobler race of men. ❧ Hubert Howe Bancroft, *California Inter Pocula* (376)

As members of the nineteenth-century Mexican Californian rancher class, María Amparo Ruiz de Burton and Mariano Guadalupe Vallejo acquired tracts of land originally ceded as mission grants in the pre-1848 era. Each also produced a literary narrative intended to address the land question as it had developed in the strikingly different sociohistorical context that followed the 1848 annexation of California. Written in the wake of the dispossession of the Californio ranchers, Ruiz de Burton's novel *The Squatter and the Don* (1885) and Vallejo's autobiography, "Historical and Personal Memoirs Relating to Alta California" (1874), stand today as foundational Mexican American literary texts.[1] Contesting dominant accounts of Southwest history during an era of consolidation of U.S. hegemony in the region, these works were among the first by members of the Mexican (American) "colony" in the newly annexed territory to examine the repressive social, political, and cultural impact of conquest that has formed a lasting historical legacy for the region's Mexican American population since the mid-nineteenth century.

I wish to expand on recent scholarship on Ruiz de Burton and Vallejo by examining the historicity of their works with reference to another set of literary narratives that in the same era similarly called into question U.S. economic and political institutions. The critique of U.S. practices in *Squatter* and "Memoirs" parallels anti-Northern discourse in Southern plantation and domestic fiction.[2] Building on this parallel, I argue that the engagement with U.S. dominance in these two early texts originates in the authors' identities as members of the Mexican Californian hacienda aristocracy.[3] For dispossessed rancher-aristocrats like Ruiz de Burton and Vallejo, the land question constituted more than a legal, political, and moral dispute with U.S. governmental authority. It also represented a struggle over the claims and conditions of hacienda community, for three centuries the dominant socioeconomic institution throughout the region that would become Mexico. Ruiz de Burton and Vallejo invoke claims to traditional hacienda community as a means of contesting injustice under U.S. rule.[4] "Remembering" the hacienda in *Squatter* and "Memoirs" thus serves an anti-Yankee ideal broadly analogous to the plantatioh myth, which similarly displaced the coercive nature of a prewar organic community in the interest of countering U.S. social depredations. But just as the plantation myth ambiguously positioned white Southerners in relation to the North, setting them apart culturally while uniting them racially with white Northerners under the banner of Jim Crow, the "hacienda" serves deeply contradictory aims in Californio writings. Ironically, identification with the "hacienda" also captures the elite's desire for integration within post–Civil War (white) society.[5] Hence the traditional conception of hacienda community in *Squatter* and "Memoirs" reflects the Californio oligarchy's divided impulses as a "colonized" and displaced aristocracy. It questions U.S. rule from the position of a marginalized elite nostalgic for the pre-1848 era of Mexican national and cultural sovereignty, when it controlled the economic and political institutions of Alta California. By invoking its pre-1848 (genteel) class and (white/Spanish) racial and caste identities through its narrative recovery of hacienda community, the Californio elite at the same time imagines a future place for itself within the newly ascendant white nation of the post-Reconstruction period.[6]

The anti-Yankee polemic in the works of such nineteenth-century Southern plantation writers as Caroline Gilman, Augusta Evans, and Thomas Nelson Page sheds light on the broad political objective of both Californio narratives. Mounting a "defense of their native or adopted region," early Southern writers, as Elizabeth Moss explains, portrayed "the South as an ordered, harmonious society governed by the aristocratic code of noblesse oblige . . . [and by a] system of reciprocal relationships that made southern society the moral superior of the individualistic North" (2). Though witness to American social and economic achievement, like early Southern writers, Ruiz de Burton and Vallejo defended their native region by redeeming its premodern social order. While neither foregrounds the "old order" in precisely the manner of Southern plantation and domestic fiction, the fluid conception of "race" in Mexican California complicates the analogy, and both Californio writers depict the hacienda as an organic "true community" set against the post-1848 landscape of capitalist modernity.[7] Having lost their land and social status, Ruiz de Burton and Vallejo drew on their hacienda identities to mold a distinctive Mexican American historical subjectivity in the post-1848 period. Their works' engagement with U.S. hegemony thus constitutes a defense of the "hacienda" in both a literal sense, as the home and patrimony of family or community, and as a sociocultural ideal identified as much with the Mexican nation as with the pre-1848 social order.[8]

My discussion consists of three parts. First I summarize biographical and textual material that establishes the context for the parallel I am drawing between the dispossessed Californio elite and the Southern ex-planter class. I highlight passages in *Squatter* that identify the shared sociohistorical status of the Californio *hacendados* and the white ex-planter class in the South. Second, I analyze *Squatter* and "Memoirs" as works that remember the "hacienda" as a means of forging an identity for the displaced Californio ranchers in the post-1848 period. Both works reestablish community boundaries to (re)define the hacienda as a social unit against U.S. material and discursive threats to its existence. Rather than expressing nostalgia for the "hacienda," both works instead affirm the attributes of the "old order" by reestablishing boundaries that once separated the (Mexican) hacienda world from U.S. society. In my conclusions, I briefly review how both narratives create the image of the "hacienda" to serve as a cultural icon for the Mexican American community, a symbolic representation in which the positive attributes of community (cohesiveness, order, stability, interdependence, and so on) are lent a kind of iconic integrity (Romine 7–8).

South by Southwest

During Ruiz de Burton's stay on the East Coast during and after the Civil War, the displacement of the plantation ruling class in the South, as Rosaura Sánchez and Beatrice Pita note in their 1995 introduction to Ruiz de Burton's first novel, *Who Would Have Thought It?* (1872), would have triggered "memories of what had taken place in Alta California, where after occupation the ruling Californios were reduced to a subaltern minority" (ix). In a more recent work, Sánchez and Pita cite Ruiz de Burton's letters to argue that she "sympathized with the defeated Confederacy, seeing in the South's defeat a mirror of the defeat of Mexico in 1848, and in Reconstruction, a clear imposition of Yankee hegemony in the Southern states" (*Conflicts of Interest* 195). But as I remark below, Ruiz de Burton made her identification with the conquered South quite explicit in *Squatter*—as well as in *Who Would Have Thought It?*—which provide ample evidence of her contempt for Reconstruction. Ruiz de Burton's motivation for drawing a South by Southwest parallel could only have become more urgent during the thirteen years between the publication of her two novels. Her fortunes declined rapidly during this period as she borrowed money to wage a legal battle to regain control of her approximately 10,000-acre ranch near San Diego. After 1870, "[f]irst the squatters, and then the rival claimants" ensured that if Ruiz de Burton "were ever to regain the rancho, it would be . . . after a long and hard-fought struggle" (Oden 164). By September 1882, after more than a decade of litigation, Ruiz de Burton was in debt to two groups of creditors and faced financial ruin. As *Squatter* indicates through its portrait of Californio (read: Spanish) landed aristocrats reduced to common (read: Mexican) laborers through dispossession, the loss of Ruiz de Burton's landed status subverted her own class and racial positioning within post-Reconstruction U.S. society.

Vallejo, Ruiz de Burton's close friend on whom she would model *Squatter*'s protagonist, Mariano Alamar, faced an equally precipitous financial decline in the same approximate period. At the height of his career in the 1840s, when his three ranchos encompassed up to 300,000 acres, Vallejo was the most powerful rancher/caudillo in the northern district of Alta California. But, as Genaro Padilla notes, "In the fifteen intervening years between the formal presentation of his 'Recuerdos históricos y personales' [in 1875] and his eighty-third year [in 1890] . . . Vallejo's fortunes spiraled downward without surcease" (103). Also forced into litigation with squatters and speculators to prove entitlement to his land, by 1880, with the exception of a small ranch in Sonoma, Vallejo's hacienda empire had been lost. Shortly after completing his narrative for Hubert H. Bancroft, according to Padilla, Vallejo "returned to Sonoma, to boredom and depression" (103). In 1878, not long after losing "another large sum of money when the Vallejo Savings and Commercial Bank failed," Vallejo "saw his own material and physical situation represented in a photograph of his once beautiful home in Petaluma" (103). "I compare that old relic with myself and the comparison is an extant one; ruins and dilapidation. What a difference between then and now. Then Youth, strength and riches, now Age, weakness and poverty" (quoted in Padilla 103–4). As Padillo describes, Vallejo's autobiographical persona evokes, as in the above self-reference, a simultaneous disillusionment with the United States "present" and solace through nostalgic remembrance of the pre-1848 Mexican era. Vallejo's close identification with his rancho suggests as well his ideological and cultural investment in the "hacienda" identities of the displaced Californio elite.

The Squatter and the Don's plot reflects the parallel experiences summarized above, now documented in the correspondence between Ruiz de Burton and Vallejo collected by Sánchez and Pita. The novel depicts the decline of the Alamars, a Californio family whose 47,000-acre cattle ranch forms part of a land grant ceded to its ancestors more than fifty years earlier. From 1872 to 1876, the Alamars lose their land and ranch as a result of laws that favor Anglo American settlers and squatters over Mexican families who acquired their ranches under the Spanish/Mexican land tenure system. The novel narrates this story through the Alamars' relationship with the Darrells, a white settler/squatter family newly arrived on the Alamar ranch. The squatter/rancher conflict develops through a series of interethnic romances involving the children of these two families.

William Darrell relocates his family to San Diego in the belief that the Alamar grant, ostensibly rejected by the courts, is public domain and therefore open to legal settlement. His wife, Mary, however, has learned otherwise, and she directs their son, Clarence, to purchase a tract from the Alamars before the family moves. Because of William's pro-squatter sentiments, neither informs William that he is a legitimate settler on land that his family owns. Just as Mrs. Darrell feared, after the family moves, William's pro-squatter sentiments blind him to the legitimacy of the Alamars' complaint against scores of illegal squatters. Significantly, Clarence and his mother's motivation for sympathizing with the Californio ranchers is influenced by Mary's Creole descent, which shapes Clarence's view of "Latin" people. The marginal presence of Tisha, Mary Darrell's African American servant, moreover, serves to remind us that, as a white Southerner after the Civil War, Mary would be sensitive to the uncompensated and unlawful seizure of property, which is the way plantation owners viewed emancipation. Hence Mary's determination to compensate Don Mariano for the land comes not merely out of the kindness of her heart but also from what Ruiz de Burton characterizes as a historical recognition of the homologous position the Californio *hacendados* and the white ex-planter class shared during this period.

While he is disabused of his misconceptions, William Darrell finds himself drawn into the sphere of Mexican American genteel society through Clarence's romantic relationship with Mercedes, Don Mariano's daughter. The squatter/rancher land entitlement conflict threatens to rend the romantic union between these two characters. Clarence's sympathy for the Alamars' plight, along with the shock of preemption by Mrs. Darrell, however, compels William to confront his beliefs and renounce squatterism. Although Clarence and Mercedes are eventually married and the Alamars are saved from destitution by Clarence's newfound stock market wealth, the resolution of the clash between the Darrells and the Alamars does not save the Californio ranchers. With countless settlers and squatters refusing to embrace Mr. Darrell's example and still more arriving to stake claims on Californio land, the era of the "Spano-American" ranchers is rapidly coming to a end. As Don Mariano must reluctantly acknowledge, "I am afraid there is no help for us native Californians. We must sadly fade and pass away. . . . We must sink, go under, never to rise" (177). Don Alamar dies of an illness as he realizes that his family's hacienda estate will be lost. A final attempt to save the family's land through the construction of a railroad, a project which the Don and other San Diego ranchers hope to broker, is thwarted by Leland Stanford and his monopolistic railroad trust, the representatives of the new capitalist order.

The railroad project serves in the novel primarily to establish a sociohistorical kinship between Mexican California and the American South, a solidarity based on a shared condition of military defeat and subjugation by the Yankee "North." Several passages illustrate this kinship by portraying Northern monopolists victimizing both the already besieged Californios and the conquered South at the height of Reconstruction. The narrator explicitly links the plight of Mexican California to the South in two chapters that depict Californio support for construction of the Texas Pacific Railroad. Connecting Southern California to the South, the railroad, according to the novel, would have benefited both regions. But in chapter 20, the Californio ranchers' representatives in Washington DC hear "strange rumors about Congressmen being 'bribed with money' and in other ways improperly influenced by a 'certain railroad man,' who was organizing a powerful lobby to defeat the Texas Pacific Railroad" (210). Confirming the rumors, the railroad monopoly controlled by Stanford terminates the Texas Pacific Railroad through political corruption in favor of its own Central Pacific line. This is in fact what occurred despite U.S. congressional action against the monopoly, the text of which is included in chapter 20 listing the frauds "perpetrated by Messrs. Leland Stanford, Huntington, Crocker, and Hopkins, under the name of 'Central Pacific Railroad Company'" (209). Conflating the contemporaneous plights of the South and Mexican California, a Californio supporter and lobbyist in Washington DC concludes: "There never can be any better argument in favor of the Texas Pacific than are now plain to everybody. So, then, if in the face of all these powerful considerations Congress turns its back and will not hear the wail of the prostrate South, or the impassionate appeals of California, now, *now*, when there is not one solitary reason under heaven why such appeals and entreaties should be disregarded, is there any ground to expect any better in the uncertain future? Certainly not" (Ruiz de Burton's emphasis, 216).

Voicing his identification with the South's condition under Reconstruction, Don Mariano Alamar decries the amoral political and business tactics used by Stanford and his monopoly to manipulate Southerners into believing that the Texas Pacific Railroad was being built for the benefit of Northerners. As he states, if the monopoly's representative "had been sent to deceive the North, to

fool the Yankees, the errand would have been — if not more honorable — at least less odious for a Southerner, not so treacherous;
but to go and deceive the trusting South, now when the entire
country is so impoverished, so distressed, that act, I say, is inhu-
man, is ignominious. No words of reprobation can be too severe to
stigmatize a man capable of being so heartless" (308–9). Echoing
the white South's grievances during Reconstruction, Don Mariano
concludes that the Yankee monopolists "should be stigmatized . . .
as corrupters, as most malignant, debasing, unscrupulous men . . .
men who are harmful to society, because they reward dishonorable
acts; because they reward, with money, the blackest treason" (309).
This sentiment is dramatized at length in chapter 33, which depicts
Don Mariano's meeting with Stanford, who peremptorily rejects
his business proposal.

In calling in the novel's final paragraph for a "Redeemer" who
will "emancipate the 'white slaves' of California," the narrator more
explicitly binds the plight of the Californio ranchers (and those
residing in Southern California in particular) to the sociohistorical
status of the "Southern States" during and after Reconstruction
(372). As she concludes:

> But these [events], as well as the blight, spread over Southern
> California, and over the entire Southern States, are historical
> facts. All of which, strung together, would make a brilliant and
> most appropriate chaplet to encircle the lofty brow of the great
> and powerful monopoly. Our representatives in Congress, and
> in the State Legislature, knowing full well the will of the people,
> ought to legislate accordingly. If they do not, then we shall — as
> Channing said 'kiss the foot that tramples us!' and 'in anguish of
> spirit' must wait and pray for a Redeemer who will emancipate
> the white slaves of California." (372)

While "Redeemer" is an ironic reference to Abraham Lincoln, the
savior of the North, it is also clearly a statement of support for the

South's Redeemers, a political party which in the 1870s and 1880s sought to dismantle Reconstruction policies in the South. As Eric Foner explains, the Redeemers "included secessionist Democrats and Union Whigs, veterans of the Confederacy and rising younger leaders, traditional planters and advocates of a modernized New South. They shared . . . a commitment to dismantling the Reconstruction state, reducing the political power of blacks, and reshaping the South's legal system in the interests of labor control and racial subordination" (Foner 588). By equating the "white slaves" of California with whites in the South during Reconstruction, the novel in the end reasserts a sociohistorical and political solidarity between the two regions — while conferring "whiteness" on the dispossessed Californios — based on a common cause against Yankee dominance. But the narrator's references to Yankee oppression and monopoly capital, here and elsewhere in *Squatter*, hardly suggest a progressive political perspective. To the contrary, if viewed in relation to Ruiz de Burton's racial, class, and caste identities as a former hacienda aristocrat, these comments instead bear a striking resemblance to anti-Yankee tracts by Southern plantation writers, such as George Fitzhugh's attack on U.S. capitalism in *Cannibals All! or, Slaves without Masters* (1857). Defending the "organic" social relations of the South's slavery-dependent plantation society, Fitzhugh called for war against a modern world dominated by capitalist competition and bourgeois individualism.

It is in this comparative context that the Californio elite's own opposition to Yankee practices must be placed, as expressed by Don Mariano's widow, Doña Josefa, near the end of the novel. Doña Josefa's elegy to her husband represents both a statement of the claims of traditional Mexican hacienda community (e.g., its fundamental "rectitude," dignity," and "equity") and an eloquent critique of the morally corrosive influence of the values of the new capitalist order:

In a mild and dignified way, her mind rebelled. She regarded the acts of the men who caused her husband's ruin and death with genuine abhorrence. To her, rectitude and equity had a clear meaning impossible to pervert. No subtle sophistry could blur in her mind the clear line dividing right from wrong. She knew that among men the word BUSINESS means inhumanity to one another; it means justification of rapacity; it means the freedom of man to crowd and crush his fellow-man; it means the sanction of the Shylockian principle of exacting the pound of flesh. . . . "Doubtless they say that they earned the money in BUSINESS . . . that one word justifies in the pursuit of riches everything mean, dishonest, rapacious, unfair, treacherous, unjust, and fraudulent." (363)

Fencing in Community

Two scenes capture the contradictory aims in *Squatter*: that is, to project integration within U.S. society through metonymic "romance," and to oppose U.S. dominance through Californio claims to traditional "true community." Even as the novel invokes the redemptive claims and conditions of separateness by establishing the boundaries of "true community," it simultaneously projects a desire for future Californio inclusion in the newly ascendant post-Reconstruction U.S. nation.

Although community boundaries may shift, they always have a geographic analogue in *Squatter*. Whether it is the boundary marking the borders of the conquered Mexican territory as set forth in the Treaty of Guadalupe Hidalgo, that which circumscribed Mexican Alta California before the war, or that which formed the property lines marking a Mexican or Spanish land grant, *Squatter* is concerned with establishing geographic demarcations that will circumscribe and define Californio community. Since boundaries form the foundation of land entitlement claims, the remapping of these lines is a central objective of the novel's argument against U.S. land tenure policy.[9] But the drawing of boundaries also functions as a way of marking a community's inside and outside and, more importantly, its conditions of inclusion and exclusion (Romine 4). By marking lines between the Californio community and the encroaching Yankee world — i.e., as the title announces, between the Mexican "Don" and the American "Squatter" — the novel works to reassert hacienda identities rooted in the region's pre-1848 "organic" ranching community.

The novel's land argument rests on reestablishing the legitimacy of boundaries based on Spanish and Mexican entitlement claims. When the narrator cites the 1848 Treaty of Guadalupe Hidalgo, which recognized the geographic demarcations established during the Spanish and Mexican periods but retreated from validating pre-1848 land grants, she refers to the history of colonization of Alta California and other northern territories by settlers from New Spain and Mexico. The novel adduces the treaty to document prior boundaries circumscribing the conquered region as well as prove, therefore, the illegality of U.S. land tenure policy. Or, as Don Mariano explains to Clarence in chapter 16, "It ought to have been sufficient that by the Treaty of Guadalupe Hidalgo . . . the nation's honor was pledged to respect our property. The treaty said that our rights would be the same as those enjoyed by all other American citizens. The [government] never thought of that. With very unbecoming haste, Congress hurried to pass laws to legalize their despoliation of the conquered Californians, forgetting the nation's pledge to protect us" (175). Similarly, in "Memoirs," Vallejo incorporates innumerable legal and political documents to establish the legitimacy of Mexican and Spanish entitlement claims and thus prove the *illegitimacy* of U.S. policy. Quoting, for example, from "Title Eleven of the Regulation and Instruction for Presidios set up by the Spanish monarch in the *cedula* of September 10, 1772," he notes that "since the regulation and its provisions had always been in force in California since the founding of San Luis Obispo Mission and since no laws were or had been passed in conflict with its provisions, it is clear that the [U.S.] California state courts acted lightly when they handed down decisions which were in open conflict with that Regulation" (5: 186).

Don Mariano's efforts to require that fences be constructed around the homesteads of squatters illustrate the key role that the marking of boundaries plays in *The Squatter and the Don*. The fences represent both a physical and figurative demarcation, one which will physically block Alamar's cattle from squatters who are shooting or capturing them when they wander onto their homesteads, as well as one that separates the "inside" Californio community of "ordered space" from the outside threat of disorder embodied by the squatters. In chapter 2 Don Mariano comments on the absurdity of the "no-fence" law, a statute ostensibly passed to protect agriculture but which in fact permits Alamar's livestock to be slaughtered or stolen by squatters who do not yet possess a legal claim to their homesteads. "By those laws any man can come to my land . . . plant ten acres of grain, without any fence, and then catch my cattle which, seeing the green grass without a fence, will go to eat it" (66). As with the piecemeal appropriation of his land, the injustices only mount, for the squatters may then "put the cattle in a 'corral' and make me pay damages and so much per head for keeping them, and costs of legal proceedings and many other trumped up expenses, until for such little fields of grain I may be obliged to pay thousands of dollars" (66).

When Don Mariano attempts to resolve the conflict by offering to cede the squatters their homesteads on the condition that they no longer grow crops but, rather, become cattle ranchers like himself, he also effectively invites them to adopt the traditional mode of production of the Californio ranchers. But he does so not because he believes the squatters are worthy of being included in the hacienda community. That Don Mariano would "invite" outsiders to become cattle ranchers when they have clearly transgressed the boundaries of the Californio social order instead reflects his growing desperation in the face of his community's imminent financial and sociocultural ruin. Agricultural and ranching products thus function here metaphorically, with hacienda products a figuration for Californio community and grain or crops (along with the more obvious symbol of guns used to kill cattle) a metonym for the threats posed by the Yankee outsiders. Since it is clear to Alamar that without fences or boundaries, between the two communities, the Yankee world will inevitably engulf Californio society, the Don tries to persuade the outsiders to leave their world for the "true community" of the Californio ranchers — as the Anglo American Mechlins, for example, have already done. It is "a mistake to try to make San Diego County a grain-producing county," Alamar explains to the squatters. "It is not so, and I feel certain it never will be. . . . This county is, and has been and will be always, a good grazing county — one of the best for fruit-raising on the face of the earth. God intended it should be." He pleads with the squatters to "devote your time, your labor and your money" to hacienda and rancho industries, "raising vineyards, fruits and cattle, instead of trusting to the uncertain rains to give you grain crops" (91).

Yet here the threat posed by the squatters represents that of a contrasting conception of culture and community as much as it does the threat of an opposing nation, race, or class. When the suspicious squatters jocosely announce that they "don't want any cattle" because they "ain't no '*vaquero*' to go '*busquering*' [searching] around and lassoing cattle" (94), the Don's tone becomes desperate. "All I want to do is to save the few cattle I have left. I am willing to quit-claim to you the land you have taken, and give you cattle to begin the stock business, and all I ask you in return is to put a fence around whatever land you wish to cultivate, so that my cattle cannot go in there" (92). Along with stock raising, the Don again pleads with the squatters to "plant vineyards, plant olives, figs, oranges; make wines and oil and raisins; export olives and dried and canned fruits" (92).

When Clarence is accused of "favoring the aristocracy" because of his willingness to be adopted into the Californio community through intermarriage, he defends the Don's proposal by pointing to the futility of efforts to do away with the Californios' traditional community and industry (96). "Plant wheat," he says to the squatter Gasbang, "if you can do so without killing cattle. But do not destroy the larger industry with the smaller. If, as the Don very properly says, this is a grazing county, no legislation can change it. So it would be wiser to make laws to suit the county, and not expect that the county will change its character to suit absurd laws" (96). As in the earlier passage, in which the existence of the hacienda order was ordained by God, here this community similarly represents the natural manifestation of geography and climate, which no laws can ever change. The immutability of land, geography, and climate confirms for Clarence the historical inevitability of hacienda community even in the face of its imminent destruction by "absurd" laws implemented by outside (U.S.) forces.

The novel's hacienda setting, where gentility and romance thrive even as the modern world steadily encroaches, forms a bastion of pre-1848 Californio community in a region and state now controlled by Anglo Americans. The hacienda's boundaries therefore serve, as in the above passages, to mark a line dividing capitalist modernity from the traditional "true community" of the rancheros. And yet the hacienda also provides a genteel space for the flowering of romantic union between Californio and Anglo, figuring the possible integration of the Californio elite into the newly dominant social order. At the beginning of chapter 8 Alice Darrell and her brother Clarence pay a visit to the Alamar rancho, where their respective partners, Mercedes Alamar and her brother Victoriano, wait to greet them. In contrast to the sordid money-centered world of the squatters and that of other representatives of the Yankee order like the Robber Baron Stanford, hacienda boundaries in this scene demarcate a realm of manners, leisure, and romance.[10] Whereas in most of the novel the pastoral motif is disrupted by the reality of occupation and violence by squatters and settlers, in this passage the hacienda, framed by the grandeur of its physical surroundings, mirrors the idealized romantic union between Californios and Anglos.

As Alice and Clarence approach the hacienda, they discern "[t]he golden rays of a setting sun," which "were vanishing in the west," and "a silvered moon," which "was rising serenely over the eastern hills." When their carriage arrived at "the foot of the low hill where the Alamar house stood," the "French windows opening upon the veranda sent broad streams of light across the garden and far over the hill." As if to extend the pastoral motif to the hacienda home itself, sounds of music and singing greet the two visitors. When the initial singing ceased, "the prelude of a Spanish song was begun. . . . A lady at the piano arose and selected another piece of music, and began the accompaniment of [an] old and well known [song]" (112). As the two watch the singer from outside the home, Alice asks her brother about the woman at the piano. " 'She is Mercedes,' whispered Clarence, glad of the excuse to whisper, and with a preparatory checking of breath and swallowing of something that seemed to fill his throat always, when her name was mentioned" (112). Mercedes sings a second song with so much feeling that "it seemed to Clarence that he could not have listened to the simple melody before now attentively enough to appreciate its pathos, for it sounded most sweetly touching to him" (112–13).

This idealized depiction of hacienda life recalls a scene in chapter 2 that similarly marks the space of the hacienda as one of romance and gentility, attributes of "true community" diametrically set against the intruding outside (capitalist) forces that frustrate Don Mariano. Troubled by the arrival of more squatters on his land, in this scene the Don is first depicted as a disconsolate figure "silently walking up and down the front piazza of his house at the rancho." He is distracted by the "sounds of laughter, music, and dancing [which] came from the parlor, [where] the young people were entertaining friends from town with their usual gay hospitality and enjoying themselves heartily" (64). The threat posed by the "outside" world distracts the Don from participating in the possible union of (Anglo American?) young people "from town" with the children of the Californios. Preoccupied with the squatter problem, as much as the Don would like to join in the festivities, he must forgo the celebration. Contrasting community "insiderhood" to the threat of disruption posed by the squatters, the narrator comments that "Don Mariano, though already in his fiftieth year, was as fond of dancing as his sons and daughters, and not to see him come in and join the quadrille was so singular that his wife thought she must come out and inquire what could detain him (64). As this brief scene suggests, as much as he endeavors to preserve the "inside" world of the Mexican hacienda, the Don cannot ignore the reality of the "outside" forces intruding upon it.

Constructing Community in "Historical and Personal Memoirs"

Literary scholars and historians have produced several studies of Vallejo's "Memoirs," a work described on the title page as "A Political History of the Country from 1769 to 1849. Customs of the Californians. Biographical Notes Concerning Notable Individuals." [11] "Memoirs" employs many of the same community-defining strategies that I have identified above in my comments on Ruiz de Burton's novel. Like *The Squatter and the Don*, the work is broadly concerned with valorizing pre-1848 Californio (hacienda) community to serve the elite's contradictory but closely allied political and sociocultural impulses to both "separate" from and "integrate" within post-1848 U.S. society. As in *The Squatter and the Don*, in "Memoirs" this project is contingent upon the inscription of boundaries that serve to draw distinctions between Californio "true community" and all of those outside groups which at one point or another threatened it (i.e., native peoples, and later, Americans as well as other immigrants who arrived during the Gold Rush). Although these boundaries may shift, as in *Squatter*, they are always at some level geographic. Depending on the period covered, they variously circumscribe Mexico, Alta California, the Hispanic

Southwest, Northern and Southern regions of Alta California, land grant territory, and individual ranchos. In the first two volumes of "Memoirs," which delve at length into the decades-long effort by colonists, settlers, and missionaries to subjugate Alta California's native peoples, the boundaries demarcate a border separating "civilized" society from "savagery." I focus below on how the concluding section of Vallejo's narrative constructs notions of Californio community inclusion and exclusion through its rendering of the Gold Rush. As in *Squatter*, the marking of boundaries between "insiders" and "outsiders" serves ultimately to reassert the hacienda identities of the displaced Californio rancher-aristocrats.

The demographic transformation of California during the Gold Rush serves as a useful reference point for considering the conditions and claims of hacienda community as depicted in Californio narratives. When in 1874 Vallejo narrated his life story to Bancroft's assistant, Enrique Cerruti, not only had he and most other Californio ranchers been dispossessed of their land, but the Mexican American population had become a minority amid a burgeoning immigrant population arriving from all parts of the United States and the world. During the period which saw this demographic shift, Mexican Americans in California increasingly became the target of racial discrimination in public institutions, objectification in popular culture, as well as violence in the form of mob lynchings. In 1841, there were between 6,500 and 7,000 Mexicans and fewer than 400 foreigners of all nationalities in Alta California. Of the 10,000 Mexicans in California in 1850 when it became a U.S. state, only 3 percent owned large ranches, illustrating the hierarchical division between high/landed and low/poor Mexicans established during the postsecularization land grab. The influx of immigrants during the Gold Rush meant that by 1851, just two years after the discovery of gold, Mexicans formed only 11 percent of the state's population (Almaguer 70–71). Between 1860 and 1900 the total number of Californians rose from 380,000 to nearly 1.5 million. [12] By the turn of the century, ten years after Vallejo's death and five years after Ruiz de Burton's, Mexicans accounted for no more than 1 or 2 percent of the state population (Almaguer 70–71).

Vallejo's desire to invoke the claims of Californio community clearly derived from the reality of a proportionately diminishing population and the concomitant loss of community land to arriving immigrants. His response, much like Ruiz de Burton's, however, captures both his expression of fear of this demographic shift and his need to (re)assert his conception of Californio (hacienda) community. Through his deferral of disorder onto the outside world (i.e., onto Gold Rush immigrants), Vallejo posits pre-1848 Californio society as a "true community" in the sense of one held together by manners and morals deriving from a commonly held view of reality (Romine 1). Framing his "Memoirs" with the idea of a "patriarchal," "healthy," "moral" Californio community subverted by the corrupting (capitalist) forces of the Gold Rush, early in volume 1 Vallejo sets up the inside/outside dichotomy by citing the harmful influence of immigrant outsiders on "our young people." This and subsequent passages I cite from "Memoirs" must be placed in the same comparative (i.e., South by Southwest) context through which I interpreted Doña Josefa's elegy to her husband in *Squatter*. Like Doña Josefa's commentary, Vallejo's criticism resembles anticapitalist tracts by Southern apologists for the "organic" society of the plantation:

> How fine it would have been, had the vaunted enlightenment which the Americans have brought to California not perverted our patriarchal customs and let down the bars surrounding the morality of our young people. For, however much it may grieve us, we cannot deny that our progeny have to a great extent forgotten the healthy maxims we taught them. This relaxation of healthy morality may be attributed to the contact they have had with people of slight scruples who emigrated to California in the first period of the discovery of the rich gold deposits which caused such a pleasant surprise throughout the world (1: 48).

Vallejo's comments thus represent more than a revisionist reading of an event in U.S. history that had already been transformed into myth by the time that Vallejo narrated his story — and one that would be romanticized by subsequent historians like Bancroft and Frederick Jackson Turner. The passage also constitutes a statement of community self-definition in the face of the all-encompassing crisis in Californio society brought about by the U.S. conquest and its postwar policies.

Vallejo returns to the same point in a lengthy passage at the end of his narrative. Although he acknowledges that the "change of government which took place . . . has resulted in benefit to the commerce and agriculture of the young state," he stresses that it damaged the "morale of the [Mexican] people, whose patriarchal customs have broken down little by little through contact with so many immoral persons who came to this my country from every nook and corner of the known world" (5: 189). Like the above quotation, Vallejo's deceptive grievance masks the intent of the remainder of the passage, which is to project disorder onto the "outside" societies and particularly the U.S. and thereby affirm the positive attributes of pre-1848 Californio community. (The United States is the central target, for it alone had become the dominant influence in California, the final arbiter of community within the former boundaries of Mexican Alta California.) Initially, the passage discusses the treatment of the insane during the early period of U.S. rule as a means of constructing notions of community inclusion and exclusion.

In California in 1849 "there was no asylum in which to care for the insane," notes Vallejo. "[M]iners and emigrants who lost their reason during the first years of North American rule in California were treated more like wild beasts of the desert than like human beings. The raving maniacs were fastened with chains to trees or posts in the stables, and the harmless lunatics were locked up in deserted ships in the harbor" (5: 188). If one interprets this comment not necessarily as historical truth but rather as an effort to assert the differences between community insiders and outsiders, one finds less surprising Vallejo's subsequent claim that "with the exception of two lunatics whom the general government had sent from Mexico," insane persons "had been unknown among us [Californios] since the settlement of Alta California" (188). Although this may very well have been the case in Hispanic and Mexican California, in the context of a lengthy passage listing each Gold Rush immigrant group with the respective social malady that it supposedly introduced to California, these comments instead seem an attempt to "restore" the pre-1848 (hacienda) social order by reestablishing the boundaries of Californio community. It was with "much wonder among us born in the country," continues Vallejo, that two native-born Californios were later deemed insane, for within the former "true community" of the Californios this social problem never existed. And as Vallejo later states, "It is in truth with profound sadness that we reflect that from '48 until '52 the sick and insane received at our hands treatment that very ill befitted the boasted civilization of the century and our humanitarian sentiments" (188). While the pronouns in this last sentence might refer ironically to a new American California collectivity of which Vallejo himself is a member, given the context of the statement it seems clear that "we" and "our" instead express the moral vision of the Californio community. Within the "organic" community of the pre-1848 era, Vallejo suggests, the sick and insane were cared for, whereas under the "modern" U.S. (capitalist) system, they were mistreated (e.g., the insane were tied to trees or locked up on ships).

By positing the Americans as only one among many outsider/immigrant groups that brought social ills to the region, the remainder of the passage illustrates this point by representing the Californio (hacienda) community quite literally under siege by outsiders *in general*. Given the politically charged politics of land entitlement, one might expect Vallejo's concluding passages to draw a bead on the Americans. Instead, Vallejo constructs a model of difference focused on establishing opposition between the pre-1848 Californio (hacienda) community on the one hand, and all of those foreign nations and societies that were represented in California during the Gold Rush on the other (i.e., those which had crossed the boundary marking "inside" from "outside"). Like the above passage, the following litany may be read as a list of actual grievances as well as a statement of the apocalyptic decline of the Californios by the mid 1870s, when Vallejo narrated his story. While the Mormons, according to Vallejo, "professed a religion which is in open conflict with good taste and with moral and political soundness," immigrants from other countries introduced more serious problems to California. "Australia sent us a swarm of bandits who . . . dedicated themselves exclusively to robbery and assault;" Peru "sent us a great number of rascals, begotten in idleness and schooled in vice;" and Mexico "inundated us with a wave of gamblers who had no occupation save that of the card table." France, continues Vallejo, sent "several thousand lying men and corrupt women," Italy "musicians . . . who lost no time in fraternizing with the keepers of gambling-houses and brothels," Chile, "laborers . . . [of whom] many were addicted to drink and gambling," and China "clouds and more clouds of Asiatics and more Asiatics . . . [who were] very harmful to the moral and material development of the country" (5: 184).

Conflating insanity with alcoholism to complete his model of the decline of traditional Californio community, at the end of the passage Vallejo points out that the "great supply of liquors" brought by foreigners created havoc in the post-1848 era. As he puts it, whereas "before the coming of Fremont, we drank only pure liquor, and that in small quantities, and everyone enjoyed good health, tenacious memories, and lively intelligence," after the war and especially during the Gold Rush the situation was very different: "[F]rom France and Germany were introduced great supplies of liquor made up of chemical ingredients and noxious herbs, and these affected the nervous system, clouded the intelligence, and undermined the most robust constitutions, sowing the fatal seeds of a multitude of diseases which were not long in sending to premature graves young men in the flower of their lives" (5: 188–89). This statement adds a new ingredient to Vallejo's discussion. Unlike the earlier comparisons, here "outsiders" not only contributed to the moral decline of community, but also undermined the "memory" and "intelligence" of post-1848 Mexican Californians. Members of the pre-1848 Californio community possessed sound memories and intelligence whereas post-1848 society must confront a tragic loss of both. Given this circumstance, Vallejo's encyclopedic multivolume autobiography thus serves the important function of repudiating this threat to Californio "memory," "intelligence," and "history" in the post-1848 era.

In "Memoirs," the Americans embody all of the social maladies listed above and something more, for not only have they permitted this invasion by outsiders, but they have controlled the discriminatory institutional apparatus which by the mid-1870s had caused the eclipse of the Californio ranchers. The Americans are thus "legal thieves, clothed in the robes of the law, [who] took from us our land, and our houses and without the least scruple enthroned themselves in our homes like so many powerful kings." As Vallejo concludes, "It was our misfortune that these adventurers of evil law were so numerous that it was impossible for us to defend our rights in the courts, since the majority of the judges were squatters and the same could be said of the sheriffs and the juries." Justice for them "was only a word used to sanction robbery" (5: 185).

Like Ruiz de Burton's criticism of capitalist practices, Vallejo's deferral of disorder onto the outside world in these passages carries with it deeply contradictory ideological and cultural meanings. At one level, Vallejo points to the Americans as the embodiment of chaos and disorder because of the very real socioeconomic and cultural threat which the Yankee order posed to the Californio *ranchero* community. As a host of historians have shown, the Gold Rush *was* a period marked by social conflict and disorder and particularly so for the landed Californios whose society was within a span of two years inundated with tens of thousands of landless "foreigners." As *The Squatter and the Don* accurately depicts, after leaving the mines, immigrants who had arrived in 1849–1850 became land-hungry squatters who, with the sanction of the federal and state governments, staked claims on land already occupied by Californio ranchers. Decades-long litigation by squatters and their supporters in the government eventually bankrupted Vallejo, Ruiz de Burton, and most of their fellow Californio ranchers.

But, as in *Squatter*, the communal boundary in "Memoirs" at another level plays a role analogous to that inscribed in Southern plantation texts in that it marks an "already ordered social space . . . inside of which order can and must be actively maintained" (Romine 6). Despite Vallejo's accommodationist politics, like Don Mariano in *The Squatter and the Don*, he was as bound to his traditional agrarian community as were most authors of plantation narratives. This does not diminish the viability and eloquence of his scathing description of U.S. practices in post-1848 California. But, let us recall, Southern plantation and domestic fiction, and the Southern Agrarian movement that in the 1930s drew on this literary tradition, formulated a critique of Northern "industrialist" (read: capitalist) ideology and praxis as trenchant as that which characterizes Vallejo's "Memoirs" or Ruiz de Burton's *The Squatter and the Don*.

Vallejo's project to restore community boundaries marking "inside" from "outside" reminds us, in another way, of the contradictory cultural and ideological impulses underlying Californio claims to "true community." Just after reconfiguring community boundaries in the above passages, Vallejo announces his willingness to integrate into the new social order if the United States would live up to the ideals that had attracted him to its republican form of government. After stating that "in spite of the Treaty of Guadalupe Hidalgo, the Americans have treated the Californians as a conquered people," Vallejo couches his grievance in rhetoric expressing a desire for conciliation with, and inclusion within,

U.S. society. In mistreating the Mexican Californians, he argues, the Americans have refused to recognize them "as [U.S.] citizens who willingly became a part of that great family which, under the protection of that glorious flag that proudly waved at Bunker Hill, defied the attacks of European monarchs who, seated upon their tottering thrones, were casting envious eyes toward California and the other regions embraced within the great federation of the sons of liberty" (5: 190).

In *The Squatter and the Don* and "Memoirs," the "hacienda" functions ultimately as a mimetic image and icon of pre-1848 Californio community. In both of these narratives the "hacienda" not only serves to circumscribe and define this lost community, but, as the elite's symbol and icon of land ownership and social power, it also constitutes the overarching image into which all of the supposed attributes of genteel Californio community have been projected. The "hacienda" as icon and myth emerges from the devastating social effects of U.S. dominance in much the same way that the pastoral icon develops in Southern writing through regional conflict with the North. The impulse to "true community" in Californio texts, as symbolized by the hacienda, constitutes an imaginary resolution to the conflictive socioeconomic processes deriving from the violent siege to traditional agrarian society carried out by the combined forces of capitalist modernity.

Notes

1. Vallejo, "Recuerdos históricos y personales tocante a la alta California" (1874). All paginations refer to the English translation, "Historical and Personal Memoirs Relating to Alta California," trans. Earl R. Hewitt (1875).

2. I draw on Elizabeth Moss's observation that nineteenth-century "southern domestic fiction essentially duplicated [plantation fiction's] setting and cast of characters" (21). As Moss explains, "The correspondences between plantation and southern domestic fiction extended

well beyond [their] superficial similarities. Both literary forms, for example, tapped into readers' apprehensions about the precarious state of southern affairs, stressing the stability of the South and the instability of the North; both lamented the materialism of the modern day; both designated the home, with woman its custodian, as the bedrock of southern civilization; both projected the South as the bastion of national virtue and the North as the nation's ruin. Most important, both the plantation novel and the southern domestic novel were quickly enlisted in the service of the southern cause as southern writers became increasingly convinced that their culture was under attack from northerners, especially northern abolitionists" (21). Examples of plantation novels include Augustus Baldwin Longstreet's *Georgia Scenes* (1835), John Pendleton Kennedy's *Swallow Barn; or, A Sojourn in the Old Dominion* (1832), and Thomas Nelson Page's *In Ole Virginia* (1887). Representative southern domestic novels include Caroline Gilman's *Oracles for Youth* (1852), Caroline Hentz's *Eoline; or, Magnolia Vale* (1852), Augusta Evans's *Beulah* (1859), and Maria McIntosh's *Charms and Counter Charms* (1848). For a recent study of the plantation novel, see Romine. For studies of southern domestic fiction, see Moss and Jones.

3. The hacienda was a semifeudal agrarian institution, dependent on a labor force controlled through debt peonage, which "produced subsistence goods as well as a market surplus and usually contained a blacksmith's shop and often a pottery and carpentry shop as well. Some of the wealthiest haciendas maintained a chapel, although resident priests were seldom present. The largest units covered many square miles and had outlying corrals, line shacks, and some dispersed housing for [laborers and] tenants." Large estates were self-sufficient (i.e., autarkic). These had crops, flocks and herds, wooded areas, flour mills, forges, and workshops. Haciendas "provided the physical focus for both social life and production. The owner's large house dominated the hacienda's residential core" (Burkholder and Johnson 184).

4. *The Squatter and the Don* and "Memoirs" accomplish this by drawing on the cultural memory of the centuries-long ranching and

hacienda presence in the Southwest and Mexico. If the plantation forms the historical foundation of U.S. Southern society and culture, the hacienda may be said to dominate the pre-1900 history of Greater Mexico, that other southern region of North America encompassing present-day Mexico and the Mexican American Southwest. Feudalistic, paternalistic, and patriarchal, from the seventeenth through nineteenth centuries throughout much of this region the hacienda's agrarian economic and cultural order shaped the character of all levels of Hispanic and Mexican society. Although it may appear more remote for contemporary Chicanos and Chicanas than the plantation has been for both white and black Southerners, the hacienda texts that I examine remind us of this colonial institution's historical proximity, illustrating its cultural role for early Mexican American writers as a site of memory and identity. Its conflicted meaning also indicates the heterogeneous historical experiences of Mexican Americans — the descendants of Spanish and North American colonialisms.

5. As John González notes, "The lingering traces of Reconstruction's dramatic restructuring of U.S. nationalism during a rapidly developing regime of capitalist expansion haunt *The Squatter and the Don's* project of renegotiating the class and racial standing of the Californios within the state's own legal, political and economic processes" (33). The novel negotiates the "treacherous parameters of race and class" of the post-Reconstruction period to "create a place within the newly ascendant 'white' nation for the Californios" (30). Hence, in González's reading, Ruiz de Burton "contests not the process of incorporation of California's economy and culture into the national core as such, but rather the social position accorded to the Californios within that capitalist order" (31).

6. Although "race did not stand as a barrier to upward mobility" in Mexican California, the frontier population "denigrated others of darker hue, and tended to 'whiten' themselves as they moved up the social ladder by denying their Indian and black ancestry." Weber points out that "the racial biases of the nouveau riche Californios actually increased . . . in part because they sought to put themselves on an

equal footing with the race-conscious Anglo-American newcomers" (Weber 215).

7. This conception of "true community" indicates contrasting ideological justifications: in Vallejo's work, a vexed relationship to U.S. republicanism, and in Ruiz de Burton's, a longing for a traditional political order modeled after a constitutional, or liberal, monarchy. Ruiz de Burton counters Vallejo's republican political views in several letters written to him in the 1860s and 1870s. See Sánchez and Pita, *Conflicts of Interest*, 215–21.

8. My analysis of Californio texts forms part of a larger study in which I explore the interplay between history and memory in the hacienda as a site of memory in early Mexican American narrative. Sites of memory are symbolic representations of the past that embody the interaction between history and memory. Forms of national or group affiliation, they include geographical places, monuments, historical figures, literary and artistic objects, emblems, commemorations, and other such "sites" of remembrance.

9. Pitt notes that "the spirit, if not the letter, of the treaty promised full protection for the conquered population" (84). Griswold del Castillo draws a similar conclusion. "In the six decades following the ratification of the treaty," he explains, "its provisions regarding citizenship and property were complicated by legislative and judicial interpretations." In the end, "the U.S. application of the treaty to the realities of life in the Southwest violated its spirit" (63). The treaty stated that Mexicans would be "admitted . . . to the enjoyment of all the rights of citizens of the United States according to the principles of the Constitution . . . [and] shall be maintained and protected in the free enjoyment of their liberty and property" (Moquin and Van Doren 185). But its final draft excluded Article X, a proviso which would have protected landowners. Article X stipulated that "[a]ll grants of land made by the Mexican Government or by the competent authorities, in territories previously appertaining to Mexico, and remaining for the future within the limits of the United States, shall be respected as valid, to the same extent that the same grants would be valid, if the

said territories had remained within the limits of Mexico" (Griswold del Castillo 182). As Rosaura Sánchez comments, despite "assurances in appended explanations that the United States had no intention of annulling land titles that were legitimate under Mexican law," without Article X the treaty provided little legal protection for land claimants (*Telling Identities* 275).

10. The novel rarely depicts the world of ranch labor. The story is for the most part set within the parlors of the Alamar hacienda and the similar ranch homes of the Alamars' neighbors.

11. See, for example, Sánchez, *Telling Identities*, and Padilla. Since Hubert H. Bancroft first solicited it as a source for his *History of California*, Vallejo's narrative has served as a key primary source for historians of Spanish and Mexican California.

12. The population of native peoples in the region suffered a more dramatic decline during the same period. In 1769, when the first colonists from New Spain arrived in the frontier north, the native population of Alta California ranged as high as 300,000. Due to introduced diseases, starvation, relocation, forced labor, warfare, and murder, under both the Hispanic/Mexican order and the American, by 1860 the population of native peoples had declined to 30,000 (Anderson, Barbour, and Whitworth 18). In the coastal region where most Spanish and Mexican land grants were located, the native population had fallen from 135,000 to 98,000 between 1770 and 1832 (Monroy 244). By the late nineteenth century, the native population had declined to only some 20,000 survivors (Simmons 48).

The Symptoms of Conquest:
Race, Class, and the Nervous Body
in *The Squatter and the Don*

JENNIFER S. TUTTLE

In the second half of the nineteenth century, physicians, railroad magnates, and real estate developers promoted the conquest and settlement of Alta California by declaring the region a health resort. Its climate and natural features, they maintained, would cure and reinvigorate even the weakest and most jaded city-dweller. Capitalizing on the dramatic rise in rates of nervous breakdown suffered by the eastern elite, the growing tourist and real estate industries constructed California as a curative, Edenic haven for the fashionably "nervous" eastern establishment. Nervousness, technically called "neurasthenia," was associated not only with upper-class status but also with whiteness, which aided the boosters of eastern tourism and settlement in cementing the Anglo American seizure of Alta California. Less immediate than military victory, less explicit than the Treaty of Guadalupe Hidalgo, such health-based campaigns nevertheless helped to solidify the military and political conquest effected in 1848.

During the 1860s, San Francisco's prestigious Lick House Hotel became one site of this phenomenon, commissioning the artist Thomas Hill to provide images of California scenery for its posh dining hall. Hill's eleven panels depicting California's wilderness "form[ed] a panorama around diners who . . . could imagine themselves on the slopes of the Sierra or in groves of mammoth trees" (Perry 117). It is poignantly ironic that the Lick House was also one of three hotels frequented by María Amparo Ruiz de Burton during the 1870s as, recently widowed, she assumed the burden of defending her Jamul ranch from the encroachments of squatters. Between 1870 and 1878, she spent time in both San Francisco and San Diego while engaging in legal struggles with individuals who had claimed over half of the land at Rancho Jamul — struggles she surely contemplated while dining beneath the Lick House's panoramic views marketing California's landscape to Anglo American tourists and settlers.[1]

Ruiz de Burton's legal and financial troubles would continue, of course, until her death in 1895. Her second novel, *The Squatter and the Don* (1885), inspired by her own experience, seeks to contest official histories of the conquest and dispossession of the Californios. It targets not only squatters, who attempted to claim land previously granted to Californios by the Spanish and Mexican governments, but also, and more fundamentally, corruption in the U.S. court system and legislature, along with monopoly capitalism. While her critique of historical and legal narratives about this conquest has been widely acknowledged (see, e.g., Goldman, "Romance," as well as Sánchez and Pita's introduction to *Squatter*), her novel also challenges medical narratives that enabled and justified conquest, particularly the theories and treatments for neurasthenia that underlay California boosterism. Though Ruiz de Burton's engagement with this aspect of conquest has for the most part gone unremarked, her invocations of medical concepts and treatments, and especially of nervousness, are a crucial part of her revisionary project. Portraying squatters, legislators, and the railroad monopoly as agents of contagion and contamination, she refutes the widespread notion that such enterprises are associated with healing and regeneration. Moreover, she appropriates explicitly the discourse of nervousness that had been used to dispossess and disinherit the Californios, revising it as part of her attempt to reclaim the race and class status that had been compromised by U.S. conquest of the region.

The discourse of neurasthenia forms a subtle but resonant frame for Ruiz de Burton's novel. She invokes it initially in chapter 2 when introducing the character of James Mechlin, a well-to-do

Anglo American banker from New York who moves to San Diego in a last-ditch effort to cure himself of this illness. "He had lost his health," we are told, "by a too close application to business," a pursuit which had left him "a living skeleton" (67). This description of Mechlin would have been entirely familiar to American readers of the 1880s, since it captures succinctly a phenomenon widespread in U.S. culture at that time. Mechlin would have been viewed as part of what was considered an epidemic of such ailments among Anglo Americans of the eastern elite classes, who suffered physical debility, it was believed, because they had overtaxed their nervous systems. In 1869, American neurologist George Miller Beard coined the term "neurasthenia" to denote this depletion of nervous energy; the terms "nervous weakness" and "nervous prostration" were also used frequently to refer to this nerveless state.[2] In his 1881 book, *American Nervousness: Its Causes and Consequences*, Beard expressed alarm at what appeared to be a disturbing increase of "American nervousness" among the elite, those white, privileged, professional classes of Americans living in the northeastern cities, whom he called the "brain-workers" (ix). Along with Beard, many physicians and lay people believed the disease was caused by overwork, especially overuse of the brain in the professions. James Mechlin's illness, then, resulting from a "too close application to business," echoes widespread warnings by late-nineteenth-century physicians about the physical costs of such intellectual and economic pursuits.

These concerns about excessive devotion to business and the professions applied, of course, mainly to elite white men. Yet women of the same social group faced similar medical warnings. White middle- and upper-class women were viewed according to medical orthodoxy as pathological by nature: Their inherently delicate and excitable nervous systems would break down from the slightest mental, physical, or emotional strain. "From the cradle to the grave," warned gynecologist H. W. Streeter, "every habit of civilized woman as a class tends to debility" (qtd. in Briggs 254). Significantly, this formulation leaves out women of color and working-class women, who generally were viewed as "uncivilized" and therefore naturally healthy, less refined, and thus immune to suffering and well suited for lives of labor.[3] These medicalized definitions of "natural" female ill health went hand in hand, then, with cultural ideals of womanhood, informing class- and race-based notions of beauty and behavior. As Diane Price Herndl explains, "The cultural norms for [upper-class white] women encouraged frailty and delicacy; robust health was thought to be the working woman's mark, not the leisured lady's. The middle-class [white] woman was encouraged from childhood to view herself as weaker and less healthy than her brothers" (23). Hence there was a profusion of pale, nervous, swooning, and dying white heroines in fiction from this period who represented a leisured, race-coded, highly romanticized model of invalid womanhood that helped to define gender, class, and racial identities.

Despite their worries over the prevalence of neurasthenia among women and men of the middle and upper classes, however, physicians viewed it as a sign of progress. Medical theories of the disease held that its high incidence among urban, white, privileged-class Northeasterners was directly related to the sufferers' positions at the forefront of American cultural and economic development. A nervous constitution signified, to Beard, "the civilized, refined, and educated rather than . . . the barbarous and low-born" (26). Neurasthenia and its milder, more fashionable form, "nervousness," were thus coded by caste: They were marks of whiteness and high class status, of a social superiority grounded in biology. Operating on an individual level to secure elite status for its sufferers, the discourse of neurasthenia was also, then, inherently nationalistic, the epidemic of "American Nervousness" providing a "scientific" justification for American national supremacy.

Not surprisingly, the nationalistic aspects of neurasthenic discourse went hand in hand with the forces of Manifest Destiny in the late nineteenth century. Ruiz de Burton was all too aware of this fact. When James Mechlin, the Anglo banker in *The Squatter and the Don*, falls ill with neurasthenia, he attempts to cure it in exactly the way that physicians of the 1880s were recommending to the leisure class. Vainly seeking "rest and relaxation" in Florida, Italy, and the South of France, Mechlin is on the point of giving up when "a friend . . . whose health had been restored in Southern California, advised him to try the salubrious air of San Diego." Once there, "his health improved so rapidly that he made up his mind to buy a country place and make San Diego his home" (67). This scenario parallels strikingly an account in Charles Nordhoff's *California for Health, Pleasure, and Residence* (1882), one of many promotions intended for an eastern audience and funded by land and railroad interests. The chapter "Southern California for In-valids" tells of a tubercular man who finds health and vigor, and therefore a new home, in California, after searching unsuccessfully for a cure in Nice and South Carolina (77–78). Dr. A. M. Shew, in his aptly titled *California as a Health Resort* (1885), attests as well that California is superior even to Europe (a popular destination for the sickly upper classes) in its effectiveness as a natural sanitarium (3). Manuel M. Martín Rodríguez has noted that Mechlin's curative move to California can be read as an invocation of this promotional literature, which "portrayed California as the land of milk and honey in order to encourage its colonization by Anglo Americans" (42).

Playing on medical rhetoric, such as Beard's, that criticized the urban, industrialized East for causing illness and cultural malaise, the marketers of California touted the state's "semi-tropical" climate, which was promised to stimulate growth and health in both human and plant life.[4] Tracts such as the railroad-sponsored *Semi-Tropical California* (1874) and *California, the Cornucopia of the World* (1870, whose cover promised "A Climate for Health & Wealth") were aimed explicitly at audiences in the East and Midwest. California developers made connections between horti-culture in the state and "advanced civilization," "moral rectitude," and "the good breeding of human stock" (Perry 88). Ruiz de Burton plays on this discourse in her novel: After moving to San Diego, "Mr. Mechlin devoted himself to cultivating trees and flowers, and his health was bettered every day" (67).

Though much of this boosterism argued only implicitly for the superiority of Anglo American culture over Hispanic and Mexican cultures, some linked the promise of health in California explicitly with such an ethnocentric viewpoint. Rodríguez cites Shew's *California as a Health Resort* to demonstrate this tendency. Dr. Shew urges his readers, eastern physicians, to send their patients west. Promising such readers that it is within their power to make California an Edenic space for individual, national, and implicitly racial regeneration, he opines, "At no distant day, when it shall have been cut up into small farms and occupied by thrifty Eastern people, we may expect a veritable Paradise on earth, and such a Sanitarium for invalids as the world has not known" (Shew 8; qtd. in Rodríguez 43). Shew links explicitly the capitalist and agricultural forms of land use, the ethnic stereotypes of Californios as lazy and spendthrift, as well as the racist philosophy urging settlement of the West by eastern (read: Anglo) racial "stock," that underwrote the U.S. conquest of California. By incorporating all of these things into a medical argument, of course, he grounds them in incontrovertible "science."

In her attempt to grant voice and agency to the conquered Californios, María Amparo Ruiz de Burton deftly invokes health tourism and the promotion of Anglo American migration to California, using the discourse against itself. For example, though settlement by Anglo Americans contributed greatly to the displacement of Ruiz de Burton and the Californios more generally, her Anglo bankers, the Mechlins, who are associated explicitly with some of the medicalized arguments for settlement, are viewed favorably in *The Squatter and the Don*. As Rosaura Sánchez and Beatrice Pita have explained, this is the case because, through their friendship and intermarriage with the Alamars (Ruiz de Burton's Californio protagonists), they help to establish the affinity between a Californio and Anglo elite during a time when the Californios' access to such status was in question (25).[5] As "settlers," not "squatters," the Mechlins have purchased a squatter's claim on the Alamar rancho, rather than contesting directly the Alamar claim to the land and simply appropriating it accordingly.[6] Some aspects of settlement, then, are viewed favorably in the novel, but only when they ensure participation of the Californios in the new economy, as Rodríguez has noted. The "Alamars' effort to retain their land," he argues, "is depicted . . . as a will to participate in the development and exploitation of the new opportunities for enrichment brought about by the U.S. economy, conscious of the fact that such action will enable them to preserve their social status" (43). What the Alamars seek, then, is social, political, and economic legitimacy as "Spano-Americans" (*Squatter* 65).

Scholars generally have concurred that this assimilation of "Spanish" into "American" is one of Ruiz de Burton's central concerns, writing as she was after the Californios' whiteness had been threatened by their lowered class status, the two being contingent categories. The "whiteness" (and hence U.S. citizenship) granted to Mexicans by the California State Constitutional Convention in 1849 was dependent, of course, not only upon claims to European ancestry but also upon such factors as social class (Almaguer 55). As portrayed in the novel, explain Sánchez and Pita, "discourses of nation or ethnicity . . . are overdetermined by discourses of class" (21). "Thus," writes John M. González, "the decline of the Californios as a landed elite by the 1880s signified not just demotion into the ranks of wage-laborers but also loss of the privileges of 'whiteness' maintained under previous negotiations of hegemony" (36). Indeed, the Alamar family, who had called themselves "Dons" and "native Californians," are forced after dispossession to share class position with those indigenous peoples whose labor had previously enabled their claims to racial and social superiority (Luis-Brown 819). The "novel's immediate cultural work," asserts González, "is to make visible the Californios as 'white' and to obscure the indigenous labor that made possible this translation" (27). Thus it is not only the Alamars' whiteness (and hence Americanness) that is threatened by their economic decline; their claim to superior "native" status, by which they established their own colonial legitimacy, is also in jeopardy. As a result, to use José Aranda's words, Ruiz de Burton is "willing to wage a rhetorical war on her conquerors but also anxious to re-assume the privileges of a colonialist" ("Contradictory Impulses" 554). In these complex maneuvers, then, Ruiz de Burton attempts to erase the Spanish and Mexican oppression of people indigenous to California by assuming the position of subaltern and "native." This gesture encompasses her appropriation of victim status for the "contaminated" and "sickened" Californios that more truthfully belonged to California's native populations lacking immunity to European diseases and subject to the violence of conquest, for whom contact with Spanish explorers and colonizers was literally deadly. At the same time, she allies her Californio protagonists with Anglo Americans and against others of Spanish Mexican descent (particularly those in the working class), belying the *mestizo* status of most Californios.[7]

While settlers like the upper-class Mechlins are welcomed by Ruiz de Burton's Alamar family because of their rhetorical function as reinforcers of the Californios' elite class and racial status, then, squatters are an entirely different matter. Along with corrupt lawyers, judges, legislators and railroad monopolists, squatters are a destructive force in the novel, the agents of the Californios' dispossession. While such corrupt individuals and organizations touted California's curative properties as a way of consolidating their own power, Ruiz de Burton reverses this discourse, marking them in her novel as malignant forces that contaminate the region and sicken its "native" inhabitants.[8] Ruiz de Burton indicates the pernicious effects of this promotional discourse by putting it in the mouths of squatters scheming to seize the Californios' land. Singing the praises of San Diego in terms that echo medical tracts, Mr. Gasbang gushes to the newly arrived William Darrell: "You never hear of any malarial fevers in San Diego, sir, never. Our perfect climate, the fine sloping ground of our town site, our eucalyptus trees, sea breezes and mountain air, make San Diego a most healthy little city" (70). As this explicit connection between squatters and health tourism suggests, Ruiz de Burton's narrative is indeed, as Anne E. Goldman has written, "at cross-purposes with the ethnocentric, blindly optimistic boosterism" so predominant during the period ("Romance" 72), notwithstanding the novel's favorable portrayal of upper-class settlers like the Mechlins. Despite Gasbang's professed interest in the health of San Diego, he, like other squatters in the novel, is precisely what makes it unhealthy for the Californios. Ruiz de Burton suggests these invaders' association with predation, illness, and contamination through descriptions of the squatter Hughes as having a "sickly smile" (211) and of Gasbang as a "malignant spirit" (212); young George Mechlin's revelation that Don Mariano "will recuperate" if "he is rid of" them reinforces the point (152). The squatters threaten to bring down the Don and his entire aristocratic family, whose fall into poverty is imagined as an illness.[9]

Victim to the squatters and, more generally, the corruption of California's legal, judicial, and legislative systems, the Alamar family faces financial ruin, the loss of its land, and thus a decline in class and race status. In addition to indicting the forces that cause such dispossession, Ruiz de Burton seeks in her novel to reassert the Alamars' elite racial and economic status in a variety of ways, not the least of which is her invocation and transformation of the discourses of nervousness that had been used to encourage and justify conquest. The Alamars' delicate constitutions, and the illnesses they suffer as a result of losing their land, mark them as both genteel and white, despite their economic circumstances. They fall ill with increasing frequency throughout the second half of the novel, along with Ruiz de Burton's sympathetic upper-class Anglo characters, a phenomenon that serves as a constant reminder of their whiteness and refinement even as they lose the outward markers of aristocratic status.

Certainly, like many elite women of their day, the upper-class Alamar women use the discourse of invalidism to negotiate and articulate family and social relationships. Though they often invoke nervousness on a rhetorical level, however, the Alamar women also fall ill in earnest. Not surprisingly, the "naturally refined" Mercedes (187), of the "pale cheek" and "golden hair" (240), is the central character in this invalid drama, since she is the blue-eyed daughter whose marriage to the wealthy Anglo Clarence Darrell will help to redeem her family's caste. Like any self-respecting heroine of nineteenth-century American literature, Mercedes swoons and falls ill with fever and delirium when faced with emotional distress — in this case, when Clarence breaks their engagement out of shame over his father's leanings toward squatterism (257). Further enervated by events equally tied to her family's legal and financial troubles, her "convalescence [is] very slow" (276).

The association of Mercedes's illnesses with whiteness and upper-class status is enhanced by the fact that in her breakdowns, she mirrors the Anglo character of Alice Darrell, Clarence's sister and the daughter of high-born Mary Moreneau Darrell. Alice, too, faints due to the trauma of Clarence's departure (249), suffers a "raging fever" with delirium, remains "so nervous, . . . that she was almost in convulsions" (262), and endures a long convalescence (276). Alice's brother confirms the pairing when he laments that "Miss Mercedes and Alice are sick — sick with grief" (263). Mercedes's delicate nervous system is agitated subsequently by her father's troubles, which, due to her hypersensitive, nervous nature, she foresees in a dream. Upon his death, of course, she is "again prostrated with fever" (305). Significantly, each of her collapses into illness is brought about by the vagaries of conquest, from her father's conflicts with squatters that threaten her own marital prospects, to his eventual defeat by the more insidious forces of monopoly capitalism. Indeed, the latter tragedy causes illness among a whole network of women: Don Mariano's death is followed shortly by James Mechlin's grief-induced suicide, and this results in the women falling ill en masse. "Mrs. Mechlin, Doña Josefa and Mercedes were . . . in their beds," we are told, "suffering with nervous prostration and night fevers" (312). Ruiz de Burton thus clearly associates her Californianas with the nervous Anglo heroines of American fiction, grounding their race and class status firmly within the elite segments of American society; in the same gesture, she manages to indict the forces that led to her characters' physical and economic decline.

Not surprisingly, Ruiz de Burton's own life was rich fodder for her portrayal of nervous women characters. Certainly, it has been widely noted that *The Squatter and the Don* was inspired by Ruiz de Burton's experiences; Frederick Bryant Oden, for example, traces several parallels between the two, explaining that particular aspects of the novel bear "an uncanny resemblance to the travails that Burton encountered at Jamul" (153). Between 1870, when she returned newly widowed to the West Coast, and her death in 1895, "she engaged in a nearly continuous saga of bitter, complicated, and expensive litigation" over land (117). Though it has heretofore been overlooked, however, the issue of nervousness is another important link between Ruiz de Burton's self-construction and her fictional characterizations. In letters to some of her major correspondents, Ruiz de Burton frequently mentions her own illness and nervousness, as well as those of her daughter, Nellie, tying this incapacitation explicitly to their struggles over dispossession. As early as 1869, writing to her longtime friend Mariano Guadalupe Vallejo, she confesses that she is "almost desperate and half sick of worry due to my business, from the difficulty I have receiving news from San Diego" (20 October 1869; qtd. in Oden 102). "I am *very, very, sad*, believe me, and there are times when the powers of suffering overwhelm me," she continues in 1870, "and I feel myself grow weak. I feel a . . . mental loss of nerve" (21 April 1870; qtd. in Oden 107).

Throughout the next two decades, she would continue to write of herself in terms of illness caused by her misfortunes. "I fret & suffer & toil & pass weary days & sleepless nights," she complained to George Davidson in 1875.[10] She wrote to Davidson in 1880: "And finances! Oh! the sick finances! how they did sicken me!" (26 July). In 1886, she reiterated that her struggles to regain her land and position, which required frequent travel away from San Diego, were "killing me slowly but sure" (2 January). If the San Diego *Tribune-Sun* is to be believed, such suffering may indeed have been on her mind while she was penning *The Squatter and the Don*, for it was reported that "[d]uring this period of writing, she 'was very nervous and went into tantrums at the slightest disturbance' " (Oden 179).

Ruiz de Burton's descriptions of her daughter Nellie's illnesses likewise span many years. Writing to Davidson from Rancho Jamul in 1880, she describes Nellie's first breakdown in terms that suggest striking similarities to Mercedes Alamar:

> She . . . has been *very ill* indeed since the 17th of February. . . . We brought her here on the 25th of March, [and] she had to be carried in & out of the carriage. . . . It was all brought about by her getting out of bed in her bare feet and taking a fearful cold, and this after being sick, weak, greatly depressed, for months before. I know that if she had not undermined her constitution by fretting and brooding over adverse circumstances, she would not have been so utterly prostrated by the shock she received when she took that violent cold. Thus, you see my dear friend, how those who have forced adverse circumstances upon us, keep on, bringing still more misfortunes by a natural sequence & result of their atrocious, inhuman, rapacity. (15 July)[11]

Ten years later, she would report to Davidson that "Nellie's neuralgia has not left her. I wish I could take her away for a while, she suffers continuously" (7 July 1890); and again, in 1891, she reiterates, "My Nellie is still a martir [*sic*]" to neuralgia (12 May). Ruiz de Burton's framing of her family's misfortunes in terms of nervousness and disease, then, not only provides insight into her fictional characterizations (particularly of her women characters), but also suggests that the discourse of nervousness was an important aspect of her own variegated attempts to construct herself and her fellow Californios in the terms of elite American whiteness.

Even more striking than Ruiz de Burton's nervous female characters are her nervous men. Sánchez and Pita have acknowledged the importance of the men's illnesses in the novel, arguing that "the crippling and freezing of the Californios is a motif woven throughout the novel and serves as a metaphor for the political disempowerment and economic choke-hold brought down upon" them (22). In addition to its metaphorical function, however, I would argue that male incapacitation is a compensatory strategy in the novel, allowing the Californios to claim precisely the class (and race) status they seemingly have lost. The patriarch Don Mariano, first weakened by pneumonia contracted while reduced to working as a "vaquero" (229), then suffers "a congestive chill" after an unsuccessful appeal for help to the corrupt Gov. Leland Stanford (300). Finally succumbing to nervous collapse, Don Mariano dies with the pitiful cry, "The sins of our legislators have brought us to this!" (304). Though this ultimate failure is a mark of his economic decline, however, it also signifies his redemption in terms of caste. Clarence makes this explicit, saying that the Don's "disappointment" over the railroad "preyed upon his mind; it saddened, worried and sickened him until it utterly undermined his health and broke down his nervous system" (331). His weak nervous system only strengthens his family's claims to whiteness and aristocratic status.[12]

Don Mariano's sons, Victoriano and Gabriel, are likewise made invalids by their fall in class status. Working alongside his father as a vaquero, Victoriano falls to hysterical, and hence nervous, incapacitation. The narrator confirms that "[w]ork broke him down" (317):

after being caught in a snowstorm while driving cattle, Victoriano loses all feeling and usefulness below his knees. Emasculated by his illness, Victoriano, dubbed "the invalid," must learn again how to walk (280). Despite these signs of recovery, however, he suffers relapses whenever he attempts any form of manual labor. Such invalidism provides ample opportunities for him to both criticize the way in which his reduction to manual laborer associates him with the subhuman status ascribed to Indians and squatters in the novel, and to reassert his aristocratic status. Though complaining frequently of "my mean, crippled legs, my ridiculous kangaroo legs" (328), he counters this slide into proletarian status with the oft-repeated line, "I am a miserable chicken from my knees down, but a perfect gentleman from my knees up" (279).

Unlike his brother and father, Gabriel suffers from a more clearly organic cause, since he was injured while pursuing a trade. Having lost his position at a San Francisco bank because of his family crises, "Gabriel was trying to be a mason, and working as a common day laborer at two dollars per day" (317), when he fell from a ladder and was buried under a pile of bricks. Much has been made of Gabriel's injury, coming as it does as a result of his slide from the position of Don to bank clerk to manual laborer. "In that hod full of bricks," reveals the narrator, "not only his own sad experience was represented, but the *entire history* of the native Californians *of Spanish descent* was epitomized. Yes, Gabriel carrying his hod full of bricks up a steep ladder was a symbolic representation of his race. The natives of Spanish origin, having lost all their property, must henceforth be hod carriers" (her emphasis; 325). Gabriel has lost outward status as upper class, which also threatens his whiteness: "The fact that Gabriel was a *native Spaniard*, [his wife Lizzy] saw plainly, militated against them. If he had been rich, his nationality could have been forgiven, but no one will willingly tolerate a *poor native Californian*" (her emphasis; 324). Lizzy comes to understand that "a well-to-do native Californian is not viewed in the same way as a poor one" (Sánchez and Pita 37). Nevertheless, Gabriel's protracted status as an "invalid" (328) has a cachet that allows Ruiz de Burton to reaffirm his inherent whiteness, refinement, and "natural nobility" (325).

The Alamar men's debilitation is, then, a device that serves both to indict those who caused the fall of the Californios and to recuperate the protagonists' lost status. Sánchez and Pita affirm that the " 'incapacitation' of men, and thus their emasculation, in the novel serves . . . as a symbolic act to reproduce the handicap of an entire collectivity" (46). Furthermore, in having all of the Alamar men fall ill as a result of overwork, Ruiz de Burton is invoking the most commonly understood cause of neurasthenia among the white upper classes. Yet while the latter were seen to succumb to nervous prostration through excessive intellectual and professional work, the Alamars break down from the inverse cause: too much physical labor, for which they are not constitutionally suited. Victoriano's illness, for example, results from his having "worked very hard, in fact, entirely too hard for one so unused to labor" (317). Thus, Ruiz de Burton's revelation that "work broke him down" is a powerful inversion of the way such a phrase was often used — to denote the "too close application to business" embodied by James Mechlin. Ruiz de Burton turns the discourse of nervousness on its head, invoking its power to ascribe elite class and race status, but appropriating it as well as a direct critique of the economic conquest of the Californios.

In making the Alamars' economic decline the cause of their physical deterioration, then, Ruiz de Burton indicts the multiple forces that contributed to her people's dispossession: "it was a noted fact, well recognized by" the Alamars and their fellow aristocrats, the Mechlins, "that misfortunes made them all more or less physically ill" (*Squatter* 315). Yet even more profoundly, in linking financial ruin with the Alamars' nervous illnesses and organic injuries, Ruiz de Burton is able to transform that which would ordinarily preclude their inclusion in elite Anglo America into evidence of their essential and incontrovertible belonging: she grounds their class and race status in their weak nerves and delicate constitutions, literally locating it in the very fiber of their being. Thus while an Eastern-dominated theory of nervousness promoted Anglo colonization of California as healthful and restorative, Ruiz de Burton's complex appropriation of this discourse identifies the same colonial process as literally "sickening," turning these symptoms of conquest toward an assertion of her own people's status as white, aristocratic, and "native," and so entitled to retain their position as a colonial elite.

Notes

My sincere thanks go to Anne Elizabeth Goldman and Amelia María de la Luz Montes for their editorial support and advice, and to José Aranda, whose insightful suggestions helped me to develop this essay into its present form. I am also very grateful for the Historical Society of Southern California/Haynes Research Stipend, which made possible my research at the Bancroft Library. Finally, I thank the Library itself for permission to quote from their George Davidson Papers.

1. For discussion of these issues, see Frederick Bryant Oden, "The Maid of Monterey: The Life of María Amparo Ruiz de Burton, 1832–1895," 99 n. 12, and 108–9.

2. For extended discussions of the cultural and medical phenomenon of neurasthenia, see also Diane Price Herndl, *Invalid Women: Figuring Feminine Illness in American Fiction and Culture, 1840–1940*; Tom Lutz, *American Nervousness, 1903: An Anecdotal History*; and Barbara Sicherman, "The Uses of a Diagnosis: Doctors, Patients, and Neurasthenia."

3. For a discussion of the ways that theories of nervousness were coded by race, particularly with respect to women, see Laura Briggs, "The Race of Hysteria: 'Overcivilization' and the 'Savage' Woman in Late Nineteenth-Century Obstetrics and Gynecology."

4. For foundational discussions of tourism and promotional discourses about California, see Earl Pomeroy, *In Search of the Golden*

West: The Tourist in Western America, and Kevin Starr, *Americans and the California Dream, 1850–1915*.

5. Although contributors to this volume refer to the Alamar family in the plural as the "Alamars," in her novel Ruiz de Burton uses the Spanish spelling of "Alamares."

6. As Sánchez and Pita point out in their 1997 introduction, Ruiz de Burton is careful to distinguish the two categories in her novel, "both on the basis of legality as well as intent" (23).

7. Ruiz de Burton's troubled relation to the position of subaltern and the implications of this for her placement in a canon of Chicana/o studies have been a question of some debate. Aranda offers a useful summary of the issue.

8. I would like to thank José Aranda for suggesting this line of interpretation to me.

9. Although Ruiz de Burton's squatters are sickening to others, they are denied nervous status in the novel, presumably as a way of confirming their lowly nature and denying them access to the whiteness she sought to reserve for the Californio and Anglo elite. She is more generous with William Darrell, whose unstable class position is acknowledged in his physical illnesses, which combine a vulnerable "constitution" (237) with injuries sustained through squatterlike behavior (228, 266).

10. Ruiz de Burton, letter to George Davidson, 4 December 1875, George Davidson Papers, box 4, Bancroft Library, University of California, Berkeley. All letters to Davidson cited in this essay come from this collection.

11. I would like to thank Anne E. Goldman for her help in tracking down Ruiz de Burton's references to Nellie's illnesses.

12. Just as Mercedes's illnesses are paralleled by those of a nervous Anglo character, it is important to note that the Alamar men's ailments are echoed in the sufferings of James and George Mechlin as well as Clarence Darrell.

❧ 2 ❧

Reading Race and Nation in
Who Would Have Thought It?

Beasts in the Jungle:
Foreigners and Natives in Boston

ANNE ELIZABETH GOLDMAN

Two Portraits of Parochial Boston

The types and faces bore them out; the people before me were gross aliens to a man and they were in serene and triumphant possession. Nothing, as I say, could have been more effective for figuring the hitherward bars of a grating through which I might make out, far-off in space, "my" small homogenous Boston of the more interesting time. ☙ Henry James, *The American Scene* (172)

The doctor's most unnatural liking for foreigners . . . was the cause of the doctor's sending Isaac to be a good-for-nothing clerk in sinful Washington, among foreigners, when he could have remained in virtuous New England. . . . [I]mpelled by that liking, the doctor betook himself to California, which is yet full of "natives." ☙ María Amparo Ruiz de Burton, *Who Would Have Thought It?* (8)

I was halfway between Cheyenne and Laramie driving east on I-80 when I saw the sign for "Little America." I remember Wyoming from the summer my family spent on a dude ranch near Jackson Hole when I was nine. Together with my brothers and sister, I rode slow ponies around a corral and wore out a pair of heavy-heeled, tan-colored cowboy boots I kept in my closet for years afterwards. Now, thirty years later, I thought I might buy another pair at this truck stop. But the view opening up around the curve of the exit smothered my nostalgia: faux colonial red brick buildings cluttered the wide horizon, disparaging its booted and hatted visitors as ill suited for the occasion — Paul Revere's ride? The battle

75

of Lexington and Concord? — the architecture revisited. Twenty-
five hundred miles away and four thousand feet higher than the
crooked Concord streets, surrounded by tumbleweeds rather than
the unfurling fronds of Boston ferns, the iconography for "America" remained faithful to what Henry James calls in *The Bostonians*
"the heroic age of New England life . . . the reading of Emerson
and the frequentation of Tremont Temple" (157).

If popular wisdom frames regionalism and urbanity as a contradiction in terms (consider the visual logic of Little America,
which grafts a New England frieze onto a Wyoming truck stop
to reassure shoppers that what they purchase here measures up to
the "national" standard), the critical imagination likewise characterizes region as rural retreat. But what happens if we regionalize
an urban center like Boston? James's "homogenous Boston of the
more interesting time" is clearly an invented geography, the sort
Amy Kaplan calls "the projection of a desire for a space outside
of history, untouched by change" (252). For the expatriate writer,
Walden Pond is a reservoir for memory and nostalgia; at the same
time, the "deep Concord rusticity" is a "medium for our national
drama" (*American Scene* 195). In *The American Scene*, by contrast,
the center is itself painted with local color. Here, as in *The Bostonians*, James eulogizes the "native" American as an endangered
species in his own birthplace: "what the old New England spirit
may still . . . give; of what may yet remain, for productive scrap-
ing, of the formula of the native Puritanism educated" (178–79).
Set in opposition to James's Italian, Irish, black, and Jewish "fla-
grant foreigner[s]" (196), the Puritan remains the "ghost of old
social orders," of "a closed circle that would find itself happy
enough if only it could remain closed enough" (*American Scene* 21),
notwithstanding its narrow political parameters, James's lament
locates the placeless "distended industrial nation" (Kaplan 251), of
contemporary critical imagining, assigning it distinct geographical coordinates. His unapologetic insistence on keeping the circle
"closed enough" corrects scholarly representations of nationalist

discourse that forget its local origins and mythify it as a master narrative.

In this essay I juxtapose James's and Ruiz's parochial portraits of Boston in order to outline a critical methodology that refuses to reduce the productive tension between American regions and the federal polity to a question of center and margin. Coupling *The Bostonians* with *Who Would Have Thought It?* encourages us to reappraise the stratified oppositions through which we conventionally interpret narrative. Read side by side, correspondences between James and Ruiz de Burton clarify themselves. However distinct their arguments, both writers satirize "the Puritan code" (*Bostonians* 36), drawing on a raced iconography to establish the city's parameters. James's "gross aliens" (figured in *The American Scene* as the "remorseless Italian," the "Jew in a dusky back-shop," and the "tatterdemalion darkies" [197, 195, 276]) have made Boston and New York uncomfortable places for Emersonian natives precisely because such "immigrants" are at home there. Like James's interlopers, the "Indians, Mexicans, or Californians" (9) of Ruiz de Burton's *Who Would Have Thought It?* are indigenous foreigners; American citizens who, from the point of view of the "blue Presbyterians" satirized here, can never be Americans. Both the New Englander and the Californian play upon the regional character of literary abbreviations for national identity, describing Boston as a parochial location from which to examine the contested term "American." The focus on movement into Boston by immigrants racialized in *The American Scene, The Bostonians*, and *Who Would Have Thought It?* and excursions out of the city by Yankees who question the equation of its parameters with national borders, clarifies the constructed nature of these dividing lines. I wish to take a closer look at the paths James and Ruiz de Burton traverse in and out of New England and the United States in *The Bostonians* (1885) and *Who Would Have Thought It?* (1872) to explore the implications of thinking "regionally" about national conflicts like the Civil War and the 1846–48 war between the United States and Mexico. In both books, national identity develops from regional formations: Basil Ransom is a pale substitute for the "tatterdemalion darkies" who migrate north after the Civil War, the transplanted southerner whom James uses to embody the nation's "black" contradictions and, in so doing, to defuse the immigrant threat. Lola Medina is also an embodiment of regional conflicts, a young Californiana who in going east occupies the paternal heart of the "blue Presbyterians" (55) of Boston and through whom Ruiz de Burton yokes together conflicts over race and land. Like James's peregrinations, Ruiz's interregional plots suggest we should look more critically at the way English departments package American literary history by assigning distinct regional coordinates to political movements.

A Foreign Beast in the (Urban) Jungle: The Bostonians

While James invokes a gendered metaphor to characterize *The Bostonians* as an American tale, his equation of femininity and nationalism is disingenuous, since Ransom's forays into his cousin's Boston drawing room are not only masculine predations but also regional agitations of "closed circles." James reminds us again and again of Ransom's "Southern complexion" (162) and of his consequent inability to cultivate "the artistic sense" so evident in the "interior" of Olive Chancellor's house, a feminine space whose "organized privacy," books, and "culture" make it "Bostonian" (15). Like *Who Would Have Thought It?* which uses the battle of the sexes to parody military exercises so as to make visible the raced contours of American life, *The Bostonians* is a novel of manners that exploits gender as an in-house metaphor for more "public" arguments between "species" (157). James's satire on the misguided adventures of the suffragettes, I wish to argue, also allows him to obliquely ward off the encroachments of black "foreigners" (26).

If the soul of New York finds concrete expression in the upraised hand of the Statue of Liberty, the mind of Boston is incorporated in spinster suffragettes like the "frumpy little missionary," Miss

Birdseye (157), and "the little medical lady," Doctor Prance, who is a "perfect example of the "Yankee female": "[s]pare, dry, hard, without a curve, an inflection or a grace" (36). This New England answer to England's Florence Nightingale is refracted through the "unregenerate imagination" (36) of Basil Ransom. But James endorses this plainness as well; to speak of the "Yankee female" in this book is to be redundant, for we don't see a single male in its environs. Doctor Prance and Miss Birdseye make up the "last link[s] in a tradition" (157), that originally masculine golden age of New England in which Emerson figures so prominently. Since New England men have migrated from the drawing room into the boardroom, Boston's interiors have become peopled only by "the sex."

This is how Miss Birdseye's frail form comes to embody Culture, and why James taxonomies her death so elaborately. When this American vestal virgin has passed, the "unquenched flame of her transcendentalism" (157) will have nothing to feed upon. Transcendentalism characterizes the "air and 'tone' " of Boston (*American Scene* 178), but Margaret Fuller is not included in the pantheon; her absence in *The Bostonians* as a reference for the "modern maidens" who cluster around Miss Birdseye speaks more loudly than does Verena Tarrant in her New York stage appearances. Like James's humiliating exposure of Olive Chancellor (meant to chastise the feminine desire for authority), the writer's erasure of the most celebrated feminist name in Transcendentalism is partial compensation for commercialism's evacuation of men from the New England drawing room.

By writing out Fuller, James prostrates suffragism at the feet of abolition, privileging the racial foundations of the "closed circle" over the gendered oversoul. Owen Wister lampoons the suffragist progressive in *The Virginian* as a "manly-lookin' " hen in a drawling anecdote that recalls Hawthorne's extended play on the ancestry of the Pyncheon family in *The House of the Seven Gables*: "There's an old maid at home who's charitable, and belongs to the Cruelty to Animals, and she never knows whether she had better cross in front of a street car or wait," the narrator asserts. "I named the hen after her. . . . I think she came near being a rooster" (Wister 55). By contrast, James provides his own "modern maiden" with a degree of dignity. Despite his derision for Miss Birdseye's myopia — her name ironically announces this — he affirms her unwavering devotion to the "heroic age of New England life": "the only thing that was still actual for her" (157). Like Ransom, who clumsily but successfully makes her his ally, Miss Birdseye is demoored, temporally adrift from the main currents of contemporary American life. Region speaks as much for racial conflict as for the battle of the sexes, for Miss Birdseye's reforming impulse is dedicated not to suffrage but to "the other slaves," "the negroes" for whom she carried the Bible (186).

Here we arrive at the novel's real cultural work, which, in spite of James's satire of Miss Birdseye, is to look longingly backward toward the closed Emersonian circle, a circle that would be happy enough if only it could stay closed enough, a circle that has been irreparably rent, in the final decades of the nineteenth century and the opening years of the twentieth, by "The Ubiquity of the Alien," with whom "there is no claim to brotherhood" (*American Scene* 91–92). Miss Birdseye's lapse of insight is not, at any rate, shared by James, who repeatedly laments the " 'ethnic' apparition" who sits "like a skeleton at the feast" (*American Scene* 101). Just as "the Hebrew conquest of New York" threatens to dilute the city's "American" value, so the "tatterdemalion darkies . . . could absolutely not fail to be, intensely 'on the nerves' of the South." Like the burgeoning population of the Jewish ghetto, the "darkies" refuse to stay within the confines of the South: waiting in a Washington railway station, the sentimental tourist visiting stateside is equally "discomposed" by this "beast that had sprung from the jungle" (*American Scene* 277, 276).

In *The Bostonians*, the beast is more tactfully and tactically hidden, but it is there, nonetheless, in the person of Basil Ransom. Like Vanderbilt's Biltmore, contaminated by the southern "niggery

wilderness" its foundation rests upon,[1] Ransom's "sultry" complexion is proxy for blackness. From the outset, with his "dark,
deep, and glowing" eyes and "his thick black hair" (6), he is a
polite expression of anxiety for the "foreigners" who are invading
The American Scene (98). Ransom is the novel's euphemism — a
ragged and rudimentary but distinctly more appealing substitute
for the "African type[s]" (*American Scene* 276) James finds in the
capital city. This nervousness is pitched at a higher note in the
travelogue than in the novel: Because the writer trains his irony
upon himself more than the objects of his (discomfited) eye, their
alienating properties stand out in bold relief. *The Bostonians*, on
the other hand, is not so highly colored. As if in obeisance to the
distaste that the city's finest have for garish portraiture, James tem-
pers his expostulations, cloaking northern feminist and southern
conservative in a satiric mist that blurs their silhouettes. Still, "the
reader . . . is entreated not to forget" that Ransom "prolonged his
consonants and swallowed his vowels, that he was guilty of elisions
and interpolations which were equally unexpected, and that his
discourse was pervaded by something sultry and vast, something
almost African in its rich basking tone, something that suggested
the teeming expanse of the cotton-field" (6).

The coded references to racial difference in *The Bostonians* also
speak for desire; Ransom's "sultry" blackness is a figure for his
aggressive sexuality, a sexuality as foreign in Olive's drawing room
as it is familiar to her sister, whom James upbraids by keeping
undressed. "Mrs. Luna was drawing on her gloves," Ransom observes, then notes he "had never seen any that were so long; they
reminded him of stockings, and he wondered how she managed
without garters above the elbow" (7). Mrs. Luna is an appropriate subject for this speculative seduction. A moon (her name, in
Spanish) to Ransom's sun (recall his "rich basking tone"), she also
registers a "foreign" difference. Tonally, both characters are too
"vast" and "basking" for the cold watercolor light of Boston's Back

Bay; too seductive to be illumined by the hesitant clarifications of the northern sun in Beacon Hill interiors.

James references blackness as a conventionally racist metaphor for uncontrolled sexuality. Ransom is "guilty" of "unexpected" "interpolations" and of suggesting the "teeming expanse of the cotton-field" (6). But the "African" (6) otherness of his speech also speaks for sexual difference. His presence in the Boston drawing room jars, not so much because of its palpable eroticism — Mrs. Luna, I have suggested, radiates this as well — as for its obliviousness to the hedging that the suffragettes wish to impose upon feminine sexuality. This refusal to accommodate resonates with Olive Chancellor's own unwillingness to mask her passionate, uncontrolled interest in Verena. While James sanctions the former, however, he does not underwrite the latter; if Ransom's observation of Mrs. Luna is a seduction, James stages Olive's intervention in Verena's life as a rape: "Olive had taken her up, in the literal sense of the phrase, like a bird of the air, had spread an extraordinary pair of wings, and carried her through the dizzying void of space. . . . From this first interview she felt that she was seized, and she gave herself up" (69). Like Leda, Verena surrenders, but what is most remarkable here is the unchecked "force of will" James registers in Olive. If Ransom's figure is, like the minstrel, oversexed, Olive's metaphorical posture recalls another bird "species" (recall Miss Birdseye!) in such a way as to frame sexual difference as inappropriately and perversely gendered. This mirroring suggests we read the intimate, potent hatred that Olive holds for Ransom in their contest over Verena as an oblique kind of self-punishment, his own (racialized) difference a way of articulating her (sexual) otherness.

Ransom's "elisions and interpolations" provide us with a troubled figure for lesbian desire, but they also speak in less ambivalent terms of James's anxiety over the "teeming" foreign interlopers who occupy the New York streets as aggressively as Ransom does Olive's Boston drawing room. Olive names Ransom an "enemy of her country" and of "the wretched coloured race" (140). Ransom is inextricably "bound up" with the "horrid heritage" of "the afflicted South" James will dwell upon in *The American Scene* (277). If the Southern black man in Washington looks "ragged and rudimentary" (*The American Scene* 276), so too does Ransom in Boston, who wonders if "there were not a prejudice against his Southern complexion . . . whether he were stupid and unskilled" (162). In fact, his Northern stay only makes his own "Africanness" more visible, for "Basil Ransom's interior" is a "low-ceiled basement, under the conduct of a couple of shuffling negresses, who mingled in the conversation and indulged in low, mysterious chuckles when it took a facetious turn" (161). The racial merging in this passage is all the more striking for the break in tone it reveals; in place of the sustained irony that characterizes the novel as a whole, readers are treated to a discomfited sentimental prose whose shaky control reflects the misgivings of the expatriate who will comment nervously upon the black and Jewish presence in *The American Scene*. Like the parody of sentimentality in minstrel theater, a spectacle that Eric Lott argues "glossed not white encounters with life on the plantation . . . but racial contacts and tensions endemic to the North and the frontier" (38), Ransom's (punned upon) "interior" and travel from the South to the North exploit this character as a stand-in for James's "darkies" and for the Great Migration to cities like Boston. Moreover, the "shuffle" James appropriates from the minstrel stage uses racial difference to indicate class distinctions. The relationship between white tenant and black proprietors is grotesque not only because it unites the races under one roof but also because of the low plane of the conversation itself. Ransom's quarters are unpardonable, so much so that James's own prose stumbles by too sumptuously insisting on the gradient of decline: He repeats the word "low," then unnecessarily underscores the cultural impoverishment of Ransom's room by locating it in the basement.

No wonder that by contrast, the unimpeachably rarified and fully enclosed spaces of Olive Chancellor's Charles Street house look so "American," her "agitation" on behalf of women "a very

American tale" (back cover, 1978 Penguin Modern Classics edition). It is this "mingling" which James will pity but not pardon, this poverty of culture which threatens and for which Ransom is made to serve, this provincialism which illustrates the raced coordinates of James's regional mapping, for Ransom's own distance from "the air of the greater world — which was the world that the North . . . had comparatively been" is a polite reminder of the distance "the Negro" has traveled from the South, the Italian from Sicily, and the Jew from the Pale.

A "Fondness for Foreigners": María Amparo Ruiz de Burton's Who Would Have Thought It?

Now, George Mechlin was making his second visit to his family. He had found New York so very dull and stupid on his return from California. ❦ María Amparo Ruiz de Burton, *The Squatter and the Don* (1993 reprint, 69)

The California skyline Ruiz de Burton delineates in *The Squatter and the Don* shares little with the topography James dismisses in *The American Scene* and *The Bostonians*. His Yosemite is a vulgar efflorescence that interrupts the sweep of western expanse, not the tempered expression of a decorous landscape. For James, the West is all Death Valley: a space rather than a place, and one characterized by absence. By contrast, Ruiz peoples California, providing the state with a mature genealogy. The southern Californians who travel east in *The Squatter and the Don* through restaurants and through opera houses (not minstrel shows) enjoy countless social triumphs, leaving a gratifying admiration in their wake. Even the railroad magnates who ruin the state's financial health are sophisticated, witty, and cultivated. With its excellent wines, its polished social life, its cosmopolitan manners, Ruiz de Burton's California — unlike the exoticized "Spanish" feudalism celebrated in Helen Hunt Jackson's *Ramona* or the dilapidated foreign glamour described by Gertrude Atherton in her California romances — is both a distinct American region and distinctly American. As if in response to estranging ethnographies like Jackson's and Atherton's, the travels of the "party from San Diego" demonstrate the class-based links that shape relations between the best of East and West.[2] The Californians of *Who Would Have Thought It?* and *The Squatter and the Don* insist on the cultural superiority of their home, it is true, by sweeping victoriously through the ranks of New England's social elites, but the paths they trace back and forth across the continent establish connections between regions framed to this day as foreign to one another.

Defending Californio claims accordingly means defending the country as a whole against those Eastern inhabitants who patronize the West as second-rate. When Clarence and Hubert praise the "flavor of the real genuine grape which our California wines have," they are really critiquing the provincial sensibilities of Bostonians like the Norval ladies, who insist that Europe provides the standard for judgment: " 'I think sooner or later our wines will be better liked, better appreciated,' Clarence said. 'I think so too, but for the present it is the fashion to cry down our native wines and extol the imported. When foreigners come to California to tell us that we can make good wines, that we have soils in which to grow the best grapes, then we will believe it, not before' " (171). Given the depredations of the railroad, whose shining rails trespass the country from land's end to land's end, the point is not to keep the circle "closed enough" but to understand how distinct "old social orders" can make class-based alliances across race and region. Both *The Squatter and the Don* and *Who Would Have Thought It?* cement interethnic affiliations through mixed marriages. In defiance of the norms of the romance genre, where marriage is idealized as a union uncontaminated by the demands of practical life, Mercedes and Elvira Alamar fall in love with Anglo American men, who, if not born to wealth and culture, at least know how to create it through wise investments. The orphaned Lola Medina, their literary precursor in *Who Would Have Thought It?* goes even further by marrying one of three well-mannered Bostonians (the other two are her fiancé's father and her mother-in-law's brother Isaac, who escapes to Mexico after release from prison during the Civil War).

This high-born young lady's stay in Boston affords as sardonic a perspective on the drawing rooms of the "blue Presbyterians" (55) as does Basil Ransom's clumsier entrance into the "organized privacy" of Olive Chancellor's Charles Street house. When Dr. Norval brings his new ward to his middle-class household, her dark skin provides his wife with an excuse to relegate her to the servants' quarters. In *Who Would Have Thought It?* as in *The Bostonians*, abolitionism is a social index that registers class pretensions and speaks to racial differences in excess of the black and white distinctions the Mason-Dixon line plots between free and slave states. Verena Tarrant's low birth is equally marked by her mother's social affectations and her father's "ignoble" position as "the detested carpet-bagger" (51). "Mrs. Tarrant," we are told, "had passed her youth in the first Abolitionist circles, and she was aware how much such a prospect was clouded by her union with a young man who had begun life as an itinerant vendor of lead pencils" (62). For James, this class status marks Verena's stay in Boston as a "foreign" agitation of the closed circle — and it is by sacrificing her at the novel's close that he can shore up the fragments of its precincts.

In *Who Would Have Thought It?* the language of abolitionism resonates with similar class values. The proof of Mrs. Norval's precarious social positioning, a woman nouveau riche at Lola's expense whose fortune she diligently siphons off, is her failure to circulate this gilded tongue with any facility. "Mrs. Norval is a good abolitionist in talk," one of her neighbors sneers, "but she ain't so in practice. . . . The night the doctor arrived with Lola, Mrs. Norval insisted that the child should sleep with Hannah, or with the cook, but as she, the cook, despises niggers, she plainly told Mrs. Norval that she 'wouldn't have sich a catteypillar' in her bed" (47). A complex language for Ruiz de Burton as for James, abolitionism defines social groups and regional affiliations as much as it signifies political identifications. The writer lampoons abolitionism as the rhetorical equivalent of a ladies' committee for the Boston Museum of Fine Arts, but she does not evacuate it of raced values. On the contrary, we are first introduced to "Wendell Phillips's teachings" (19) at the same time we are introduced to the child Lola, that is, through the diseased imagination of Mrs. Norval and her daughters, who mistake the "Spanish" child for a "nigger girl" (15). Ransom is figuratively associated with the South's "tatterdemalion darkies," but Lola, born into an Indian captivity, is literally blackened by her mother to ensure her safety. Her "black skin" (31) moves the Norval daughters to revile her, using standard racist tropes; she is a "specimen" of the "animal kingdom" (16) whose dark skin entitles her to share the kitchen and the "blackened pillow" (38) of the Irish servants but not the front rooms that the family occupy.

In the hands of some writers, translating "blackness" to the Irish workers would destabilize it as a racial signifier, but Ruiz's exploitation of blackness, like James's play on "African" speech in *The Bostonians*, does not liberate it from racist hierarchies. Instead, the physical begriming of the servants in *Who Would Have Thought It?* mirrors their comportment. The brogue of the "sensitive Irish ladies" (31) is audible in the novel, as is their distaste for the girl they think is black. Their lack of hospitality toward Lola resonates with their lowly social station, which Ruiz naturalizes through metaphors that play upon color. Divested of her feminizing hoop skirts, the "repulsive" (38) cook stands in the center of her fallen clothing "like a stubby column in the middle of a blackened ruin" (37). Her stockings, similarly soiled black . . . had the privilege of ascending to her ankles, where they modestly coiled themselves in two black rings" (37).

The "blackening" of the Irish is not idiosyncratic to Ruiz, of course. Eric Lott notes that even before the massive waves of immigration from Ireland at midcentury, "Irish and black tended to share the same class niche . . . 'smoked Irishman' was nineteenth-century rural slang for 'Negro' " (95). Clearly, the raced metaphors of *Who Would Have Thought It?* play off of such discursive conventions. But Ruiz de Burton's besmirching of the Irish also indicates her desire to foreclose upon potential affiliations between two populations whose Catholic practices have afforded others an opening for vilifying them both as "foreign." Yet despite their shared position as a religious minority in the land of the "blue Presbyterians" — Ruiz calls our attention to this when she satirizes the cook's hostility toward Lola ("being a good Catholic and a lady of spirit, [cook] crossed herself earnestly but hurriedly, shook her fist threateningly at Lola, and bolted into bed" [31]) — the gap between Irish servant and Californiana ward is unbridgeable in the 1872 novel. Ruiz's anxiety about the possibility of a religious cross-racial alliance is serious enough that she distinguishes Lola from the kitchen workers she is forced to sleep near with a metaphor that threatens to locate the aristocrat in the position of the black slave — another elision she is at pains to deny throughout the novel. Forced by Mrs. Norval to sleep with the Irish servants, Lola chooses instead to throw herself down in the hall on a mat positioned directly outside the bedroom door of the matron herself.

But Lola's blackness is only skin deep, and Ruiz de Burton, writing from a racially defensive position herself, is impatient for it to wear off. If, according to Eric Lott, "those who 'blacked up' and those who witnessed minstrel shows were often working-class Irish men" (35), the feminine "minstrel" of *Who Would Have Thought It?* figures the conventional massing together of different Catholic populations in New England in order to distance herself from just this "servant" class. So we are reminded by Dr. Norval, who has rescued Lola from captivity, that her "blood . . . is as good as, or better than," his own; that she is "neither an Indian nor a negro child" but that her blood "is pure Spanish" (29, 33). Ruiz de Burton insists upon the ignominious social position of "Indians" and "Negroes" to celebrate the "highly born" Lola (33). Like the dismissive stance taken by California's 1856 Colored Convention movement, whose newly inaugurated black newspaper, *Mirror of the Times*, desired to "tell [white] Californians that Negroes appreciated and understood [the principles of republican government] more than many of the state's foreigners and [Irish] illiterates" (Lapp 220), Ruiz de Burton's own unattractive representation is designed to undermine the assumptions that white Americans hold about Mexicans. Nevertheless, it distinguishes one California population only to demean others en masse.

Yet as Amelia de la Luz Montes indicates in "Reading the Nation in Nineteenth-Century American Literature," Lola's whiteness points also to the vexed relation between Native Americans and Mexicanos. "Like [Lydia Maria] Child," whose novel *Hobomok* "does not quite describe a world where the Indian and Puritan can coexist equally . . . Ruiz de Burton subsumes her own indigenous heritage when she insists upon the 'whiteness' of Mercedes's skin in *The Squatter and the Don* as well as Lola's whitened skin in *Who Would Have Thought It?*" Lola's transformation from "little black child" (46) through the "spotted" condition that makes the Reverend Hackwell think she "must belong to a tribe of Mexican Indians called 'Pinto' " (78) to the woman whose skin is so "white and smooth" it made the doctor's "kind heart beat with pleasure" (79) is remarkable even within the forgiving network of intimacies and disaffiliations that characterize American race relations. However, Ruiz de Burton's use of blackface complicates Eric Lott's argument that "minstrelsy . . . reinstit[utes] with ridicule the gap between black and white working class even as it reveled in their (sometimes liberatory) identity" (71). In so doing, it calls our attention to the insufficiency of bipolar models of race relations.

When the Norval ladies cast (and cast off) Lola as black, they allow the writer not only to exploit the value of abolitionism as a social currency but also to undermine its regional coordinates in a manner unavailable to the satire of provincialism afforded by a text like *The Bostonians*. By comparing the political repercussions of the Mexican War with the unjust civil conflict that follows it,

Ruiz de Burton suggests that defining the United States and its citizens using the rubric of North over South is itself a misapprehension of grand proportions — a misreading of all the people, at least, of all the "Roman Catholic" (8) people who live and work in the West. It is the Civil War booster Beau Cackle (of whom the narrator comments that "a long war was good for the Cackle family") who defines the western region as preyed upon by federal policies designed to favor the Puritans residing on the other edge of the continent. "[A]s soon as we take their lands from them they will never be heard of any more," this worthy predicts, "and then the Americans, with God's help, will have all the land that was so righteously acquired through a just war" (9).

What is politically radical about this book happens here, when Ruiz de Burton unhesitatingly juxtaposes two American wars — critically segregated to this day — to undermine both as national values. The ironic cadence strips the Mexican War of glamorous rhetoric. It is not, after all, a peaceful annexation (under the terms of Manifest Destiny) or a "just" and glorious conquest (the elegy at the Alamo). Instead, the war is a prosaic matter of gaining real estate for the personal betterment of the New England incompetents who control the federal machine. While Ruiz de Burton is not the first to censure U.S. imperialism during the war against Mexico — recall that in New England this conflict was, if not roundly condemned, at least partially contested — her insistence that readers acknowledge the relationship between this conflict and the Civil War opens a space for comparing, and so reevaluating, a wide range of nationalist discourses. Lazy military men like Beau Cackle, who use the sectional turmoil that follows in the wake of the Treaty of Guadalupe-Hidalgo to line their pockets and to further their political careers, do a lot of cultural work in this novel, because they allow Ruiz de Burton to move beyond the indictment of discrete actions to expose systemic flaws in the federal government. The capsule description Ruiz de Burton provides of the first "just war" of 1846–48 anticipates the extended ironic treatment she will give the second. It is the interpretive key through which readers gloss the military exploits and domestic squabbles that will occupy the rest of the novel, and a briefer version of the argument embodied in the person of Lola Medina, whose journey east and north reverses the geographic and gendered descriptions of Anglo American travel and whose presence undermines the ostensible centrality of "virtuous New England" (8).

The domestic triumphs Lola enjoys over the provincial prejudices of the Bostonians remind readers of the regionalized and raced frame through which the Civil War is filtered in this sardonic parody of northern virtues. We leave the shores of California behind us when Dr. Norval rescues Lola from her Indian captivity, but her graceful drawing-room victories inevitably resonate with the fumbling military exploits of the Yankees in the Civil War. Their own veniality during this apparently sectional crisis is in Ruiz de Burton's satire of nationalist rhetoric indistinguishable from the imperial fantasies that motivate the appropriation of Mexican land; the logical extension, that is, of systemic federal corruption. We can see her exploitation of military metaphors for the social battles fought over the daughter of California as a reminder of the contiguities between these two conflicts, traditionally distinguished as foreign and domestic policy. When Ruiz likens the conflicts between the Presbyterian Norval ladies and the Catholic daughter of Mexico to the military conquests that the descendants of the "Pilgrim fathers" enjoy over their southern neighbors, she conflates "separate spheres" in two senses: that of gender and that of the nation's political life.

Just as James uses Ransom's regional forays to figure the violation of national borders, so Ruiz de Burton's "blue Presbyterians" are chastised by western eyes to foreground relationships between imperial designs and sectional tensions. In *The American Scene* and *The Bostonians*, ethnic Americans are "foreign" precisely because they exist beyond the pale of the Emersonian circle, and it is this geographical confusion which Ruiz de Burton plays upon in *Who Would Have Thought It?* Provincialism in her book does not characterize national identity so much as corrode it. Mrs. Norval dismisses California residents as beyond the pale, presciently laments her son Julian's "fondness for foreigners" (18), and identifies her brother Isaac's penchant for "gallantry . . . Havana cigars . . . and those miserable sour wines to a good drink of whiskey" as "tastes . . . which the well-regulated mind of a New Englander repudiates" (72–73). It is this kind of regionally defined prejudice which makes honorable soldiers like Julian and Isaac expatriates in twin removals that leave the American political field open to the misappropriations of Bostonian philistines like the Cackles.

Granted, Ruiz de Burton's satire of New England manners celebrates the superior culture not only of Mexicanos native to California but also of Mexico itself. Isaac's international pilgrimage following his release from prison destabilizes the authority of the Mason-Dixon line as regional index; rather than return to his Boston home, he opts for further travel in the South. This move deconstructs New England authority from within the nation, of course, but it also recontextualizes the imperial agenda of the United States. Through the vision of a reformed Yankee, Ruiz de Burton develops a political critique that is itself articulated using culture as metaphor. Compared with their Mexican social equivalents, the best citizens of New England have few social resources. Like Henry James, who exploits house and garden as metaphor for the quality of consciousness that its inhabitants enjoy, Ruiz de Burton's novel of manners describes interiors in order to sit in judgment upon the ethical conduct of American homeowners.

James may call Washington DC, the "City of Conversation," as Susan Luria indicates in "The Architecture of Manners," because of its "social indifference to the vulgar vociferous Market" (303–4), but for Ruiz de Burton, Lincoln's federal seat is merely tacky, as is the Boston home of the Norvals. Their overstuffed mansion looks tawdry when glimpsed from the well-appointed haciendas of Mexico's upper classes. While the president of the United States chews on tobacco and thumps his foot "like a ballistic pendulum" in time with the "base drum" of the band music he admires, California's relations *del otro lado* "sit in the library" reading "papers, books, reviews" and "pamphlets" in four languages and dining on "the best wine" their guest Isaac "had ever tasted in his life" (279, 286).[3] If the Mexican elite were less well mannered, one suspects they would enjoy a guffaw at the expense of their plebeian neighbors to the north.

Ruiz de Burton's comparative reading of culture accords a select few of Mexico's citizens a prestige hitherto unregistered in the American literary landscape, but it would be a mistake to assume that the Californiana writer's critical location is synonymous with that of Lola's relatives. The domestic tableaux in *Who Would Have Thought It?* register the social altitude of the Mexican elite, yes, but they do so from the vantage point of a Californian who, after living for a decade on the East Coast as the wife of a military officer, was intimately connected with the highest authorities of the U.S. federal government. It was she, after all, who obtained a promotion for her husband by appealing personally to President Lincoln, as her letters document.[4]

Originally published in Philadelphia in 1872, *Who Would Have Thought It?* was produced out of this social milieu; the portraits of systemic incompetence and corruption are accordingly indigenous representations, not the musings of an armchair traveler.[5] Put another way, the glimpses we get into the drawing rooms of the two nations are interior ones not only because they use a domestic metaphor to describe political conflict but also because, along with the California-based historical romance Ruiz de Burton will publish out of San Francisco in 1885, they are internal critiques designed to make readers reconsider the legislative and cultural monopoly that northern cities like Boston and Washington enjoy over U.S. citizens as a whole. When "the people of California take the law in their own hands in order to seize the property of . . . these monopolists" (*Squatter* 366) — legislators whose corrupt policies remake national policy into a provincial image — then the nation will be home not only to the descendants of emigrants like the Pilgrim Fathers but also to its regionally defined "natives."

Notes

1. James writes to Wharton in February 1905 of Vanderbilt's Asheville, North Carolina, estate: "one's sense of the extraordinary impenitent madness (of millions) which led to the erection in this vast niggery wilderness, of so gigantic and elaborate a monument to all that isn't socially possible there," as cited in Luria (298). The conflation of such racist language about the South with a classically northern template (the language of the Puritan errand invoked by "vast" and "wilderness") suggests that James is parodying Vanderbilt's secular mission over and against the northern spiritual quest that forms the bedrock of ideas of the United States.

2. See also Dana's condescending *Two Years before the Mast* and Prescott's *History of the Conquest of Mexico* as well as the extensive histories of California by Hubert H. Bancroft. For more sustained attention to Anglo American representations of Californios, see Padilla, *My History, Not Yours*, and Sanchez, *Telling Identities*.

3. It is useful to stress here that the focus is on culture, or rather, as Genaro Padilla points out, Mexican cultural authority is counterpoised against the political weight of the United States (literalized in the thumping foot of the president keeping time to the bass drum of the band). The latter, as Padilla argues, "is power, the other is the affectation of power in the refinement of reading and fine wine" (correspondence with the author, June 1996).

4. Letter to Mariano Vallejo, 8 March 1861, as cited in Montes, "Es Necesario Mirar Bien," 18.

5. For additional background on Ruiz de Burton's stay in the East, see Sanchez and Pita's comprehensive introduction to *Who Would Have Thought It?*; Aranda's essay "María Amparo Ruiz de Burton"; Montes's "María Amparo Ruiz de Burton Negotiates American Literary Politics and Culture," as well as Montes's "Es Necesario Mirar Bien."

"Thank God, Lolita Is Away from Those Horrid Savages": The Politics of Whiteness in *Who Would Have Thought It?*

JESSE ALEMÁN

As with most historical romances, *Who Would Have Thought It?* has its share of contrived plots, melodramatic moments, stock characters, and crucial misunderstandings that help and hinder the narrative's national nuptials. First, the novel recounts the coming of age of Lola Medina, a wealthy Mexican American orphan born in Indian captivity, raised in New England by the Norvals, and eventually reunited with her father in Mexico, where her Yankee lover, Julian Norval, joins her following the Civil War. The novel also covers the rise and fall of Mrs. Norval, the cruel republican mother who treats Lola miserably, plots against Mr. Norval to exploit Lola's wealth, and, in the process, falls into an affair with the Reverend Hackwell that endures until the matron succumbs to brain fever. The cross-country relations mirror the book's geopolitical context as the narrative, which is mostly set during the Civil War and Reconstruction but includes significant events from the war with Mexico, collapses the regional borders between the Southwest, the South, the Northeast, and Mexico to generate a critique of Northeastern colonial culture and provincial jingoism.

New England native Mrs. Cackle, for instance, literally and figuratively recounts the complex legacy of conquest in the West when she exclaims: "To me they are all alike — Indians, Mexicans, or Californians — they are all horrid. But my son Beau says our just laws and smart lawyers will soon 'freeze them out.' That as soon as we take their lands from them they will never be heard of anymore, and then the Americans, with God's help, will have all the land that was righteously acquired through a just war and a most liberal payment of money" (11). Never mind their own differences based on region, cultural practices, colonial history, nationalisms, or racial caste categories. Mrs. Cackle has no problem homogenizing Indians, Mexicans, and Californians: They are simply "horrid." The order in which she lists these groups is likewise important: "Indians, Mexicans, and Californians" recounts the order of conquest as a result of Anglo westward expansion. Moreover, while she recognizes expansion as a literal legal process and capitalistic venture, she nevertheless upholds the figurative construction of Manifest Destiny as divine intervention — God willed it; Yankees bought it. Mrs. Cackle, in other words, expresses the mainstream racist and colonialist logic promulgated by many Northerners during the nation's most rapid period of expansion.

But if Mrs. Cackle is unsympathetic to the plight of Indians, Mexicans, or Californios, she herself is treated unsympathetically, as her name suggests. The novel goes to great lengths to disprove Mrs. Cackle, hoping to show instead that "the natives" of Spanish descent, as the narrative often describes them, are not at all like those "horrid" Indians or Mexicans that Mrs. Cackle imagines. Rather, Californios are white. Certainly, the history of Mexican and Mexican American racialization in relation to Indian removal, westward expansion, and the shifting colonial powers of the mid-nineteenth century help explain the white racial politics of Ruiz de Burton's novel.[1] Even though Mexico recognized Indians as full citizens with land rights after the 1821 War of Independence, the secularization of California's Spanish missions created a distinct hierarchy between landowning Californios and lower-class Indian and mestizo laborers, as Rosaura Sánchez points out (*Telling Identities* 6–41). After 1848, however, Mexican territory became subject to the laws of Manifest Destiny. The United States thus rescinded Mexico's 1821 landownership policies and reintroduced racialized codes of citizenship status, voting rights, and property titles that fully denied land rights to Indians and questioned the rights of Mexicans, whose racial ambiguity made them dubious representatives of the United States' citizenry. "Given the nature of the U.S. racial system and its laws," Martha Menchaca explains, "the conquered Mexican population learned that it was politically expedient to assert their Spanish ancestry; otherwise they were susceptible to being treated as American Indians" (587).

Indeed, the contradiction between Mexican American dispossession and claims to white citizenship rights remains the thorn in the side of Chicana/o literary history. From the critical ambivalence with which Genaro Padilla introduces his study of Californio narratives in *My History, Not Yours* to Rosaura Sánchez and Beatrice Pita's strong readings of María Amparo Ruiz de Burton as a subaltern subject in their introductions to *Who Would Have Thought It?* and *The Squatter and the Don*, Chicana/o scholars struggle to resolve the problem of Mexican American whiteness. Carey McWilliams called it the "fantasy heritage" of Mexican history, and Raymund Paredes dubbed the emphasis on white Hispanicism an example of "hacienda syndrome." Tey Diana Rebolledo has convincingly shown how early Nueva Hispana texts — products of the Southwest's layered colonialisms — deploy "narrative strategies of resistance" that, among other things, blend genres, record "unofficial" history, and act as cultural and linguistic translations (134–46). Yet there is still the problem of whiteness, for even as Rebolledo's discussion emphasizes the importance of women's literary and cultural resistance, her analysis elides the conspicuous construction of white hispanidad that informs early Chicana/o literature.

Paredes's "hacienda syndrome" is not a flippant analogy — it likens Mexican American writers to Southern whites, whose constructed position of white racial power rested on the reality and legacy of black slavery. The alternative georacial cartography Paredes invokes challenges the subaltern strain of Chicano/a studies by seeing whiteness as the link between the cultures of Southern slavery and the Spanish/Mexican colonial history in the Southwest. "[F]ollowing established Spanish practice in New Spain," José Limón explains, "large-scale economic activity depended on the extermination of local Indian societies or, whenever possible, on their appropriation as what amounted to racially defined and restricted quasi-slave labor under conditions not unlike those of African-Americans in the U.S. South, with its increasing focus on the plantation system" (10).[2] In both the South and the Southwest, white privilege depended on the economy of slavery or indentured servitude, but following the war with Mexico, when Northern market capitalism displaced the Southwest's economy and brought the issue of black slavery to a crisis, Old World notions of whiteness gave way to a new definition of racial privilege based on free wage labor, industry, and citizenship status. Especially after the Civil War, Southern whites and landed Californios felt themselves equally victimized by Yankee imperialism, equally excluded from the emerging discourses of Anglo American socioeconomic privilege, and equally white.

Ruiz de Burton's life and work thus capture the colonial contradictions of nineteenth-century Mexican American whiteness, the paradox of being caught between the rapid growth of the nation and its attendant politics of land displacement and cultural dislocation. Already established in the Californio ruling class, Ruiz de Burton, as with many of her upper-class criollo contemporaries, had to negotiate a new position within an emerging American ruling class that by no means readily embraced California Mexicans. Californios distinguished themselves from Native Americans and blacks at the 1848 California Constitutional Convention, for instance, in an attempt to align the landed Californio gentry with the colonial ideologies that threatened to displace them racially, economically, and legally in the United States.[3] As with *The Squatter and the Don, Who Would Have Thought It?* reveals the fissures of racial categories created after 1848 and exposes white racial identity as a category contingent on geography, labor, and class status. "Who ever heard of a blue-eyed Mexican?" Reverend Hackwell asks after meeting Lola Medina's father (253), and his question gets to the complexity of racial politics in general. Señor Medina poses a threat to Hackwell's sense of white privilege, which he constructs at the expense of Lola and her family, but the novel's emphasis on Mexican whiteness itself comes at the expense of Native, Irish, and African Americans, who all remain on the racialized margins of white Mexican privilege. The narrative redistributes white privilege from the North to the South by the Southwest, consolidating the Confederate states with greater Mexico and its far northern frontier to chart the emergence of Mexican American whiteness as a contradictory identity created in response to Anglo American imperialism but ultimately (per)formed in contrast to nonwhite racial others.

Consider the plight of Lola Medina, for instance. Dyed dark while in Indian captivity, Lola arrives in New England under the paternalistic protection of Dr. Norval, a geologist whose colonial expeditions led him out to the southwestern borderlands in the first place. When Lola passes the Norval gates, Mattie Norval, Mrs. Norval's daughter, offers an initial reaction that captures the sentiments of the rest of the group: "Goodness! What a specimen! A nigger girl!" (17). Mattie sees Lola first as a geological artifact with a racialized body but soon recants her response when she notices the "pretty pink shade" of Lola's white hands (17). For Ruth Norval, however, Lola is no better than a "baboon," since she is the daughter of "Indians or Negros, or both. . . . Anyone can see that much of her history" (17). Lavinia Sprig, Mrs. Norval's spinster sister, fears Lola "might be Aztec" (20), while Mrs. Norval sees Lola as a "disease," "a true emanation of the black art!" (17). Finally, confusing things further, Dr. Norval explains that "Lolita's blood is pure Spanish blood, her mother being pure Spanish descent and her father the same, though an Austrian by birth, he having been born in Vienna" (28).

As a way of establishing their own Anglo identity, the provincial New Englanders share the same racialization of the nation's cartography. They see themselves as civilized in contrast to Indian, Mexican, and Californio savages; they define their freedom in opposition to black slavery in the South; and they consider the political, religious, and governmental practices of the South, Southwest, and Europe as foreign to the Northeast's Anglo American culture. The series of oppositions constructs the New Englanders' sense of whiteness, but as Anne Goldman explains, "Ruiz de Burton recirculates all of the stereotypical traits of the Yankee, using parody to turn the Anglo American racial aesthetic on its head" ("Blue-Eyed Mexican" 63). Indeed, Lola's civility during such a savage reception not only reverses the dichotomy between the Northeast and Southwest, between civilization and savagery, but it also collapses the imaginary distance between the North and the South, showing that, despite the Mason-Dixon line, the North's racism is not far removed from Southern slavery.

As with Lola's arrival in the North, the expansion of the United States' borders after 1848 means the expansion of the nation's racial signifiers, and through the story of Lola Medina, Ruiz de Burton challenges the definition of whiteness in the United States to include Mexicans. Going from black to white, and seen as Indian and Spanish, Lola passes through various stages of racial identity — black, Indian, brown, "spotted" white, and finally "pure" white. The narrative's plot emphasizes Lola's "pure" whiteness, but as Lisbeth Haas explains, in colonial Spanish America, "Whiteness was . . . not a singular or static category but included a range of color. 'White' lineage could be purchased from the crown with gold or other goods through a decree called *gracias al sacar* (thanks to be taken out, removed, or freed)" (31). In this sense, Ruiz de Burton is not working to include Mexicans within the category of Anglo American whiteness, as John M. Gonzáles suggests; rather, she situates the ambiguous racialization of Lola's body — and the Mexican body politic she represents — against Anglo America's white/black paradigm and within the Spanish/Mexican process of *gracias al sacar*, suggesting that the post-1848 Mexican American population in the Southwest has the potential, legally at least, to become white citizens.[4]

And the ideal white citizenry in the novel — Anglo American Northerners — reacts poorly to such a possibility. Their racism is both cruel and capitalistic as they treat Lola's "spotted" skin as a disease yet negotiate their racial hatred with class envy (78). Mrs. Norval hates Lola, and even after Lola's skin turns pure white, her republican stepmother nevertheless insists on calling Lola a "spotted mongrel" (149) for fear that the "little nigger should be so rich, and her girls so poor" (49). The daughters Norval, who give Lola a miserable reception when she first arrives, have no problem using her money to tour Europe and enter New York's more fashionable circles of new rich, fully equipped with Lola's handmade French jewelry. Despite his aversion to Lola's skin, as well as his marriage to Mrs. Norval, the duplicitous Reverend Hackwell orchestrates an underhanded legal scheme to trap Lola in marriage and claim her wealth. On a more paternalistic level, Dr. Norval sympathizes with Lola, but he also brings her home with a wealth of natural resources — gold, diamonds, and emeralds — that he quickly converts into stock and legal tender. Even Julian Norval, the hero of the romance narrative and Lola's Yankee lover, initially finds her dark skin unattractive: "Lola was decidedly too black and too young for Julian Norval to take a fancy to her, whilst she, the poor, lonely little soul, idolized Julian" (51).

Yankees, in other words, are more concerned with their class status than they are with refined — even "civil" — cultural practices, which is ultimately how the narrative distinguishes between déclassé Anglo Saxonism and genteel Mexican whiteness. Lola and her father, for instance, couldn't care less about the mineral wealth Dr. Norval turns into ready cash for Lola. Money means very little to Lola; cultural gentility is her capital. Her manners are impeccable in contrast to the rude Northerners. She never responds to racist comments made directly to her; she follows Mrs. Norval's orders, despite the animosity between the two; and she returns from Catholic boarding school even more polite than when she entered it. Even in romance, Lola is quite a contrast to Mrs. Norval, that matronly "Yankee Popocatepetl" or volcano of passion, as Hackwell calls her (177). "[I]t must be stated," the narrator explains, "that [Lola] had passed the greater part of the night tracing for herself a 'prospectus' of her future conduct towards Julian, which was so strict and circumspect that Mrs. Norval herself could not have found a single fault with it" (146–47).

The narrative constructs Mexican whiteness as a refined identity category that contrasts with the vulgar Anglo Saxonism of the novel's Northerners, but ironically, Lola's identity as a rich, white Hispana emerges at the expense of the narrative's nonwhite racial others. The richer Lola gets, for instance, the whiter she becomes, culminating with Emma Hackwell's envious comment: "I think Lola might teach us the secret of that Indian paint that kept her white skin under cover, making it whiter by bleaching it" (232). Her secret is Spanish/Mexican colonialism in North America. After all, Lola and her mother are dyed dark because they are Indian captives, and even though the war with Mexico made Mexican citizens vulnerable to native attacks, as Aranda has shown, not just any Mexican citizens were targeted. The Indians carried Doña Theresa off her Sonoran hacienda. Intersecting colonial conflicts thus make up the secret of Lola's Indian paint: the United States' expansion into Mexico displaced Mexican landowners and made them vulnerable to Native American attacks, but indigenous groups attacked landholders such as Doña Theresa in the first place because they dispossessed Native Americans of their land, labor, and natural resources.[5]

The history of Lola's wealth bears this point out, since her money comes from her mother's use of Indian labor to mine native resources. The doctor explains: "She picked it up, and, as she had some knowledge of precious stones, she saw it was a large diamond, though only partly divested of its rough coating. Then, she looked about for similar pebbles, and found many more. . . . Afterwards the Indians brought her emeralds and rubies, seeing that she liked pretty pebbles. Thus she made a fine collection, for she took only the largest and those which seemed to her the most perfect" (28). Enacting in miniature the history of Spanish colonization of the Americas, Doña Theresa uses the wealth she gains from indigenous exploitation to rescue (*sacar*) Lola from the threat of Indian identity. And for Doña Theresa, this threat to Spanish "purity" is both biological and cultural. She implicitly fears the fate of Lola's sexual interaction with Indians, but she is equally concerned with Lola's religious fate: "Thank God, Lolita is away from those horrid savages! Please do not forget that she must be baptized and brought up a Roman Catholic," she explains to Dr. Norval (36). As Californios put it, Doña Theresa wants Lola to grow up *gente de razón* instead of *gente sin razón*, the two opposing cultural markers that distinguished Spanish criollos from Native Americans, white citizens from dark-skinned laborers, in Spanish colonial California (Haas 31). Mirroring the racialist logic that Mrs. Cackle and the rest of the Yankees apply to the "horrid" Indians, Mexicans, and Californios, Doña Theresa's Spanish/Mexican caste system allows Lola to "purchase" her whiteness from Northern bankers rather than from the Spanish Crown, as was usually the case with the *gracias al sacar* process. In other words, Californio colonial mentality in the novel is akin to Anglo American colonialism when it comes to fashioning whiteness by racializing and oppressing others.

While the confluence of religion and labor distinguishes Lola from Indians, though, Catholicism is not the sole harbinger of white *razón*. The narrative must still negotiate the anti-Catholicism of the Protestant Northeast, where the influx of Irish immigrants created a host of alternative Anglo American anxieties regarding "savagery." Thus, Ruiz de Burton must also work to distance white Mexican Catholics from the Irish Catholic maids Lola encounters in the Norval house. Relegated to the servants' quarters by Mrs. Norval, Lola would rather sleep on the floor outside of Dr. Norval's bedroom with the family dog than share a bed with one of the Irish servants: "Lola had refused to share the bed with either of the two servants, and both had resented the refusal as a most grievous insult. . . . Hannah, the chambermaid, was not so repulsive to look upon. Still, the thought of sharing her bed was to Lola very terrible" (30). Lola cringes from having to share a room, let alone a bed, with Irish servants; she is after all the daughter of a Don. The Irish maids, however, with their broken English, dirty socks, "corrugated" knees, and loud snoring are racialized whites who, although meant as comic relief, put in relief the natural, genteel whiteness concealed by Lola's dyed skin (31).

And this is exactly the dubious distinction Ruiz de Burton is making. As Noel Ignatiev argues, Irish immigrants learned to become white by making conscious political choices that collectively situated them within white supremacist discourses and practices. Labor politics and economic competition in particular, Ignatiev notes, created racial tension between Irish Americans and blacks in the United States, ultimately leading many Irish Americans to support slavery as a way of protecting their own positions as wage laborers in free territories such as Boston and Philadelphia. In 1844, they helped elect President James K. Polk, a Democrat who led the country to war with Mexico; they often contributed to the mobocracy of violent voting arenas to help maintain slave states; and many Irish, according to Ignatiev, generally supported an ideology of "white solidarity" (77). As a way of overcoming the racism and anti-Catholicism they encountered in Anglo America, Irish Americans, Ignatiev concludes, established their whiteness at the expense of black freedom (87).

As servants in the Norval house, the Irish maids have thus secured a wage-labor status that distinguishes them from free blacks in the North, but as laborers, they have yet to establish themselves fully as "whites" vis-à-vis the nouveau riche Norvals. Lola outclasses them economically, culturally, and racially, as she does many of the Northerners in the narrative. Lola is already white, Ruiz de Burton would have us believe, and is just beset by her blackface; her grace, gentility, and language perform the "natural" whiteness beneath her dark skin. Just as whiteness in general erases its cultural formation as a racial category, the narrative conceals its construction of white Mexican identity. Much like the Irish, Californios had to reposition themselves as white in Anglo America to secure the country's real and imaginary citizenship rights. They did this by distinguishing themselves from Indians and blacks, whose status as indentured servants or slaves left them with no rights in the United States. Californios also brokered on their class status, hoping that their material and cultural capital would buy them entry into the emerging Anglo nation. This class hierarchy ultimately informs the racial hierarchy that distinguishes Lola from the Norvals and the Irish maids. Lola's status as white depends on the degree to which she is economically distant from the Irish servants, and even though Mrs. Norval sees no difference between Lola's racialized status and the economic status of the servants, Lola finds the comparison repugnant. Rather, the novel implies, the Norvals and the Irish maids have much to learn from Lola about being white.

Blackness, though, is the prevailing anxiety of Ruiz de Burton's narrative about whiteness. Along with her class envy, Mrs. Norval, as with many of the book's Northerners, hates Lola because she looks black. "And would that little nigger be so rich, and her girls so poor?" Mrs. Norval thinks to herself (49). Put off by Lola's refusal to share her bed, the Irish cook likewise responds, "Niggers ain't my most particlies admirashun" (30). While Lola never utters such blatantly racist comments, she regrets her dark skin because she rightly thinks Julian finds it unattractive. Explaining the "stain" of her skin, Lola tells Julian, "I wanted to tell you this many times, for though I didn't care whether I was thought black or white by others, I hated to think that you *might* suppose I was Indian or black" (100). Lola's dark skin exposes the North's racism, but her blackface also enacts a peculiar Mexican racial anxiety for being categorized as Indian or black. As Eric Lott contends, blackface performances in the nineteenth century reveal white, male working-class fears and desires of blackness that crossed racial boundaries while simultaneously reinforcing them in contradictory public displays of black cultural appreciation and appropriation. "What was on display in minstrelsy," Lott explains, "was less black culture than a structured set of white responses to it which had grown out of northern and frontier social rituals and were passed through an inevitable filter of racist presupposition" (101).

Lola's blackface undermines Anglo American racism but replaces it with a Spanish/Mexican racial caste system that nevertheless situates whiteness as the highest identity marker. It thus resolves the fear of Californio racialization by enacting it and resolving it through a process of deracination that positions Mexicans within the nation's white imagined community. For Ruiz de Burton, though, low-down, scheming Anglo politicians and socialites determine the nation's modern political policies from the North, so the South, with its attendant racial codes, becomes the last bastion of national honor and Old World whiteness in the United States. The narrative, for instance, valorizes the nameless Confederate soldier who befriends and releases Isaac from prison based on his promise "not to bear arms against the Confederacy" (191). The virtue, honesty, and trust that the nameless soldier extends to Isaac contrast with the cowardice of the Cackles, the duplicity of Reverend Hackwell, and the political shenanigans of Congressman Le Grand Gunn, who is responsible for Isaac's overextended stay in the Southern prison camp in the first place.

This might explain why the narrative conceals the hard condition of the prison camps in the South, as Sánchez and Pita point out (xxiii–xxvi). Short of being openly pro-Confederacy, the novel goes to great lengths to see the South as a victim of the North's liberal capitalism and politics. The plight of Dr. Norval makes this point clear. A Northern democrat, Dr. Norval finds himself run out of the country after he advocates an alternative to Southern succession and civil war. Representative of the Peace Democrats, Dr. Norval supports the Union but also sees the hypocrisy behind its claim to democratic liberty. He considers Lincoln's suspension of the Writ of Habeas Corpus as an infringement on the right to free speech and finds the racism behind Northern abolitionists, including his wife, doubly hypocritical, leading him to believe, as with many Southerners, that the government is securing the freedom of blacks at the expense of white citizenship rights. As Dr. Norval puts it when he explains his sympathy for Lola, "I — a good-for-nothing Democrat, who doesn't believe in Sambo but believes in Christian charity and human mercy — I feel pity for the little thing" (18).

The absence of slavery in the novel more tellingly reveals the narrative's attempt to valorize the South. It is difficult to imagine why a novel set during the Civil War includes very little about slavery, unless the issue of slavery raised problems for the text's larger cultural work of reimagining Mexican whiteness. The novel may eschew slavery to take on issues of national racism, but in the process it recirculates its own racist paradigms of blackness by aligning Mexican whiteness with the whiteness of displaced Southerners. Take Caesar ("Sar" for short), for example, Ruiz de Burton's version of the "happy darky" who whistles "merrily" as he cleans "his master's pistols" (190). Indeed, as Isaac finds "a friend in [the] rebel" soldier, he also gains Sar as a personal body servant: "Spring did not find it necessary to tell Sar to go for the clothes. Sar had been an attentive listener to the officer's recital, and started off after him at a trot. 'Here, massa, put 'em on, for do Lo's sake, an look like a gin'leman ag'in'" (190). Sar in effect remakes Isaac into a Southern gentleman, as the narrative participates in the Reconstructionist myth that the Old World order of the South, especially for blacks, was much better before the Civil War. Her argument with the Colossus of the North, then, leads Ruiz de Burton to romanticize the South as a way of symbolically aligning the Old World Hispano culture of the Southwest, built by the exploitation of Indian labor, land, and resources, with the South's Old World slavocracy. In a move that remaps the nation's georacial landscape, Ruiz de Burton connects the victimization of Mexicans in the United States with the violation of Southern white citizenship rights, hoping to participate in a reconstruction of whiteness that includes upper-class Mexicans in the nation's white citizenry. It is thus fitting that, disheartened with the North, Isaac leaves for Mexico following his release from the Southern prison camp. And there he finds the same hospitality and gentility that the anonymous Confederate soldier extended to him. He also finds more body servants: "On arriving home, Don Felipe ordered his servants — all of whom were male, with the exception of an old housekeeper — to take the best care of the *Señor Americano*" (200). As Anne E. Goldman explains, "The hospitality Isaac enjoys in Mexico reproaches the hostile treatment Lola suffers in New England, just as the worldliness of [Don Felipe and Don Luis] indicts the provincialism of their counterparts in Washington" ("Blue-Eyed Mexican" 74). Yet Ruiz de Burton's cross-national critique of the North relies on the South by Southwest displacement of class and racial others.

Mexico represents the last bastion of white national consolidation and serves as a racial and cultural corollary to the United States that positions Mexicans, not Anglo Americans, as the ideal white citizenry. Consider Lola's father and grandfather. One is Austrian-born; the other is a Mexican criollo. Both are well-educated, trilingual representatives of Mexico's landed, old-world gentry whose whiteness derives as much from their bloodline as it does from their land tracts. They are enlightened and en-whitened citizens who debunk popular stereotypes of Mexicans as a degenerate race and instead reverse the stereotype to highlight the moral and social degeneracy of Anglo Americans. The two enlightened Mexicans, however, also signal an alternative national whiteness, one bordering on monarchist sympathies for an ordered form of governance that ensures the privileged status of upper-class white Mexicans.

This is why the romance between Lola Medina and Julian Norval is so significant to the narrative's racial politics. Their ethnoracial romance unites Julian and Lola at the end of the narrative, a magical solution to the novel's sociosexual conflict that deports Julian's republican ideals and Lola's wealth back to Mexico. *Who*

Would Have Thought It? deploys the Norval-Medina romance to introduce an alternative Mexican republic, one that consolidates the political ideals of the United States with the cultural capital of rich landowners like Lola's father and grandfather. The reunion of Julian and Lola in Mexico, then, counters the rise of "Cacklism" in the United States and offers a sense of hope for the restoration of republican ideology and its attendant ideology of whiteness. Ironically, though, the narrative's resolution reproduces the racism Lola encounters in the North. We might even say this is the contradictory price for remapping the nation and its geoliterary cartography. Ruiz de Burton reimagines the nation's social, racial, and literary terrain as a way of positioning Mexicans at the forefront of the formation of the United States. Yet positioning Mexicans within the nation means positioning Indians, blacks, mestizos/as, and the working class without it in a process of racial formation that undermines Anglo Saxonism but reconstructs its exclusionary logic to ensure the whiteness of Mexican Americans.

Notes

1. Several recent essays examine the historical significance and problematic politics of Ruiz de Burton's construction of whiteness. My article on *The Squatter and the Don* and Helen Hunt Jackson's *Ramona* argues that Ruiz de Burton relies on a cultural rather than biological notion of race to place Californios within a category of whiteness while distinguishing them from Native and African Americans (Alemán 63). Margaret D. Jacobs makes a similar point by comparing *Who Would Have Thought It?* with Jackson's novel (213), while Peter A. Chvany maintains that Ruiz de Burton's strategic use of whiteness critiques Anglo American racism but reproduces it (109). Deploying different analyses, all three essays understand that race in general and whiteness in particular are arbitrary constructs that change over time, especially during national or economic crises.

2. While Limón's connection between the South and the Southwest

remaps the nation's geopolitics, it also creates some historical gaps. Limón upholds the slavocracy theory of the war with Mexico without fully considering the North's expansionist interest in Greater Mexico. He also collapses the entire Southwest under the rubric of Texas, but California and the New Mexican territory share more regional differences than similarities to the embattled history of Texas. Nevertheless, his discussion is one of the first to understand the historical and cultural exchanges between the South and the Southwest.

3. Genaro Padilla argues that Mariano Guadalupe Vallejo's account of the 1846 Bear Flag Revolt, when Anglo American thugs got drunk and attempted to take over California, is a double-voiced discourse that troubles the outright complicity of the Californios. Vallejo "demonstrate[s] a strategic manipulation of multiply coded statements that, on the one hand, assured his American captors that his intentions coincided with their own and, on the other, exposed their violations of trust and their violent abrogations of the democratic rhetoric they mouthed while they were forcefully taking the country" (23). Nevertheless, Vallejo welcomed American expansionism before the Bear Flag Revolt. As Richard Henry Dana notes in his popular 1840 travel narrative, *Two Years before the Mast*, "The *commandante* of the presidio, Don Guadalupe Vallejo, a young man, and the most popular, among the Americans and the English, of any man in California, was on board when we got underway. He spoke English very well, and was suspected of being favourably inclined to foreigners" (187).

4. Gonzáles argues that the trope of marriage in *The Squatter and the Don* consolidates Californio whiteness and allows them to secure a privileged class position in the emergent Anglo American nation. His argument is akin to David Luis-Brown's analysis of white citizenship rights in the novel. Both authors, however, conflate "whiteness" with "Anglo American" without accounting for the cultural and class distinctions Ruiz de Burton creates between Anglo Americans and white Mexicans.

5. As Aranda notes, the Indian abduction of Lola's mother speaks volumes about the historical moment of her captivity, since it occurs on

the eve of the war with Mexico: "This is undoubtedly a very deliberate use of irony to mark the disruption of regional power that enabled Native American groups to take action against Mexican settlers. Dr. Norval's rescue of Lola Medina figures as poetic justice, since it was his nation that made Mexican citizens vulnerable to native retaliation in the first place" ("Contradictory Impulses" 577). It is also important to realize, though, that in rescuing Lola from Indian captivity and returning her to Mexico, Dr. Norval is following the provisions of Article XI of the Treaty of Guadalupe Hidalgo, which makes a clear distinction between U.S. and Mexican citizens and Indian "savages" (Griswold del Castillo 190–91).

Captive Identities: The Gendered Conquest of Mexico in *Who Would Have Thought It?*

JULIE RUIZ

Within the first pages of María Amparo Ruiz de Burton's *Who Would Have Thought It?* (1872), New Englander Dr. Norval describes his 1857 rescue of a Mexican child, Lola Medina. She was born in captivity in the Colorado River region after her mother had been kidnapped from her home on a hacienda in Sonora, Mexico, by Apache Indians during the Mexican War in 1846. Lola's subsequent escape from Indian captivity in the Southwest symbolizes the cleansing of Mexican national identity from the "stain" of U.S. imperialism during the Mexican War.

Like Ruiz de Burton, other California authors such as Angustias de la Guerra Ord conflate national and domestic invasion in Alta California. In *Occurrences in Hispanic California*, Ord describes the collapse of the public and private through the invasion of her home and the plundering of the missions. However, it is her upper-class position and claim to a Spanish-Mexican whiteness that allow her to depict herself as the heroine in her narrative. While both Ruiz de Burton and Ord long for the redemption of a fallen Mexican nation, both of their narratives reveal the limits of appealing to a nostalgic Mexican past to solve the realities of a Mexican American present.

Chicana poet Lorna Dee Cervantes addresses these realities by connecting this Mexican American past to the Chicana/o present in "Poema para los californios muertos" [Poem for the Dead Californios]. Here she describes Los Altos, California, as a "bastard child," lost and separated from its indigenous mothers and Californio fathers. This Chicana narrator, who describes herself as the "hija pobrecita" [poor daughter] (24), speaks for the upper-class Californios and Californias, filling the void left by the erasure of Mexican American history in a California where only "yanqui remnants" (30) and not those of Californios remain. Trying to see into the invisible realm, the narrator asks if the Californios still "live here in the shadows of these white, high-class houses?" (23). Certainly their presence persists in their descendants: those Chicanas and Chicanos who provide the menial labor that have run these homes and communities since the turn of the century (5).

Cervantes's poem also connects the Californios to the land as "husbands de la tierra" [of the earth] (9) to create a sense of legitimacy. María Viramontes in *Under the Feet of Jesus* (1995) will also transform images of Chicanas and Chicanos as a bastard race and orphaned people through Petra, who tells her children as she points a "red finger" coated with dust to the earth: "Tienes una madre aquí [You have a mother here]. You are not an orphan." Yet simultaneously Viramontes describes the alienation and exile Chicanas and Chicanos experience through Petra's daughter, Estrella, who fears La Migra at the most "American" of past times, while watching a baseball game from outside the ballpark (63).

Ruiz de Burton's novel anticipates the alienation and marking as "alien" of Chicanos and Chicanas through her configuration of the border at the end of her text as a "black dividing line" (284). For Ruiz de Burton, the color black signals immobility as symbolized by the captive Lola, who doesn't gain mobility until her skin is lightened. Thus, this border symbolizes the lack of social, political, and economic mobility that Mexican Americans experienced after the war.

Just as her novel foreshadows the shift between mobility and immobility for nineteenth-century Mexican Americans, so too does María Amparo Ruiz de Burton's life story replay a similar trend. In *Conflicts of Interest*, Rosaura Sánchez and Beatrice Pita deftly trace the contradictory aspects of Ruiz de Burton's life from 1848 to 1895, through an analysis of her letters. Descended from the Carrillo and the Ruiz de Apodaca families who came to Sonora and Sinaloa, Mexico, from Spain, the Ruiz de Burton family, while not wealthy, did have "political recognition and social status" (Sánchez and Pita 6). Her voluntary relocation to Alta California from Baja during the Mexican War in 1848 and her marriage to New Englander Henry Burton also endowed her with social mobility. Thus, although she was an outsider culturally and politically, her "status as a citizen with access, through Burton, to the seat of power also made her an insider of sorts." In this position, she stood with "a foot on each side of the border" as both a citizen and resident-alien (184).

So too does her racial and cultural essentialism complicate her position as an outsider and insider. In identifying as one of the conquered from the Mexican War, Ruiz de Burton connects her colonized status with the Southerners from the Civil War, "seeing in the South's defeat a mirror of the defeat of Mexico in 1848, and in Reconstruction, a clear imposition of Yankee hegemony on the Southern States" (Sánchez and Pita 195). Ruiz de Burton's sympathy for the demise of southern slavery demonstrates her derogatory views of African Americans as well as a blindness regarding the connection between slavery and imperialism. In *Who Would Have Thought It?* Ruiz de Burton's lack of vision causes her to denigrate African Americans and indigenous peoples and to denounce "a nation ostensibly opposed to slavery" but "willing to enslave those south of the border and to subject its own people to the mandates of the railroad monopolies" (201–2).

Her vacillations between colonizer and colonized positions led to an incredible trail of contradictory stances. Yet despite her contradictions, Ruiz de Burton, along with the majority of Mexican Americans living in the conquered territories after the war, lost their wealth and status and became part of the laboring classes. Thus, Ruiz de Burton is a "forerunner of Chicana/o writers" not only because she is the "first person of Mexican origin to write fiction in English and to have her work published" (Sánchez and Pita 551) but also because she speaks for and is a member of this marginalized collectivity. As Genaro Padilla in *My History, Not Yours: The Formation of Mexican American Autobiography* insightfully argues, many Mexican American writers, like Ruiz de Burton, "mimicked an Anglo-American discourse that romanticized the Spanish Southwest" while their "writing nevertheless also operated as a vital form of resistance to Anglo-American ethnocentrism" (21).

In *Border Matters: Remapping American Cultural Studies*, José Saldívar cogently argues that it is this collectivity in the twentieth century, located on the margins of the nation, which will mark the "U.S.–Mexico border as a paradigm of crossing, resistance, and circulation." With a designated "inside" and "outside," the movement between these positions "must always be a process of hybridity" (84). Yet this migration between nations and national identities has a price. As Saldívar astutely notes, Arturo Islas in *Migrant Souls* (1990) defines the cost of this migration through the "central consciousness," Miguel Chico, who describes migration as that constant coming but never arriving, where border crossing symbolizes unequal markets, competition and opportunity (J. Saldívar 80).

In the Chicana/o novel, that originless, unstable in-betweeness of Islas's "Children of the Border" becomes the space for the expression of a dialectical, Chicana/o subjectivity. According to Ramón Saldívar, "It establishes itself upon the unstable borderline of difference between Mexican and American social ideologies. . . . Chicano subjectivity . . . is both Mexican and American and also neither one nor the other, completely" (175).

In her novel, Ruiz de Burton provides the antecedents of this Chicana/o subjectivity. If what Islas's character says is representative of Chicana/o subjectivity — "we don't know who we are because we don't know where we are" — then Ruiz de Burton begins to map where "we" have been by providing a coherent, unified, criolla Mexican soul in her first novel, *Who Would Have Thought It?* which marks a return to origins. In her novel, Ruiz de Burton redefines the formation of the border in the Southwest resulting from the Mexican War. The dialectic within Chicana/o identity assumes a border as that position between national identities. For Ruiz de Burton, the fractured borders persisting between the United States and Mexico after the war represent the lack of a coherent Mexican national identity in the nineteenth century. It is this border which Ruiz de Burton seeks to figuratively mend, thereby refashioning that in-between border space within the pages of her text that will come to symbolize a dialectical, Chicana/o subjectivity in the twentieth century.

The republishing of *Who Would Have Thought It?* and *The Squatter and the Don* marks an important intervention into Chicana/o Studies that is initiating the reevaluation of what we consider resistance literature in which a "working-class ideology" has been central to the construction of Chicanismo since the late 1960s and early 1970s. Consequently, the majority of criticism on María Amparo Ruiz de Burton's texts subordinates gender issues to those of class and emphasizes middle-class resistance to U.S. colonialism as the most important factor in determining the "recovery" status of her texts. When gender is included in an analysis of Ruiz de Burton's writing, it is usually viewed only in terms of romance and marriage where gender is the bridge to racial homogenization in creating a white nation and in guaranteeing class privilege.

As José F. Aranda notes in "Breaking All the Rules: María Amparo Ruiz de Burton Writes a Civil War Novel," the adoption of postcolonial theory in Chicano/a studies has helped foster "resistance strategies of reading Chicano/a texts" but has reduced the "field of analysis to only one colonialism, that promulgated by the United States" (70).[1] This largely ignored colonial past is embedded in Chicana/o history and nationalism: "Chicano/a scholars consistently mark the Mexican-American War of 1846 and the Treaty of Guadalupe Hidalgo of 1848 as that geopolitical and psychic rupture that made possible the internal colonization of 100,000 Mexican citizens. While this assessment is irrefutable, what is ironically lost upon most Chicano/a scholars is the prior colonialist status of these same 100,000 Mexican citizens" (71). And yet this southwestern land, like many of these recovered texts, is attached to a colonial past. The romance of Aztlán, then, and Chicano nationalism by extension, is the erasure of criollo origins in favor of a romanticized national unity that eliminates a nineteenth-century Mexican and Mexican American past incongruous with twentieth-century Chicano ideologies.

Pita and Sánchez argue that Ruiz de Burton's privileging of criollo whiteness is due to her sense of "Latinidad" — the defense of the Latin race by the infusion of French culture and the elimination of Euro-American hegemony (194). In describing U.S. imperialism, Ruiz de Burton depicts this threat in both gendered and racialized terms: "Es necesario que yo no me entusiasme por el progreso del continente. ¿Para qué? Ni mi raza ni mi sexo van a sacar mejora alguna (2-15-69)" [It is necessary that I do not get too excited about the progress of the continent. And why? Because neither my race nor my sex will improve"] (195). Because she views the Civil War as a struggle between Franco-Latin and Euro-American races, Ruiz de Burton considers the South an extension of Latinidad and thus, for her, a "white" nation is designed to prevent the immersion of South America by North America.

Ruiz de Burton's writing enters into a body of nineteenth-century literature immersed in this gendered conquest and Spanish/American colonial origins. In *The History of the Conquest of Mexico with a Preliminary View of the Ancient Mexican Civilization and the Life of the Conqueror Hernando Cortés* (1843), William Hickling Prescott connects the aristocratic, Spanish male conquerors with the Puritans. Aligning racially pure origins with consent, Prescott ends his narrative just before the birth of the mixed-blood Mexican. In James Fenimore Cooper's *The Prairie* (1827), Cooper, like Prescott, separates the Indian from an aristocratic Spaniard and removes a foreign "obstacle" from the fluidity of a male, Euro-

American national identity. In Cooper's text, it is the prairie, with its "same waving and regular surface, the same absence of foreign objects, and the same boundless extent to view," that represents the fluidity of identity. The aristocratic, Spanish Inez, or the "Louisiana Lady," disrupts this oceanlike western prairie. Captive to the squatters, the foreign Inez is hidden in a tent that disturbs the visual continuity of the prairie. In one scene in which Inez is captured by the Sioux, Cooper juxtaposes her face with that of an Indian woman, separating the Spanish criolla and aristocratic "beauty" from the Indian just as Prescott separates the Spaniard from the Aztec in his text. As Prescott makes this separation to merge the Spanish colonial with the American, so too does Cooper separate Spanish and Indian to reappropriate a pre-Mexican Independence, criollo Spanish claim in the New World by marrying the Louisiana Lady (Inez) to the Protestant, Euro-American Middleton (13, 293).

This is the literary tradition of Mexican dispossession that Ruiz de Burton is writing within. Like Prescott and Cooper, she privileges a Spanish whiteness at the expense of African Americans and American Indians. But unlike these writers, it is a post-Mexican Independence criolla identity. In *Who Would Have Thought It?* Ruiz de Burton genders this whiteness as female. In her text, she aligns Prescott's racially adulterated Mexican origins with the adulterous Puritan New Englanders. Through Lola's feminization of the New Englander, Julian, and subsequent marriage in Mexico, Ruiz de Burton reverses Cooper's subsuming of a criolla by Euro-American identity. Rather, in *Who Would Have Thought It?* the Euro-American Julian is engulfed by a feminized, aristocratic Spanish/Mexican identity. The unification of Lola's Mexican family as a coalescence of the Mexican nation represents Mexico's repossession of its Spanish borderlands — that land Don Felipe claims Spain was "cheated" out of by Louis XIV's "intrigues," which includes Cooper's Louisiana and, by extension, Texas (197).[2]

Ruiz de Burton begins her text by mixing the domestic and

the foreign within a New England home to critique U.S. Puritan origins. In chapters 1 through 28, the Norvals' Massachusetts home seems to be a model of the cult of domesticity, where the corruptions of the public are kept separate from the private. However, this separation of spheres collapses when the Norvals move to their New York mansion in chapter 29. Ruiz de Burton critiques these domestic spaces by showing that lurking behind both Norval homes is the mixing of the domestic and the foreign through Mrs. Norval's imperialistic designs — an adulteration Ruiz de Burton connects to the United States' Puritan origins.

In moving from the opposition between public and private to the domestic and foreign, Ruiz de Burton critiques what Amy Kaplan calls "manifest domesticity": a trend in domestic literature of the 1850s to mix the domestic and the imperial. Shifting from a contrast between men and women as inhabiting separate public and private spaces to an opposition of the domestic and the foreign, nineteenth-century domestic discourse could unite men and women as "national allies against the alien, and the determining division is not gender but racial demarcations of otherness" (Kaplan, "Manifest Domesticity" 582).

Along with Rev. Hackwell's hatred of things foreign, Mrs. Norval operates within a domesticity that allows her to expand her influence beyond her home and nation while simultaneously contracting this sphere to "police domestic boundaries against the threat of foreignness both within and without" (Kaplan 585). This play between the domestic and the foreign allowed for the envisioning of nation as home and fostered national expansion by encouraging the domestication of the foreign beyond the bounds of the nation through female influence — such as adopting native children. It also entailed the policing of that racial "other" within the bounds of the home by civilizing the foreign (Kaplan 601–2). Domestic novelists depict this negotiation between the domestic and foreign through the breakdown between the internal and the external in which "the privileged space of the domestic novel" — the interiority of female subjectivity — holds "traces of foreignness that must be domesticated" (Kaplan 600).

Unlike most domestic novels, *Who Would Have Thought It?* shows how the contraction and expansion of manifest domesticity — that play between the domestic and the foreign, civilized and savage — does not lead to the fortification of the domestic and the national, but to their division. By endowing Mrs. Norval with nativist stereotypes, Ruiz de Burton creates a nineteenth-century female domestic subject who is incapable of domesticating the "alien" within herself. As an extension of her interiority, Mrs. Norval's Massachusetts home reflects this savage, New England subjectivity that is unable to civilize or be civilized. Extending this problem of domesticity to the nation, Ruiz de Burton depicts the interiority of the nation as incapable of union, and the North, as the "savage" other, incapable of domestication by its more "civilized" southern counterpart.

In chapters 1–28, the Norval household follows the trajectory of manifest domesticity as Mrs. Norval both contracts and expands the bounds of her home. She hates "foreigners and papists" (92), laments Catholic-church attending Isaac, and criticizes Julian's fondness for foreign things, particularly Old World things: "Julian is perfectly ruined by his unfortunate trip to Europe . . . and, like Isaac, he will never get over his fondness for foreigners" (18). Contracting the bounds of her family by excluding the foreign, Mrs. Norval polices the domestic sphere. Bringing what she thinks is a black and possibly racially mixed child into her household, Mrs. Norval simultaneously extends the imperializing reach of female influence as her "Christian" duty while constantly fearing contagion from that "uncivilized" child she must domesticate.

Yet it is her attempts to extend her domestic empire through Lola's wealth that most "infect" her. Lola's Mexican gold becomes her god — "she was so subdued, so humbled, before the yellow god!" (26) — and allows her to extend her influence beyond the domestic domain and into the fashionable society of New York. She at once buys a mansion and sees that her daughter, Ruth, and Reverend Hackwell's sister, Emma, attend the opera arrayed in "costly silks (all bought with Lola's money)" (167). Financing the Norvals' rise from middle to high class, Lola's gold corrupts Mrs. Norval, making her feel as if her soul were "floating over those yellow, shining lumps of cold, unfeeling metal" and transforming her from a "sedate, severe, sober, serious lady of forty" into a "playful, laughing child again" (25) — hardly the mother in control of an unruly, domestic empire.

Her loss of self control and restraint parallel her fall into the "unruly" and "uncivilized" savage she had attempted to tame. It is this decline that Ruiz de Burton links to Mrs. Norval's Puritan origins in which her seduction and adultery stem from the adulteration of the national origin. Ruiz de Burton's critique of nineteenth-century U.S. origins links her text, *Who Would Have Thought It?*, with Nathaniel Hawthorne's novel *The Scarlet Letter* (1850). Within his text, Hawthorne debunks the myth that the Pilgrims and Puritans were the first democrats by depicting their condemnation of Hester's dissent from patriarchy — her adultery — as an act of intolerance. By exposing this hypocrisy, Hawthorne explodes the myth of pure origins by showing that the United States is not a regenerate breed that dissented from its forefathers to foster freedom of opinion. Puritan origins are adulterated, not pure, and Hawthorne uses adultery to represent U.S. origins as an imperfect union. Hawthorne links Catholicism, as an adulterated mixing of flesh and spirit, with impure Protestant origins through Pearl. As the product of Hester's adulterous act of dissent, this child represents a "Catholic" mixture of the material and immaterial. [3]

In her novel *Who Would Have Thought It?* Ruiz de Burton, like Hawthorne, couples the political and the sexual through the adulterous union of the Protestant minister Hackwell and Mrs. Norval. This mismatch represents the continued adulteration of seventeenth-century U.S. origins in the nineteenth century. Before a sermon by Hackwell, the narrator notes that it was a day "in which the Pilgrim fathers had done one of their wonderful deeds. They had either embarked, or landed, or burnt a witch, or whipped a woman at the pillory, on just such a day. The reverend gentlemen [Hackwell and Hammerhard] of our acquaintance were to hold forth their respective congregations, who idolized them, and would have mobbed and lynched anyone daring to hint that the two divines solaced themselves with a jug of whiskey after those edifying sermons" (62). Thus, just like their Puritan forefathers who silenced dissenting women, these two reverends preach intolerance by criminalizing any act of dissent.

Ruiz de Burton also Catholicizes this nineteenth-century intolerance stemming from U.S. Puritan origins. But she, unlike Hawthorne, takes the nativist stereotypes of Catholicism and aligns them with the barbarous, New World Puritan while separating an Old World Spanish Catholicism from this mixture.

In placing nativist stereotypes of New World Catholicism onto a Protestant mother and reverend in the domestic sphere, Ruiz de Burton critiques the convent captivity genres that equated imprisonment within the "savage" New World wilderness with captivity to the seductive interiors of the Catholic convent. These nativist narratives domesticated the colonial Indian captivity narrative which, according to Jenny Franchot, "became a drama, not of being kidnapped into the American wilderness, boundless and frightening, but of being entrapped by spaces — cathedral, confessional, and convent" (*Roads to Rome* 112). While their colonial ancestors encountered "the satanic within the popish denizens of the wilderness; so too did these nineteenth-century 'maidens' claim to have met savagery behind the religious guise of priest and nun" (118). With the closing of the frontier in the nineteenth century and numerous limitations of property, gender, and ethnicity, the Protestant sovereign self transcended these limitations by "imagining a recurrent escape from Romanism, whose spaces, infinitely bounded by rules, costumes and religious practices, were, further-more, capable of exhibiting fascinating transformations from 'in-laid casket' to 'sublime cathedral' " (184).[4]

The domestic space of the Norval home substitutes for the enclosed space of the convent. Within this Massachusetts home lurks that "lecherous father confessor" of the convent captivity narrative who usurps the place of the Protestant father and seduces young maidens within the confessional where unsupervised dis-course between the sexes is tantamount to illicit sexual intercourse (Franchot 125). Within Ruiz de Burton's narrative, it is the former lawyer-reverend-captain, Mr. Hackwell, who is to be Mrs. Norval's "father-confessor," displacing her husband, Dr. Norval (44).

Mrs. Norval's seduction occurs through the reading of Dr. Nor-val's will within the enclosed domestic space of the Norval library rather than the convent. Violating Dr. Norval's sanction that his will not be opened until Lola turns twenty-one, Hackwell and Mrs. Norval pour over the "forbidden document" just two weeks after the alleged death of Dr. Norval (122). As the medium that connects the two through their greed, their joint reading of the will creates a physical reaction in both: "His face was pale as he read; hers was flushed; the hands of both trembled, and they spoke in whispers" (122). This adulterous union first manifests itself through hand-holding, making Mrs. Norval tremble "like a young maiden," and then kissing, where Hackwell conquers Mrs. Norval: "she felt so weak in his arms, so powerless to resist, that she did not resist. The stately lady, paragon of propriety, was as morally weak as — as — *what?*" (123).

Hackwell's ability to change identities enables him to seduce Mrs. Norval. This mix of identities is hardly the sovereign, Protes-tant self but the adulterated, mixed, "Catholic" savage. Safe to "be anything he pleased" (136), Hackwell claims to be her Ithuriel — an angel from Milton's *Paradise Lost* who was able to detect deception with the slightest touch of his spear (140). So too does Hackwell claim to have "penetrated" the surface of Mrs. Norval: "I am an *Ithuriel*! . . . *Ithuriel*, to be sure, and without any spear, but with a single kiss I caused the mask to fall" (140).

Through her seduction, Mrs. Norval is transformed: "She felt a thrill through her whole frame, just as might have felt one of those creatures — whom she so abhorred — . . . . she liked, she enjoyed, this antithetical position with her former self" (173). Ruiz de Burton associates this changed self with Mrs. Norval's "frozen-up soul" (174): "She rejoiced that she had kept this volcano in her heart, closely covered over with layer upon layer of snow, which the devotion, the generosity and the kindness of the doctor had failed to melt, but which her 'Ithuriel' had charmed away in one instant!" (174). In describing Mrs. Norval's frozen heart as a volcano, Ruiz de Burton combines the Yankee trait of "cold dignity and propriety" (84) with the warm passion of those "irreverent women with foreign, loose notions" that Mrs. Norval, ironically, criticizes (174).

Thus, Mrs. Norval embodies the "mongrel" mix (179) that she detests: "Lola might be now all black or all white, no matter which, only not with those ugly white spots" (78). Ruiz de Burton aligns the adulteress, Mrs. Norval, with the racially mixed origins of Lola and Mexico through Hammerhard's comparison of her to Popocatépetl, a volcano outside Mexico City: "Who would have supposed such a Vesuvius covered over with New England snows, eh? A Yankee Popocatépetl!" (177).

Ruiz de Burton couples regional divisions between New England and the Southwest with the national division between the North and South through hypocritical Northerners, like Mrs. Norval, whose desire for southwestern wealth and her refusal to take care of Lola, "the little black child," speaks, as Dr. Norval notes, "very highly for New England — abolitionist New England, mind you" (19). Like Mrs. Norval's greed, northern motivation for invading the South is not to free blacks but to dispossess the South. Ruiz de Burton exposes this New England hypocrisy by claiming that the Puritans came to the New World to dispossess its inhabitants, not to free themselves or others. In chapter 24, she connects seventeenth-century and nineteenth-century duplicity through Mr. Cackle, as he lectures on the meaning of a painting representing "the embarking of the Pilgrims" (109) at the same time he proudly ruminates over the role of his four sons in dispossessing the South. Here, Ruiz de Burton couples northern greed over southern wealth with Puritan greed over New World wealth.

In a nation led by adulterers like Hackwell and lower-class social climbers like the Cackles, U.S. Manifest Destiny becomes an extension of adulterated Puritan origins. In *The Scarlet Letter*, Reverend Dimmesdale praises New England origins in his election day sermon, a jeremiad designed to manifest the "divine destiny" of the New England people in North America. For Hester at the scaffold, this eloquent speech on Manifest Destiny reaches her as an "indistinct, but varied, murmur" of "indistinguishable words" (164).

Like Dimmesdale's election day sermon on Manifest Destiny that degenerates into a murmur, Manifest Destiny becomes cackling in *Who Would Have Thought It?* If Hawthorne writes the "dimmed" seventeenth-century voice of Dimmesdale as carrying within it the adulterated origins of the United States, where the voice of the adulterer fades into a mix of indistinguishable sounds, Ruiz de Burton aligns this adulterated speech with cackling by placing the words of Manifest Destiny in the mouth of Mrs. Cackle: "She was a good American woman, she believed firmly in 'MANIFEST DESTINY,' and that the Lord was *bound* to protect the Union, even if to do so the affairs of the rest of the universe were to be laid aside for the time being" (159).

For Ruiz de Burton in *Who Would Have Thought It?* the Civil War is an extension of Puritan barbarity stemming from its impure origins in which the conquest of the South means the silencing of dissent through forced union. She aligns this Manifest Destiny with northern savagery through the Yankee practice of starving the South and their northern prisoners, a "barbarous policy" that one congressman denies: "When it comes to killing our brave boys with slow torture, then the American heart and mind revolt" (117). Yet it is this policy which another congressman claims has been sanctioned by the people since the American Revolution, that "time of Washington" (116).

While Ruiz de Burton depicts the Civil War as a conquest and extension of Manifest Destiny, it is the Mexican War and the continued dispossession of the Mexican nation which parallels southern dispossession in her text. Doña Theresa represents the fall of Mexico after the invasion of 1846 and the violation of the Mexican nation through her capture by Apache Indians from the domestic space of her bedroom in northern Mexico. It is her offspring, Lola, born five months after Doña Theresa's capture and sale to the Mojave Indians in 1846, who symbolizes the promise of renewal of that Mexico of 1848 — that violated body of Doña Theresa and continued plundering of Mexican territory and wealth along the weakened borders of the Mexican nation.

As the representation of the Mexican nation after its defeat by the United States in 1848, Lola is born into that space of violation, that ruptured Mexican border greatly weakened by the invasion. Ruiz de Burton equates the captivity of Lola by Apache "savages" and the "staining of her skin" with the continued violation of Mexican borders by the United States during the Mexican War and the denigration of Mexican national origins. She further aligns this staining of Mexican nationhood with New England through Lola's captivity to the "savage" Mrs. Norval and Hackwell. Ruiz de Burton couples the southwestern Native American with the New England "savage" through antinativism. Transplanting the nativist stereotypes of the convent captivity narrative into the New England Norval home, Ruiz de Burton writes Protestant domestic captivity as convent capture. In her text, it is a Protestant minister, and not a Catholic priest, who is the seducer, and it is a Puritan matron, not a mother superior, who is the figure of a deviant, masculinized femininity and motherhood.

Lola's flight from Indian and domestic captivity and into the freedom of the convent parallels her conversion from black skin to white, from racial and national ambiguity to certainty, as she strips off the captive influence of U.S. New World domestic savagery in favor of the aristocratic and genteel Spanish Old World convent. Thus, it is through her captivity that Lola and Mexican origins will become "purified." As Emma Hackwell remarks, "I think Lola might teach us the secret of that Indian paint that kept her white skin under cover, making it whiter by bleaching it. I would bargain to wear spots for a while" (232).

It is Lola's flight from the domestic captivity of the Norval home and into the convent that parallels her whitening. Fulfilling the wishes of her dying mother, Doña Theresa, that Lola be taken away from "those horrid savages" and "baptized and brought up Catholic" (36), Dr. Norval once again saves Lola from captivity by placing her in a convent. Moving from being Mrs. Norval's "despised black child" (30) to the convent where she is "received most kindly" by the mother superior (101), Lola escapes from the inhumane and middle-class New England home to the security of an Old World aristocratic and genteel domain. It is here that she regains title to her "pure blood" through her whitening.

Ruiz de Burton links Lola's white skin and beauty with the power to influence by transforming the contagion feared from her black and spotted skin (17) into the seductive force of her gender as Lola's appearance metamorphosizes from the despised skin of the "black child" to the "lovely white skin" of womanhood (100). Aligning Lola's power to influence with the unveiling of her "lovely white skin," Ruiz de Burton invests Lola with the privilege of Mexican/Spanish whiteness at the expense of Indians and blacks. In doing so, Ruiz de Burton replaces the threat of racial contamination through the contagion of disease with the power of sexual attraction which Julian experiences through her gaze: "His gaze became fixed on hers, and a thrill went through his whole frame from the little soft hand he held in his" (91).

If whiteness is the mark of civilization and power, then in chapter 39, "Julian Carries the War into Africa," the Norvals do wear "spots" for a while. Lola's "whitening" through her New England captivity allows her to reenter the New York Norval domestic realm as the civilizing force against Norval savagery where civilizing means repossession, not dispossession. While Lola's stay in the Norval home in Massachusetts represents the contraction of her power through her captivity, it is in the New York mansion, bought with the dispossessed wealth of the Mexican Southwest, that Lola experiences an expansion of her power. Simultaneously, Mrs. Norval suffers the constriction of her domestic realm through her subsequent fall into insanity.

Through the domestic realm of the New York mansion and Mrs. Norval's insanity, Ruiz de Burton shows how New England Manifest Destiny collapses into its own interiority. Thus, the very thing Mrs. Norval fears upon Lola's entrance into her mansion in chapter 39 is what leads to her downfall. As Julian reads the paper, Mrs. Norval is overcome with dread that something might be published there about "Lola's friends looking for her, or about her husband not being dead" (178). Within the space of the New York mansion, funded by southwestern wealth, both Julian and Lola are repossessed of their lost lineages.

This union causes the collapse of Mrs. Norval. Her demise begins with the arrival of Dr. Norval's letters announcing his impending return and culminates after the reading of Doña Theresa's manuscript and the arrival of Lola's father, Don Luis. Thus, shortly after marrying Hackwell, Mrs. Norval is bereft of any power she had gained from this adulterous union and she loses her "short twilight of reason" (267). This loss of reason links her to the New World "savages" whom nineteenth-century thinkers like William Hickling Prescott considered irrational. It is that "superstitious mind" attributed to New World natives and Catholics — that "primitive mind" which cannot separate reality and fantasy, verging on lunacy and collapsing on its own interiority (Franchot 45) — that Ruiz de

Burton invests in Mrs. Norval. Thus, she is struck with a "violent brain fever" that "might deprive her of reason, if not of life" (267). Her demise is described as an invasion as the Mexican manuscript and African letters (which represent the repossession of both Lola and Julian's paternal lineages) invade her home and her mind: "For a whole hour the poor woman raved about her darling buried in the sand, and the horrible negroes and ugly Indians" (269).

Ruiz de Burton extends this division represented by Mrs. Norval's loss of reason to the U.S. government through Mrs. Norval's "imps." These internal voices, which result from Mrs. Norval's adulterous union with Hackwell, represent her impending mental collapse. They are the voices that Ruiz de Burton aligns with Washington, the base of the federal government: "Her gang of unbottled imps . . . laughed and skipped about in joy, and clapped their hands, knowing that the madam would take them all to Washington, which is a city very congenial to all unbottled imps, and where the jolly crew would have abundant fun" (148). This is a government now run by adulterers like Hackwell who cater to "unbottled imps" through their seductive promises. Hackwell plunged "into politics and became the warmest friend of the Cackles" (292). Forming their own party, the Cackles exhort their followers to treat the South with ill will and to violate the national union represented by Grant's kind treatment of Lee. Ruiz de Burton's Republican Cacklism reflects the fragmentation of a government collapsing into its own interiority: "The Democratic party is dissolving. Now is the time for us to catch the falling pieces and join them and shape them into *Cacklism*" (298).

Ruiz de Burton contrasts Mexico with the fall of the U.S. government symbolized by the demise of Mrs. Norval and her domestic space. In her text, the U.S. invasion of Mexico in 1846 destroys Mexican borders and leads to the capture of Doña Theresa from her home in northern Sonora. Depicting the denigration of the Mexican nation through the violation of this domestic space, Ruiz de Burton aligns the fracture of Mexico with the Medina family.

The return of Doña Theresa's manuscript to her husband, Don Luis, and her father, Don Felipe, correlates with the cleansing of Mexico's pre-1848 origins. Describing the Mexico City as the "classic ground of Montezuma the timid and Cortez the daring" (194) while also protesting against the Mexican government for letting "Indians live as they please" while its "more civilized citizens take care of themselves as best they may" (194), Ruiz de Burton shows her desire to "cleanse" her "white" Mexico of its racially mixed heritage.

Through Doña Theresa's narration from beyond the grave, Ruiz de Burton purges Mexican womanhood of its mixed racial origins beginning with the sixteenth-century conquest of Malinche by Cortés and ending with the nineteenth-century conquest of Mexico, symbolized by Doña Theresa's capture in 1846. Cleansed in heaven as a "beautiful radiant face," Doña Theresa redeems her purity through her death and "resurrection" during the reading of the manuscript. Reading releases her captive voice, long silenced by her violation: "I am an angel now. I was always pure, for my soul did not sin, although I was insulted by a savage. I was a martyr; now an angel" (202). At the expense of its indigenous past, Ruiz de Burton "purifies" the origin of Mexican nationhood through its attachment to criolla roots.

Joining Doña Theresa's voice with that of her husband, the Austrian-born Don Luis, as he reads the words of Doña Theresa, Ruiz de Burton also connects the unified Mexico to its future, which she believes lies in its rule by an Austrian prince, Maximilian. So too does Ruiz de Burton promise the repossession of Spain's dispossessed lands through Maximilian, a descendent of the Habsburgs. It is this lineage which both Don Luis and Don Felipe associate with the "legitimate and lawful heirs of the glorious Isabella and the great Charles V" (197). For Ruiz de Burton, resurrecting this genealogy means restoring the lands that the pro-Spanish Habsburgs were "cheated" out of by France during the seventeenth century. This land includes Louisiana — that land stolen by France from Spain and then purchased by the United States in 1803 (197). Ruiz de Burton blames the Mexican government for the fate of Doña Theresa in not protecting its frontiers from "savages" (201). However, through the words of Don Luis, she places the blame on U.S. imperialism: "this *fatal* influence *which will eventually destroy us*" (198).[5]

With the reunion of Don Luis and Lola, Ruiz de Burton reunites a pre-1848 Mexico (represented by Don Luis, Don Felipe, and Doña Theresa) with the Mexico of post-1848 (represented by Lola). The unification of the "Mexican" family, through the "purification" of its lineages as well as the repossession of its plundered southwest wealth, correlates with the fall of the "U.S." family: the Norvals. Ruiz de Burton depicts the Medinas' flight from Hackwell as the end of a national captivity narrative. Their return to Mexico represents the restoration of Mexico's fractured borders through the "black dividing line" from the steamer carrying Lola and her father away. As Mattie notes to Hackwell, this border has been traced by "Providence" to separate Hackwell from Lola and, by extension, the United States from Mexico (284). It is this blackened border which heralds the racialization and criminalization of the half million Mexican Americans living in the territories acquired from the Mexican War and the millions of Mexicans who will join them in the years following 1848.

Notes

1. In their introduction to *Reinventing the Americas: Comparative Studies of the Literature of the United States and Spanish America*, editors Bell Gale Chevigny and Gari Laguardia distinguish between Spanish and American colonialisms. For them, the Spanish conquest "obscures the fact that once the Amerindians were subjugated . . . the feudal and corporative mentality of the Spaniards demanded that they be

incorporated in some way into the social hierarchy." Conversely, the Puritan "conquest" of the New World did not involve incorporation where "egalitarian political positions for Europeans" were backed by "aggressive anti-Indian policies" (4).

2. Taking place in 1804, just one year after the purchase of Louisiana from France, *The Prairie* represents a turn back to Spanish colonialism in order to undo Mexican claims to southwestern land. Ignoring the Adams-Onis Treaty of 1819 through which the United States gave Texas to Spain, many U.S. political thinkers in the 1830s, like Democratic representative Robert Walker, asserted that the 1803 Louisiana Purchase included Texas in order to lay claim to a pre-Mexican Independence (1821) Spanish borderlands. Cooper's 1827 text represents this line of thought, which would erase Mexican title to southwestern land by laying claim to a pre-Mexican Independence Spanish origin.

3. From a lecture given by Jenny Franchot, University of California, Berkeley, 1996.

4. See also " 'Who Ever Heard of a Blue-Eyed Mexican?' Satire and Sentimentality in María Amparo Ruiz de Burton's *Who Would Have Though It?*" where Anne E. Goldman insightfully notes that Ruiz de Burton uses the captivity genre to refute racialized conceptions of sexuality (64–65).

5. In privileging Maximilian as the savior for Mexico, Ruiz de Burton displays her support of Latinidad — that Latin race opposed to Euro-American hegemony. Her idea of Latinidad includes the French culture, and Maximilian, as a French subject, is part of her ideal Latinidad (194).

ɛᴏ 3 ɛᴏ

Critiquing the Conquest
of California

A Europeanized New World: Colonialism and Cosmopolitanism in *Who Would Have Thought It?*

GRETCHEN MURPHY

María Amparo Ruiz de Burton's 1872 novel *Who Would Have Thought It?* poses a problem for recent critical efforts to decenter Anglo American literature. These efforts have included Lawrence Buell's idea to "refashion American studies as a hemispheric project" (479), which Janice Radway has proposed to name "Inter-American Studies" and which Eric Cheyfitz would call "Americas Cultural Studies." Carolyn Porter has suggested that this project might help critics to "grasp how the cultural, political, and economic relations between and within the Americas might work to reconstellate the field itself, reinflecting its questions in accord with a larger frame" (510). While this reframing would perhaps make a text like *Who Would Have Thought It?* central instead of marginal, the novel's remapping of "America" resists such a hemispheric project. Instead, the novel emphasizes the larger frame of transatlantic culture in which Ruiz de Burton wants to place the Americas — a frame that she uses to undermine claims of New World identity. *Who Would Have Thought It?* reimagines the New World as a space of transatlantic cosmopolitanism and renders meaningless the geographical division of the globe into Eastern and Western Hemispheres.[1] Unlike the writers of "Our America" that Kirsten Silva Gruesz and José David Saldívar examine in order to imagine "a broader, more oppositional American literary history" (Saldívar, *Dialectics of Our America* 17), Ruiz de Burton not only decenters Anglo American culture and politics but also deconstructs the utopic concept of a New World with radical transformative power.

Her "remapping" specifically opposes the Monroe Doctrine, a nineteenth-century foreign policy statement that justified U.S. nationalism and imperialism through its construction of a politically unified Western Hemisphere and its utopic concept of a New World. *Who Would Have Thought It?* most obviously and didactically criticizes the discourse of the Monroe Doctrine during a scene set in Mexico in which two Mexican characters discuss the possibility of Austrian Archduke Maximilian accepting the newly created Mexican throne, a historical event that marked Mexico's brief switch from democracy to monarchy.[2] One character, Don Felipe, says that although he is a liberal, he "will be happy to be the most loyal of subjects" to Maximilian (197). He justifies his loyalty by projecting another history of Mexico wherein monarchy triumphed rather than democracy. Although an election will determine whether it is the will of the people that Maximilian be king, Don Felipe argues that the Austrian has a claim to the throne of Mexico by right of succession. Maximilian, he explains, is not a Bourbon but one of the Habsburgs, "the legitimate heirs of the glorious Queen Isabella and the Great Charles the V," and had the Habsburgs remained in power, Mexico might never have declared independence from Spain in 1824. "The Mexicans did not want a republic," Don Felipe says, "they just wanted a good and just prince. . . . Under a different dynasty, we might now have been an independent kingdom" (197).

This alternate history challenges the ideas in James Monroe's 1823 Presidential Message that subsequent statesmen and writers would call the Monroe Doctrine. Monroe, writing soon after many Latin American countries declared independence from Spain, claimed that the Western Hemisphere's move toward democracy and away from monarchy was inevitable and one that the United States was bound to protect. His message stated that "the American continents, by the free and independent condition that they have assumed and maintain, are henceforth not to be considered as subjects for future colonization by any European powers" (328).

Anticipating that Spain, in its "Holy Alliance" with France and Austria, might attempt to recapture the new American republics, Monroe wrote that "it is impossible that the allied powers should extend their political system to any portion of either continent without endangering our peace and happiness, nor can anyone believe that our southern brethren, if left to themselves, would adopt it of their own accord" (341). For the next twenty years this statement in Monroe's Message was virtually ignored in American politics, until James K. Polk, in his 1845 Presidential message, told Congress that it was time to "reiterate and reaffirm the principle avowed by Mr. Monroe" by refusing to allow "the European system" to control Oregon and Texas (Polk 14). "The American system of government is entirely different from that of Europe," Polk explained, for American republics share "a system of self-government which seems natural to our soil, and which will ever resist foreign interference" (5). According to Dexter Perkins, the first major historian of the Doctrine, by the end of the 1860s the Doctrine was "consolidated and vindicated" in U.S. political discourse and had become a "catchword" whose meaning had "taken deep lodgment in the American mind" (546).

Monroe's Message and its subsequent reinterpretations as "Doctrine" declared a categorical division between Old World tyranny and New World democracy, and justified U.S. prohibition of European intervention in the Western Hemisphere with this binary. Monroe's message was motivated by a need for the newly formed nation to ease postcolonial anxiety of influence and to assert its status not as a satellite of Europe balancing Old World power struggles but as the center of an entirely separate system.[3] Don Felipe, however, explicitly challenges democracy as the "natural" and destined mode of government in the Americas. "Of course the ideas of this continent are different from those of Europe," he momentarily concedes, echoing the language of the American statesmen, "but we all know that such would not be the case if the influence of the United States did not prevail with such despotic

Gretchen Murphy

sway over the minds of the leading men of the Hispanic American republics. If it were not for this terrible, this *fatal* influence — *which will eventually destroy us* — the Mexicans, instead of seeing anything objectionable in the proposed change, would be proud to hail a prince who, after all, has some sort of claim to this land, and who will cut us loose from the leading strings of the United States" (198). For Don Felipe, the obvious difference that separates New World from Old, Western Hemisphere from Eastern, is a sham that "everyone knows" results from the dominance of Anglo American ideas in Hispanic America.

These passages have troubled many critics because they raise the question of whether Ruiz de Burton was speaking through her character in this instance to express what might be her own monarchist loyalties. Rosaura Sánchez and Beatrice Pita sidestep the question by stating that "whether Ruiz de Burton herself favored liberal monarchy in Mexico is not clear nor really at issue," insisting that more importantly, the author uses the scene to demonstrate that U.S., not European, empire was the greater threat to Mexico (lvi). José F. Aranda Jr. builds on their point by arguing that Ruiz de Burton uses this monarchical legacy "as a subtle reminder of Mexico's eighteenth-century enlightenment credentials" and the possibility of an alternative to the corruption and demagoguery she depicts in U.S. politics (571). Aranda sees in Ruiz de Burton's novel an indictment of Spanish and Mexican colonialisms "for failing to secure North America for their white, educated, European elite," and an urgent cry to Americans that it is not too late for them to achieve this ideal (573).

Both Sánchez and Pita's and Aranda's arguments seem to me correct in that Ruiz de Burton was primarily interested in criticizing the United States rather than in proposing monarchy as a real alternative for Mexico or other Latin American states. But reading Ruiz de Burton's novel in the context of the U.S. debates about the Monroe Doctrine in the 1860s demonstrates that her interest in Maximilian's right to rule Mexico is not merely an effort to legitimate herself as "a daughter of the Enlightenment" in the New World (Aranda 573). Instead, this scene is part of the novel's sustained opposition to a powerfully emerging statement of foreign policy and cultural identity. It is one element of a narrative that strives to reveal the hypocrisy of the Monroe Doctrine's proprietary isolation of the Western Hemisphere.

Officially the United States did not oppose French intervention in Mexico: Henry Seward, Lincoln's secretary of state, never mentioned the Monroe Doctrine in his diplomatic correspondence with Napoleon III, and he never threatened to use force to drive the French out of Mexico. But many Americans of the 1860s wished that he would, and their desire for the United States to stand behind the Monroe Doctrine created a widespread and vocal public discourse that professed a new, post–Mexican American War relationship between the two North American countries.

The events in Mexico interested Northerners, many of whom wrote articles and attended meetings to promote awareness of the events in Mexico. Matías Romero, a lobbyist assigned to raise support in Washington for Mexico's republican government, worked throughout the early 1860s to keep the phrase "Monroe Doctrine" an active part of public discourse. This was a difficult task, as most Americans were primarily absorbed in the domestic strife of the Civil War, but Romero succeeded in getting a number of influential Americans, William Cullen Bryant among them, to support U.S. intervention in Mexico. As the Civil War neared its end, this support grew; some Americans even feared that secessionists would join Maximilian's forces rather than rejoin the Union. Lew Wallace, the best-selling author and Civil War general responsible for the exotic Zouave costumes that Ruiz de Burton pokes fun at in her novel, took up the cause and was sent by General Grant in 1865 to explore possibilities of sending U.S. troops into Mexico to fight for the democratic government. That mission failed, but after the Civil War, Wallace resigned his post and received a commission in the Mexican army with the assignment of raising U.S. support for

Mexican republicanism. He traveled around the Midwest signing up men for service, founding Mexican aid societies and "Monroe Doctrine committees," and finally leading a mission to bring arms across the border to Juárez's men. [4]

The Monroe Doctrine was widely discussed in congressional debates, editorials, speeches, and pamphlets, and the language of these texts reveals an interest in Mexico that slid back and forth between a desire to protect and foster democracy in the New World and a desire to control Mexico's land and resources. Articulations of the Monroe Doctrine often differed from previous expressions of Manifest Destiny, which called for the complete annexation of Mexico. Instead, a new partnership was envisioned between the United States and Mexico. Lancelot Everitt, an essayist whose work was published in pamphlet form by one of the Monroe Doctrine committees, writes that a partnership between the United States and Mexico was logical because the two nations have "met together in deadly conflict, and each opponent has found the other worthy of his steel; hence the mutual regard and love existing between us, ever ready to expose itself on proper occasions" (7).

Yet Everitt makes clear that this partnership was an unequal one: "Prostrate Mexico invites us to her aid — to her country — to her gardens — to her table — to her fertile lands — and to her rich inexhaustible mines; and she invites us to associate with her people as brothers and sisters of one common family; to be a mutual protection from fraud — from robbery — from tyranny" (6). The two flags will float side by side, but Everitt's gendered imagery and language clearly naturalizes their inequality. This partnership will benefit Mexico through racial and cultural influence, Everitt argues: The races will intermingle as the "energetic American type" marries "the beautiful, chaste, affectionate, truthful Mexican," and as America's "superior taste and accomplishments will influence Mexico," creating "a desire for knowledge and general literature that would destroy [Mexico's] low condition of society, and engender a wish for higher pursuits" (8–9). Everitt makes it clear that this is not simply a matter of the Anglo Saxon improving the native or mestizo through assimilation; he spends the first few pages of his essay explaining the important evolutions that have taken place in the New World, and especially in the United States, since its settlement. The partnership that Everitt envisions is one unique to and expressive of New World freedom and productivity; only in the Americas, he argues, can such a partnership occur.

There is no evidence that Ruiz de Burton read or was influenced by Everitt's essay, but his is only an extreme example of arguments that were made in numerous places and that formed part of a wider discourse of New World partnership of which Ruiz de Burton was undoubtedly aware. The key characteristics of this partnership were not inevitable territorial expansion but political and cultural influence, with the United States as senior partner, husband, or big brother protecting a distinct American "system." As another pamphleteer writes, the United States' new responsibility was to "reassert our highest self-respect as the leading republic of the New World, and the ready representative of the Political System of America, with which European politics had no business to interfere" (Leavitt 48). For Ruiz de Burton, the question was not only by what right the United States declared itself the leading republic, but whether there even existed a "Political System of America." The conversations in the Almenara home are thus significant not primarily as a blueprint for monarchy in Mexico but as alternatives to the historic and geographic assumptions that grounded a U.S. foreign policy gaining ascendancy in the 1860s. She does not only attack these assumptions in scenes dedicated to Mexican politics, however. Her narrative strategy is more indirect, and it demonstrates her awareness that the idea of New World difference was crucial to cultural as well as political representations of American life. Concepts of "America" as essentially different than Europe were articulated not only through the political discourse of foreign policy but also through constructions of American culture and character that circulated in U.S. literature since before the Revolutionary War.

The ruthless satire of Anglo American culture in *Who Would Have Thought It?* has been ably pointed out by Sánchez and Pita and Anne E. Goldman, but my interest is specifically in the way the novel depicts the United States as a space enmeshed in transatlantic cultural influences, caught in an inferior relation to Europe from which one escapes only through genteel improvement that is not mere imitation. The myth of New World difference is her target as she represents the Americas as outposts of European culture that risk chaos, tyranny, and gauche manners in their attempts to turn their backs on the Old World.

The novel opens in an unnamed town in New England, a space that seems to its inhabitants to be separate from and superior to the rest of the world. Dr. Norval, his son Julian, and brother-in-law Isaac Sprig initially appear to be the only members of the community with a desire to travel the world, desires that lead Mrs. Norval to worry repeatedly "that Julian is perfectly ruined by his unfortunate trip to Europe" (18) and to decry "Isaac's corrupted love for drama and foreigners" (87). The narrator, who repeatedly mocks New England characters like the Cackles for not knowing the classical and continental literary allusions that pervade the text, makes quite clear that such provincial knowledge and preferences are the result of poor taste: Isaac simply prefers "Havana cigars to a pipe or a chaw of tobacco, and those miserable sour wines to a good drink of whiskey" (55). When Dr. Norval proposes to send his daughters to Europe during the Civil War, Mrs. Norval lets "her buckwheat cakes drop to the floor" in shock and protests that she will not send her girls to foreign countries "when we have a better one of our own — a *great deal* better one!" (51).

These scenes set up a binary between agrarian isolation and urbane worldliness that would have been quite familiar to readers. Following in the tradition of the Yankee type popularized in

Royall Tyler's famous play *The Contrast* (1784), and updated for later generations in countless plays like Anna Cora Mowatt's *Fashion* (1845), we see Mrs. Norval as a caricature of the thrifty and uncultured Yankee, one who financially "minds the main chance," as did Tyler's Van Rough, and rejects foreign modes of fashion and manners in favor of homespun simplicity.[5] In these stories foreign contamination threatens to corrupt American virtue, and frequently provincialism is valorized. Colonel Manly, Tyler's hero, proudly announces that he "was never ten leagues from the continent [of North America]," and he eschews travel as a means of improvement, preferring "the laudable partiality which ignorant, untraveled men entertain for everything that belongs to their native country" (Tyler 45).

But Ruiz de Burton has inverted this genre by putting Mrs. Norval, one of the least sympathetic characters, in this role. And the superiority of America, and especially New England, that Mrs. Norval professes is tested as the family begins to travel — Ruth and Mattie Norval to Europe and then to New York with their mother, and Julian, Isaac, and his sister, Aunt Lavvy, to Washington and the front during the war. While Julian, like the others traveling to corrupt Washington, concludes it would be a long time before "he should again believe that in America there is not as much despotism as in Europe" (244), the travelers to New York reveal that virtuous domestic isolation, like the superiority of the American government, is a mythic and self-deluding ideal.

Mrs. Norval protests her daughters' trip to Europe, but Ruth Norval seizes on the opportunity, not because she wants to see the art or history of Europe, but "because in her two trips to New York she had learned that it was genteel to talk of having been to Europe, and that you were not considered tip-top exactly until you spoke of Paris and the Coliseum, . . . and of being presented to crowned heads" (51). Mrs. Norval gives in, and after the move to New York, they begin a life of conspicuous consumption in which the authority of European culture figures heavily. Ruth attends operas with the cream of New York society, but she finds she has "seen too many real princes and danced with too many *bona fide* dukes and counts of aristocratic foundation to care for these whom a tumble in the stocks might dethrone tomorrow" (167). Instead of finding foreigners "horrid," as her New England neighbor Mrs. Cackle had, Ruth is pleased to have Lola's father stay with them for his "*distingué* look which would bring *éclat* to the Norval mansion" (255). Mrs. Norval adapts more hesitantly to the life of conspicuous consumption they lead in New York, finding the opera a "Chinese din" that she attends only to please her lover, Major Hackwell. Indeed, the move to New York seems to enact a generational as well as a geographic transition. Ruth becomes more fully the "power" of the family in New York, and Mrs. Norval defers to her daughters on most matters. The ostentatious house they move into offends the mother's thrifty habits, but she considers that her daughters, "who had been in palaces," must know best: "The Empress of France had spoken to them, and complimented them on the sweet way they spoke French. They knew all about genteel society" (125).

Again, these scenes reference and invert the popular genre of nationalist drama. Like the Tiffany family in *Fashion* and Billy Dimple in *The Contrast*, the Norvals slavishly worship European ways, but unlike in these plays, there is no redemptive return to the New England countryside for the Norvals at the story's end. Sánchez and Pita read this move to New York as symbolic of the economic transformation occurring in the United States after the Civil War, as increased industrialization combined with the lands and resources taken from Mexico created wealth for a new generation of capitalists. The Norvals are, after all, quite literally living off of Mexican Lola's inheritance. But the change in their household economy also suggests a shift in what could be called the global location of the United States toward the core of production. Thus Ruth Norval ceases to claim postcolonial difference and virtue in agrarian isolation as her mother did, and instead works out her own imitative relation to European authority. The narrator ironically describes Dr. and Mrs. Norval's courtship on the Sprig farm, depicting the young Norval unable to kneel down to propose because his industrious girlfriend was surrounded on all sides by apple peelings. But what Ruth's and to a lesser degree her mother's aspirations in New York most fully reveal is that the thrift and industry of that New England farm life was a mode of economy born out of greed and necessity, not virtue. "Foreign" and extravagant ways are eagerly accepted once the means to achieve them appears.

Indeed, if Ruiz de Burton is inverting a popular convention in nationalist drama that champions provincialism, she is also developing a version of the popular literary figure of the new American abroad, the subject of numerous Gilded Age essays and novels. The popularity of this figure was in part merely a reflection of the trend among a growing class of wealthy Americans to travel abroad where they encountered (and occasionally married) Europeans. But the figure is also a site where writers struggled to make sense of American identity at a time when the myth of agrarian isolation had lost some of its power to narrativize and represent a rapidly industrializing United States with global economic and political interests. Especially in more popular versions of this story, the traveling American typically proves himself or herself in European society by negotiating or rejecting the aristocratic social mores.[6] In these formulations, the difference of the New World is not compromised by a United States that has lost its agrarian isolation and that traverses the globe as a world power. For Ruth Norval, however, the loss of her mother's pretense of agrarian isolation renders the myth of American difference entirely irrelevant. Ruth's only aspiration is for power in the elite circles of New York, Washington, and Hampton Beach, where European cultural authority is fully recognized but only crudely imitated.

Through Ruth's quest for power, Ruiz de Burton seizes upon uncertainty about the shifting identity of the United States vis-à-vis Europe by depicting the change as one from xenophobic and uncultured isolation to laughable imitation. Her emphasis on these two unsavory options is crucially emphasized in the comic relief she provides through her two ex-Zouave characters, Scaly Wagg and Sophy Head. The two soldiers are stationed in New York to assist Major Hackwell, where they occupy their time in different ways. Scaly Wagg, an alcoholic besieged by delirium tremens and his love for the octoroon prostitute Lucinda, drowns his sorrows and entertains Sophy with his skills of grunting like a pig, crowing like a rooster, and braying like a donkey (185, 223). The gruff Scaly's crude manners contrast with those of the sentimental Sophy, who attempts to imitate romantic, foreign ways. Sophy pines for Ruth's French maid Mina, whom he mistakes for one of the Norval sisters, composes songs to her in "broken French, bruised Spanish, and maltreated Italian," and longs to serenade her "like a good knight of old." Indeed, his error in mistaking Mina for a Norval emphasizes his comic pretensions. When he meets Mina, he decides that "her lovely foreign accent" must have been "acquired in speaking foreign languages," and he attempts to impress her with his knowledge of French (186). When her true identity is revealed, Sophy is at first shocked that he's been courting a maid, but he later decides her class status is unimportant. Wagg, absorbed in corruption and mis-cegenation, develops what seems to be the uncouth art of barnyard imitations, while the pretentious Sophy emulates foreign culture but is unable even to distinguish ladies from maids, a dire mistake in the world of Ruiz de Burton.

In fact, because of his romantic pretensions, Sophy bears certain similarities to Lew Wallace, the creator of the Zouave regiment in which Sophy and Scaly fought. Wallace modeled the dramatic uni-forms for his regiment of Indiana soldiers after that of the French foreign legion, with baggy trousers and kepi hats. The regiment was famous for its dashing uniforms, which Winslow Homer sketched for *Harper's Weekly* in 1861, and for its elaborate drilling techniques. Wallace described their drills as "the rush and tear of a thousand men advancing, retreating, taking and closing intervals, charging front and centre, firing in all positions, and doing anything on the run and double-quick," creating for spectators "a downright show" (*Autobiography* 274). Surely this must be the model for Sophy's elaborate horsemanship, in which he parades in front of the Norval house, "taking a half-hour to go the length of three blocks," while having his horse go "sideways like a crab, and [stand] on his hindlegs like a circus bear waltzing" (183–84).

Ruiz de Burton seems to use Sophy to satirize a United States that pretended and performed culture without actually having any. Toward the end of the novel she even explodes the distinction between Sophy and Scaly by having her narrator relate that Sophy eventually learns to outdo his companion in the skill of barn-yard imitations, explaining ironically that "[n]o other of the glorious and immortal host — and I don't expect Columbus, Vasco de Gama, Newton, or any other of the glorious and immortal host — was ever so proud or elated with his newly found world as Sophy. He would now eclipse Wagg!" (260). This equation of Sophy's skill with a "newly found world" emphasizes the provincial concerns underlying his shallow admiration for foreign cultures, and perhaps it also hints at a tendency to overestimate the value of newly found worlds as simpletons like Sophy define them.

Then what is the New World to Ruiz de Burton? Certainly not a hopeless cultural backwater. Her Mexican characters evade New England's proud isolation and New York's fashionable imitation, instead embracing transatlantic ties with genuine cosmopolitan urbanity. The Almenara household in Mexico is represented as a place of graceful hospitality and genuine learnedness. During the conversation about Maximilian, for example, Don Felipe and Don Luis sit "in the library by a table loaded with paper, books, reviews, pamphlets etc." and read "with great interest" letters composed in Spanish, French, German, and English. They treat their visitor Isaac with the greatest consideration, giving him delicious meals and "the finest wine he had ever tasted" (199). Anne E. Goldman points out that this contrast self-consciously differentiates Ruiz de Burton's Mexico from stereotypical accounts and corrects "a literary cartography which fetishized New England and pushed the rest of the Americas off of the map altogether" ("Blue-Eyed Mexican" 75). I would add that with it Ruiz de Burton is also correcting a cartography that constructed the Western Hemisphere as an isolated and unified space in order to radically separate Europe from the Americas. Mexico is a cultural center insofar as Lola and her relatives recognize and live up to European cultural authority.

This European cultural authority, however, is also racial authority. Examples of racism in *Who Would Have Thought It?* range from Ruiz de Burton's dramatic demonstrations of Lola's "pure" whiteness, to the negative treatment of Native Americans, to repeated implications that American politicians are "courting" African Americans at the expense of justice to whites. This last miscegenated union is symbolized by corrupt politician Le Grand Gunn's affair with prostitute Lucinda, but is more literally described when Julian asks if by supporting Lincoln he has "surrender[ed] his freedom to give it to Sambo" (241) or when the narrator complains that power-hungry politicians are persecuting Ulysses S. Grant for the exaggerated crime of snubbing Frederick Douglass (298).

By mocking the racial mixing and pretensions to racial equality that mark U.S. society, Ruiz de Burton goes beyond merely envisioning an alternative and racially superior colonial destiny for the Americas. She also pointedly protests the complicated racial identifications that structured U.S. national identity. Cross-racial bonds that cast Mexicans as sisters, wives, or brothers were a crucial part of the Monroe Doctrine's construction of the Western Hemisphere. Both Eric Wertheimer and Kirsten Silva Gruesz have identified an imagined unity between the United States and pre-Columbian South American civilizations as a common theme in late eighteenth- and nineteenth-century U.S. poetry, and both critics have linked this identification with the developing political discourse of the Monroe Doctrine. In this trope, American colonists are destined to follow a pre-Columbian tradition by creating "the preeminent agricultural and political culture of the New World," the survival of which is, "like the South American civilizations, . . . profoundly threatened by the meddling of the illegitimate European empires" (Wertheimer 26). The obvious contradictions and hypocrisy of this imagined bond between New World empires were, in Wertheimer's argument, crucial to burgeoning U.S. nationalism. "The story of exceptionalism," Wertheimer writes, "required New World others to emulate and then revile" (97).[7]

These romanticized and self-interested myths of cross-racial identification are clearly evident in Lew Wallace's first novel, which he completed shortly after his commission in Juárez's army ended. *The Fair God*, published one year after *Who Would Have Thought It?* identifies Aztecs as true Americans in contrast to Cortés and the invading Spaniards. The story is framed as a long lost manuscript written by Fernando de Alva Iztlilzochitl, a real historian of Tezcucan descent who lived in the early sixteenth century. Wallace pretends to be merely translating the manuscript that de Alva, "anxious to rescue his race from oblivion," wrote in Spanish for the emperor of Spain to read (*The Fair God* xi). Thus representing the text as one that gives the Aztec perspective on the invasion of Cortés, Wallace further invites his reader to identify with the Aztecs by repeatedly calling them a "nation" of "New World men" and creating a hero, Guatamozin, whose fight against colonization is fueled by his nascent conception of democracy. During Montezuma's death scene, Wallace has the king prophecy eight generations into the future to see his "tribes newly risen, like trodden grass, and in their midst a Priesthood and a Cross! An age of battles more, and lo! the Cross but not the Priests; in their stead Freedom and God!" (459–60). The novel thus identifies the Aztecs with the Anglo Americans, but it encourages these readers to see themselves not as heirs to Aztec legacy but rather as executors carrying out a long forgotten Aztec will.

When one is aware of Wallace's political investment in Mexico, it makes sense to read his historical romance's self-motivated constructions of New World unity and destiny as narrative versions of the Monroe Doctrine, which he was politically so active in propagating. These contradictions are evident in his life as well: Only a few years after writing *The Fair God* from the perspective of the colonized, Wallace was directing military operations against the Mescalero Apaches as the governor of the New Mexico territory. This kind of self-interested and hypocritical cross-racial identification is precisely what *Who Would Have Thought It?* attacks, in the form of Mrs. Norval's phony abolitionism or Hackwell's empty sermons on freedom and democracy. The epigram by John Greenleaf Whittier that Ruiz de Burton selects for her work makes clear this central intention: "But, by all thy nature's weakness, Hidden faults and follies known, Be thou, in rebuking evil, Conscious of thine own" ("What the Voice Said," st. 15). Defining and defending the virtues of the New World requires an exaggerated binary between democracy and tyranny, equality and hierarchy, freedom and oppression that Ruiz de Burton devotes her novel to debunking.

Recognizing the ways in which *Who Would Have Thought It?* contends with the particular terms of the Monroe Doctrine should not mean sidestepping Ruiz de Burton's own racist and colonialist agendas, however. As my argument makes evident, destabilizing the category of nation and exceeding or transversing the traditional, Anglo American cultural spheres are not necessarily radical textual acts — in the case of Ruiz de Burton they are often quite reactionary in their reproduction of the conventional constructions of race and civilization that impelled European colonialism in the New World and elsewhere. Furthermore, for critics interested in reorganizing American literary study within hemispheric rather than national boundaries, *Who Would Have Thought It?* provides another warning. The novel's specific challenge to the concept of "America" as a meaningful, unified, and democratic space reminds us that "reconceiving American studies as a hemispheric project" is an effort that always risks conceptually replicating the Monroe Doctrine's ambivalent and hegemonic constructions of "the Western Hemisphere." It reminds us that not unlike the category of nation, the geographical construct of the hemisphere has its own contested history.

Notes

1. By using the term "cosmopolitanism," I do not intend to invoke the new meanings attached to the term by contemporary theorists attempting to outline an emancipatory project of global consciousness. Rather, I am drawing on older Eurocentric conceptions of the term described by Harvey and Malcolmson as a form of enlightenment universalism enmeshed in the globalizing world market and "civilizing" intentions of nineteenth-century colonial expansion.

2. See this edition's chronology for an explanation of the French intervention in Mexico and the events leading up to Maximilian's election to the throne in 1864.

3. May describes this political situation.

4. On Romero, see Schoonover. On U.S. support for Juárez, see R. R. Miller, "Arms across the Border." On Wallace's role, see Morsberger and Morsberger.

5. The parallels between *Fashion* and *Who Would Have Thought It?* as romantic comedies of New York are striking: Mrs. Norval and Ruth clearly resemble the scheming Tiffany women. Both plots hinge on libertines attempting to trick the heroine into marriage and include mistaken identity scenes with a French maid, and both plots include a comic old maid who is sister to a scheming mother.

6. I'm referring to James's *Daisy Miller* (1877) or Christopher Newman (in James's *The American* 1878); to the St. George daughters in Wharton's unfinished manuscript for *The Buccaneers*; to the title characters of Archibald Gunter's wildly popular *Mr. Barnes of New York* (1887) and *Mr. Potter of Texas* (1888); and to Frank Stockton's New England matrons in *The Casting Away of Mrs. Lecks and Mrs. Aleshine* (1886).

7. According to Wertheimer, these New World identifications be-

came "obsolete" around the mid-nineteenth century, as real transatlantic power made fantasies about "the nativeness of nationalism" no longer necessary. I would complicate this time line by pointing out that the popular political discourse of the Monroe Doctrine and Wallace's revision of Prescott emerged in the 1860s. In my analysis this obsolescence was a much slower and more gradual process, and the vacillation between identification and disidentification, or emulating and reviling, was an ongoing instability in U.S. relations with Latin America during and after the nineteenth century.

The Whiteness of the Blush: The Cultural Politics of Racial Formation in *The Squatter and the Don*

JOHN M. GONZÁLEZ

The historical romance makes nations in making families, but in María Amparo Ruiz de Burton's 1885 novel *The Squatter and the Don*, the romantic dream of national unity is dispelled by another allegory that ominously promises the disappearance of family and nation altogether. Late in the narrative, the patrician son of a once wealthy Californio landowner is forced by declining family fortunes to accept "the pitiful wages of a poor hod carrier" (353). Working to build the mansions of San Francisco's newly minted Gilded Age "railroad millionaires," the stoic Gabriel Alamar "never complained," comments the novel's narrator, but "the eloquence of facts had said all that was to be said. In that hod full of bricks not only his own sad experience was represented, but *the entire history* of the native Californians *of Spanish descent* was epitomized. Yes, Gabriel carrying his hod full of bricks up a steep ladder, was the symbolic representation of his race. The natives, of Spanish origin, having lost all their property, must henceforth be hod carriers" (352). As in national allegory, an individual character represents a specific group within an imagined national whole; but in contrast to national allegory, what gets produced through this allegory of proletarianization are racially marked noncitizens. Far from ensuring the integration of Californios into the nation, national allegory in *The Squatter and the Don* can no longer provide stable registers of racial and class hierarchies that would ensure the familial production of citizenship.[1]

The decline of the Californios as a landed elite by the 1880s signified not just demotion into the ranks of wage laborers but also the loss of the privileges of "whiteness" maintained under previous regimes of racialization.[2] Proletarianization is thus not the only resentment at work in this novel, or rather not the only way this resentment is expressed. Race indexes this fall in class status as wage labor transforms Gabriel from a *criollo* into a California Indian: "The fact that Gabriel was a *native Spaniard*, [his wife Lizzie Mechlin Alamar] saw plainly, militated against them. If he had been rich, his nationality could have been forgiven, but no one will willingly tolerate a *poor native Californian*" (351). This change in class status is linked to a change in racialization, so that a proud white genealogy of "Spanish descent" becomes transformed into the demeaning experience of laboring under the racial markers of colonial difference. Even the fact of fair complexion, which makes Gabriel and his brother Victoriano "look like Englishmen," is insufficient to arrest their social refiguration as California natives or, in other words, as indigenous Californians (89).

As a "poor native Californian," Gabriel Alamar stands not as a (white) citizen of the United States but as the indigenous colonized of post–U.S. conquest California. As this example demonstrates, the only begrudged difference between an Indian day laborer and a "Spanish Don" was indeed the "whiteness" which decades of forced Indian labor on Californio *ranchos* had purchased. Precisely this renewed figuration of "whiteness" is what *The Squatter and Don* attempts to renegotiate for the Californios in the years following Reconstruction. The novel works to mark national identity as the inevitability of family ties, ties which established racial difference as social agency within the post-Reconstruction intertwining of race and nation.

But if *The Squatter and the Don* posits a renewed class-based whiteness for the Californios, then it also suggests how national allegory could no longer refurbish the cultural logic of imagining nation as (white) family. Ultimately, the ruined project of the book's national allegory symptomatically traces the disarticulation of whiteness from earlier national hegemonies of organic moral fitness (epitomized by white families) and its rearticulation to prosthetic corporate enterprises. Unable to celebrate nationally (re)productive unions, *The Squatter and the Don* foregrounds the inability of national allegory to reestablish the racialized terms of national hegemony in the aftermath of the U.S. conquest of 1848 and the ascension of a new cultural logistics of nationalism modeled not by the family but by the corporation.[3]

I

There is a sense in which *The Squatter and the Don* secures a tentative form of whiteness for the Californios. Clarence and Mercedes eventually *do* marry. This does not prevent the loss of the Alamar *rancho*, but it does halt the Alamar family's precipitous slide into a rapidly coalescing *mestizo* and indigenous working class.[4] Ruiz de Burton's historical romance figures their marriage as the romantic union of two "white" people, thus working to mark, however provisionally, the Californios as "white." These ties are made possible by the constant circulation of sentiment communicated between the two lovers through numerous blushes. Mercedes blushes repeatedly "like a rose," while Clarence, not to be outdone, reddens "to the roots of his hair" continually throughout the narrative (101, 182).

In *Telling Complexions: The Nineteenth-Century English Novel and the Blush*, Mary Ann O'Farrell traces the signification of the blush as the human body's infallible indicator of moral character. Unlike the possibly undetectable deceptions of speech, the body's involuntary betrayal of individual will ensured that moral character would always be rendered self-evident. As an unscripted bodily practice, the blush makes visible the social reading frame itself, according to O'Farrell: "The use of the blush in the nineteenth-century novel . . . can be thought as articulating the tension between a sense of the blush as expressive of a deep personal truth . . . and a notion of the blush . . . as a mechanism . . . of the workings that forward the grander social work of legibility and manners"

(111). In this cultural logistics, the blush functions as a bodily discipline that ensures the individual's role in the service of reproducing the gendered division of labor in a patriarchal social order, even when the apparently demure blush would announce the presence of an excessive, seductive desire (which, of course, typically leads to marriage, as in *The Squatter and the Don*).

But insofar as this understanding of the cultural work of the blush separates individual agency from its social context, something of the cultural work of the blush in confirming *collective* agency is lost. The blush's betrayal of an individual's sense of agency ultimately matters less than what that betrayal affirms; the blush is not so much the denial of individual agency as much as the confirmation of collective agency. In the context of the United States, the articulation of individual subjectivity and collective agency finds perhaps its canonical expression in Thomas Jefferson's *Notes on the State of Virginia*.

In that 1784 treatise, Jefferson postulates that the racial differences of color "fixed in nature" between white masters and African slaves determined a self-evident distinction in each race's capacity to screen moral character (186). Identifying the ability to blush as "the foundation of a greater or less share of beauty" in the white race, Jefferson links the visibility of sentiment displayed by the blush across the white face to an aesthetics of racial legibility: "Are not the fine mixtures of red and white, the expressions of every passion by greater or less suffusions of colour in the one, preferable to that eternal monotony, that immovable veil of black which covers all the emotions of the other race?" (186–87). A profound epistemological uncertainty confronted Jefferson in reading the emotional states of (his) African slaves; their emotions existed, he concedes, but the "immovable veil of black" confounded the colonizers' ability to interpret the emotional or moral states of this conscripted colonial workforce (187).[5] Jefferson's anxiously rhetorical interrogative only fitfully casts this epistemological challenge to colonial knowledge as the self-evident truth of racial ontology. By positing the blush as a kind of racialized writing that makes morality legible, Jefferson desperately sutures the gaps in colonial knowledge.

Denying the human agency of enslaved Africans, Jefferson confirms the collective agency of white people. For Jefferson, the legibility of the blush corresponded to the racialized subjectivity proper to the new nation's political and economic circumstances of democratic openness and laissez-faire mercantile capitalism. The white body's apparent ability to screen emotions upon the face indicates the capacity to place private sentiments into public circulation, in contrast to the aesthetically displeasing and morally suspect stoppage of emotional economies found in the "eternal monotony" of the African slave's face. Insofar as the inability to make invisible moral character visible upon the body indexed their position as racialized objects within the national economy, African slaves, as the antithesis of agency itself, seemingly confirmed the social power of whiteness in the new nation. As read in blushing white faces, moral character stands as the emotive marker of social agency; the white ability to blush legibly, self-evidently, indicated, rather than any suspension of individual agency, an ascension to a national-collective agency.

But precisely this nationalized conjunction of blushing white bodies and positional agency is both deployed and contested in *The Squatter and the Don*. In the coalescing of post-Reconstruction nationalism around "whiteness" as the imperative category of civil rights and political agency, Ruiz de Burton's historical romance creates an affective economy of circulating sentiment that enables Californio claims to "whiteness" by inscribing within Californio bodies the very structure of a laissez-faire, entrepreneurial capitalism that might ensure continued Californio social standing among the nation's elites.

Tellingly, the initial meeting between Clarence and Mercedes arises from Clarence's true reason for visiting the Alamar *rancho*: to purchase the Darrell home site from Don Mariano. With "the business proposition" literally bracketing and enabling the courtship, the latter mirrors the former's consensual circulation of economic value with its own legible circulation of consensual affect. Even as the Don and Clarence mutually recognize each other as fellow citizens through the land deal, the blushing love affair between the squatter's son and the Don's daughter confirms what the business transaction implied: The business of citizenship is an affair of the (white) heart. Already thinking of union, Mercedes "blushed anew; her blushes being immediately reflected on Clarence's forehead, made them both look like a couple of culprits" (97, 100). Establishing the grounds of moral legibility rather than legal culpability, their blushes identify Californios and white "settlers" alike as having the properly laissez-faire subjectivity for nation-building sentiment. Put differently, the circulation of blushes and blanches within the text establishes properly "white" subjectivities, thereby enabling the Californios' ascension to allegorical status within the national allegory of the historical romance.

In appealing to the national aesthetics of whiteness, the narrative works to regain for *mestizo* Californios the privileged political and economic subject-position which they had enjoyed under previous negotiations of national and regional hegemony. By claiming Californio whiteness through the blush, the narrative can posit the making of a truly national, bicoastal family union through marriages that no longer pose the specter of miscegenation. Bereft by the 1880s of the material base of cattle ranches, which had hitherto enabled a begrudged status as "white" within post-annexation California, the Californios found their racial identity as "white" ever more precarious as they collectively became wage laborers, an "indianized" proletariat. But backed by the financial and cultural capital of their white in-laws, the Alamar family can figuratively shift the material base of their "whiteness" from a failed pastoral economy hounded by legal and political enemies into an entrepreneurial enterprise based upon professional employment and speculative investments in real estate, mining, banking, and stocks.

So if by the novel's close Gabriel Alamar no longer can claim the patriarchal inheritance of the *rancho* as the eldest son of Don Mariano, as a banker he no longer must work as a hod carrier either. With the Alamar siblings married into the entrepreneurial bourgeoisie (embodied by their brother-in-law Clarence), Gabriel is able to convert a renewed class status into "whiteness," and "whiteness" into "white-collar." Through the historical romance's marital unions, Californio claims to whiteness allow access to class positions which might ensure continued Californio economic and political viability on the white side of the national color line.[6] In short, the wholesale transfer of the Alamar family from landowners to the professional classes through intermarriage highlights the process by which Californios could claim whiteness after 1848.

II

Yet the postponed wedding of Mercedes and Clarence stands symptomatic of the contradiction between the narrative's insistence upon Californio whiteness and the ultimate corporate denial of that social agency. That their wedding is abruptly canceled, severely jeopardized, and only belatedly performed suggests the ultimate dissolution of the Anglo Californio hegemony, which allowed the Californios to retain some measure of political and social power after the U.S. conquest. Indeed, the very structure of white nationality itself remains quite tenuous in *The Squatter and the Don*, which ends not with the success of a reunited nation in which Californios enjoy their properly elite place but with a desperate plea for "a Redeemer who will emancipate the white slaves of California" (372).[7] Titled "Out with the Invader," the last chapter calls for a mass uprising to restore the nation and release California from an imperial subjugation imposed by the Central and Southern Pacific Railroads.

Throughout the novel, the vampiric railroad monopoly has ignored its larger responsibility to the national good by arresting the invisible hand of the market, thereby reducing the Californios, and indeed all Californians, to "poverty, overwork and discouragement" or, in other words, to the slavery of low-paying wage labor without the prospect of upward mobility (319). Don Mariano's speculative property investments in San Diego collapse in value following the Big Four's successful efforts to block the southern-route Texas Pacific Railroad. By refusing to allow the struggling port of San Diego to become the nation's second transcontinental railroad terminus upon the Pacific Ocean, the railroad monopoly ensures that "San Diego must be strangled" and along with San Diego any possibility that the Alamar family might enjoy continued economic viability as an independent national elite (314). Ignoring "the wail of the prostrate South, or the impassionate appeals of California," the Southern Pacific in particular had interfered with "the rights of the Southern people" to partake of the rapidly expanding post–Civil War economy by not allowing ready access to a burgeoning Pacific Rim trade market (216, 316). In effect, enforced underdevelopment of Southern California's economy completes the dispossession of the Californios, which had started with the U.S. conquest and had been greatly accelerated by the 1851 Land Act. Without the Texas Pacific, relates Don Mariano, "the work of ruining me begun by squatters will be finished by the millionaires" (311).

The plea for liberation from "white slavery" in *The Squatter and the Don* thus is not a condemnation of capitalism, or at least of the mercantile or entrepreneurial sort (such as Clarence's) which ultimately saves whiteness for the Californios. Rather, the approbation is for a government-corrupting monopoly corporate capitalism that would chaotically erase racial distinctions in the pursuit of profit. The stranglehold the Southern Pacific Railroad has upon California's economy creates a narrative crisis of embodiment in which the markings of racialized servitude have been improperly transferred from the pre-emancipation South's black bodies to the post-Reconstruction West's "white" ones. What enables "white slavery" in California is the extent to which corporate proletarianization indiscriminately interpolated whites and nonwhites alike into a wage-labor economy in a way that eroded racial distinctions. Elevating the wage-labor relationship over any and all racial distinctions, the corporation monstrously endangers the "white" status of white people, as in the case of Gabriel Alamar.[8] In essence, the narrative protests the erasure of "race" in the railroad monopoly's suspension of the mercantile or entrepreneurial economy in which and from which the positions of political and economic agency accrued to nationalized white bodies.

If the irony of the novel is that a railroad corporation devoted to the transportation of goods and people, symbolic of westward U.S. progress itself, has become the agent of economic stagnation and stoppage, then what is perhaps even more striking is how the corporate monopoly corrosively dissolves the legible connections between moral sentiment and white bodies. Casting "white" Californios and white settlers alike as victims of the railroad companies, the narrative traces this immoral enslavement of "whites" to a peculiar lack of affect on the part of the corporation and its agents: "That soulless, heartless, shameless monster," says Mr. Mechlin, "has no soul to feel responsibility, no heart for human pity, no face for manly blush" (320). Likewise, the Southern Pacific's chief representative, former California governor Leland Stanford, remains unmoved by the impassioned pleas of Mr. Mechlin, Don Mariano, and Mr. Holman, noting, "Corporations have no souls, gentlemen, and I am no Carlylean hero-philanthropist. I am only a most humble '*public carrier*'" (318). Identifying with the corporation to the extent that he appears as the calculating effect of self-interested corporate logic rather than as a moral person independent of that logic, Stanford is the narrative's projection of post-individual subjectivity in the corporate era. Immune to morality, Stanford becomes less the capricious tyrant than a mere cog in the corporate machinery.

In supplanting the laissez-faire circulation of mercantile capitalism, the monopoly corporation disarticulates what had been the earlier linkage between "free" market agency and the white body, destroying the legibility of "race" and thus national white privilege. Legally embodied yet morally unaccountable, this corporate empire transforms the economic and political agency of white U.S. citizens into the subjection of abjectly racialized human commodities; "white slavery" becomes the logical result of erasing racial legibility. The railroad monopoly's apparent lack of commitment to the white nation is not limited to the domestic erosion of whiteness; draining capital from California as well as from the South to "build railroads in Guatemala and British America," the monopolies encourage the flight of capital across national borders (370).

More concerned with transnational circuits of labor and capital than with the (white) national welfare, corporations replace the collective agency of blushing white people with that of disembodied, deterritorialized, and depersonalized entities which defy even their national origins. In short, the railroad monopoly functions as an *imperium in imperio* that threatens to replace the nation's white citizenship with the corporate empire's white slavery. Delinking class difference from racial difference, corporations transform white Californios into Indians, white workers into the structural equivalent of black or Chinese workers, and U.S. citizens into colonial subjects.

Ultimately, *The Squatter and the Don* abandons the historical romance narrative altogether, as if that genre could not negotiate these restructurings of race and class. Yet in some sense the supersession of the national allegory by the allegory of proletarianization may be not so much a refutation of the nation's earlier racial formations but rather a transformation of colonial power. Transnational in its reach, the Southern Pacific Railroad operates as what Bill Brown terms "a prosthetic extension of America — not a 'natural' expression of westward expansiveness, but the mechanical institution of hemispheric domination, the technological and technocratic control over the global flow of goods" (134–35). The experience of the Californios anticipates what would become the dominant twentieth-century mode of U.S. imperialism after the Spanish American War of 1898. The blushing individual may embody the racialized subject formation of a nationalized mercantile capitalism, but the unblushing collective of the "deadly, soulless corporation" enacts the mechanics of colonialist and neocolonialist agency in the corporate age of U.S. empire.

III

The allegorical mappings of *eros* and *polis* in *The Squatter and the Don* register the imperial presence of monopoly corporations as they traverse national boundaries and exceed national sovereignties. This novel focuses upon the invidious corporate delinking of race and class, but the narrative also obliquely registers the subterranean resistance of racialized labor to either *ranchero* or corporate exploitation. These communities are the Indian and *mestizo* ranch laborers whose presence is taken for granted and whose racialization frames Californio agency before and after 1848. Before the U.S. conquest, *rancheros* often enslaved Indians to work as ranch hands; afterwards, the *rancheros* helped block citizenship status for indigenous peoples at the California state constitutional convention in order to retain a large pool of disenfranchised laborers.

Rancheros were subsequently able to influence the passage of laws that guaranteed a vulnerable labor force for exploitation at a moment when labor shortages hampered their ability to profit from the boom in cattle prices brought about by the Gold Rush. Anglo settlers readily joined the *rancheros* in availing themselves of a legalized form of quasi-slavery in a "Free Labor" state. In a rehearsal of the New South's notorious convict lease system, vagrancy laws such as the so-called 1855 "Greaser Act" allowed for the lease of offenders (usually Indians or very poor *mestizos*) for a specified time as cheap, no-wage labor granted only room and board. Similarly, the Indenture Act of 1850 allowed for the involuntary bonding of Indians to citizens for at least a decade with no remuneration but subsistence.[9]

While the few appearances of Indian servants in *The Squatter and the Don* serve mainly as opportunities for the Alamars to complain about Indian "laziness," the general invisibility of Indian labor in the narrative belies the degree to which the wealth *mestizos* and Indians produced also manufactured Californio whiteness before and after 1848. The Spanish colonial order of racial hierarchy, largely maintained during the Mexican period despite the formal extension of citizenship to Indians, had emphasized *limpieza de sangre*, or "purity of blood," despite this gesture's easy effacement of the Californios' historically *mestizo* origins. In danger of losing their hegemonic status as white after the U.S. conquest, the Californios traded upon their status as class elites in post-1848 California to construct an Anglo Californio hegemony that at some fundamental level granted them rights and privileges as white citizens, and these political concessions resulted in real material advantages from the resulting increased control of indigenous labor.

Grave as the danger posed by the transnational corporation to Californio social agency, the threat posed by racialized labor may be greater yet. Indeed, an Indian ranch hand at the Alamar *rancho* single-handedly derails the national allegory as completely as any monopoly corporation. Clarence's hasty departure from a distraught Mercedes after his father's rude assault upon Don Mariano is made possible by Chapo's studied neglect in following Victoriano's orders to groom and stable the horses immediately: " 'Yes, *patroncito*, I'll do it right away,' said the lazy Indian, who first had to stretch himself and yawn several times, then hunt up tobacco and cigarette paper, and smoke his cigarette. This done, he, having had a heavy supper, shuffled lazily to the front of the house, as Clarence was driving down the hill for the second time" (278). The resulting cancellation of the lovers' wedding jeopardizes the dream of national unity, but in a way different from Californio imaginings of corrupt post-national corporations.

In this case, the immediate cause of narrative and national crisis alike is traced to the ranch hand's sense of time, as "the *Americano* went off with his horses before he [Chapo] had time to put them in the stable" (279). The narrative implies that Victoriano could have overtaken Clarence on the way to the San Diego ship docks and hence averted the Alamars' financial disasters if only Chapo had followed orders without delay. The narrative links Chapo's deficient sense of time to the racialized disposition of Indian "laziness," a racialized trait which casts the entire project of national allegory in doubt. If the mark of premodernity lay in "laziness," then the Indian was simply too primitive in the narrative's terms to have yet internalized the bodily discipline vital to work regimes under a developing capitalism. [10]

From *within* the logic of the narrative, in no way could Chapo's actions be interpreted to signify an all too clear understanding of capitalism's restructuring of work relations along the color line, nor could "laziness" be read as resistance to the colonizer's imposed narrative of modernity. This narrative instance demonstrates the ideological necessity of denying the foundation of Californio whiteness upon the labor of subaltern communities. Whiteness triumphant or imperiled can only be imagined as the result of the actions of true agents of history: white individuals, nations or transnational corporations. The narrative reveals no possibility that in coming to share the same structural and symbolic positions within the corporate U.S. imaginary, Californios and *indios* might also share a similar historical consciousness of their racialized class positions.

The call for the redemption of white slavery, then, is what remains of the failure of national allegory. No longer able to imagine nationally hegemonic families, *The Squatter and the Don* is also unable to suggest alternatives to a reinscription of the wages of whiteness. The possibility fails to register that, far from superseding the nation and its racialized order, transnational corporations trade upon the racial and gendered division of labor at the heart of the nation. Likewise, the possibility cannot be brought to fruition that the very flows of labor across borders and (sometimes) color

John M. González

lines might provide a new basis of imagining communities. In relying upon the racialized national claims of citizenship through white descent, *The Squatter and the Don* demonstrates the dead end of national allegory in contesting corporate restructurings of everyday life.

Notes

1. The Californios' "dispossession by due process" resonates with Carl Gutiérrez-Jones's characterization of Chicana/o narrative's refiguration of U.S. liberalism's consent/force dichotomy into the hegemony/coercion parameters of power. With the "consent" supposedly represented by legislation so clearly aligned with the violence of "conquerors," *The Squatter and the Don* accurately diagnoses the racialized operation of the United States. Yet the novel's critique fails to imagine viable strategies of communal resistance along lines other than whiteness.

2. Ruiz de Burton was likely aware of an 1859 petition to Congress signed by more than fifty Californios. Outlining many of the same circumstances that had already economically devastated the *rancheros*, the petitioners pleaded for Congress to "respect, protect, and uphold the treaty of Guadalupe Hidalgo." This text is reprinted in Robert Glass Cleland's *The Cattle on a Thousand Hills*, 243.

3. Like *The Squatter and the Don*, Ruiz de Burton's 1872 novel *Who Would Have Thought It?* charts the complicated incorporation of Californios into the national imaginary. In this narrative, a Californiana rescued from Indians experiences racist contempt against Mexicans after she is adopted into the very Yankee Norval family. Lola Medina and the family scion Julian fall in love during the Civil War, but their union finds acceptance only after the dye (applied by the Indians) that had darkened her fair skin wears off. While critiquing a bankrupt middle-class domesticity and a morally corrupt mode of government, *Who Would Have Thought It?* (like *The Squatter and the Don*) nonetheless envisions the desirable possibility of a united Californio and Anglo national elite. Unlike *The Squatter and the Don*, this novel does not

yet articulate a critique of the process of racialization brought about through the economics of a nascent monopoly capitalism.

4. The novel's aesthetic resolution to the Californios' proletarianization cannot remedy the unresolvable historical process, as Sánchez and Pita have argued in their introduction to *The Squatter and the Don*. Yet the specific way this aesthetic resolution is enacted and legitimated outlines the historical limitations (as well as possibilities) of imagining resistant practices.

5. The same epistemological uncertainty confronted British inquiries into how blushing might index the emotional state of colonial subjects. In his 1872 treatise *The Expression of the Emotions in Man and Animals*, Charles Darwin reported that a British colonial official in India was constantly foiled by those under his surveillance. The colonial official "attended to the expression of the inhabitants, but found much difficulty in arriving at any safe conclusions, owing to their habitual concealment of all emotions in the presence of Europeans" (21).

6. As David Roediger and George Lipsitz have shown for the nineteenth- and twentieth-century United States, respectively, a white proletariat gained material and symbolic advantages over a nonwhite proletariat.

7. The uneasy ambivalence of the term "redeemer" in the post-Reconstruction period suggests the treacherous parameters of race that *The Squatter and the Don* attempts to negotiate in creating a place for the Californios within the newly reconstituted white nation. On one hand, "redeemer" invokes topological imaginings of Christian salvation and, more specifically in the immediate post–Civil War era, Lincoln's venerated status as the signer of the Emancipation Proclamation. On the other hand, "the Redeemers" also refers to the group of Whiggish Southern Democrats whom early historians of the New South enshrined as the liberators of a distraught white South from the ravages of "black misrule."

8. The narrative's trajectory from decrying Gabriel Alamar's racializing wage labor to protesting the monopoly's white slavery stands in marked contrast to Roediger's description of the nineteenth-century

U.S. white working class's rhetorical trajectory. Before emancipation, Roediger details in *The Wages of Whiteness*, "white slavery" denoted not a challenge to capitalist labor relations but rather *herrenvolk* Republican objections to the capitalist mistreatment of white workers as if they were black slaves. "Wage slavery," on the other hand, implied bondage as the permanent condition of a capitalist system of wage labor, a viewpoint gradually adopted by the white working class after the Civil War. The term "white slavery" reemerged during the late nineteenth century to denote the lurid, alleged international conspiracy to force white women to become prostitutes for nonwhite men in foreign lands.

9. Heizer and Almquist have noted the similarity between the Indenture Act and the notorious Black Code laws enacted during Presidential Reconstruction. Revised in 1860 to allow for an indenture period of twenty-five years, the Indenture Act was repealed only in 1863 after this legalized quasi-slavery in a supposedly "Free Labor" Union state became too much of a political embarrassment during the Civil War.

10. See Hurtado for a more detailed account of how California Indians negotiated their lives after the U.S. conquest.

Rescuing the Past: The Case of
Olive Oatman and Lola Medina

ANDREA TINNEMEYER

Upon the narrative of Olive Oatman, an Anglo American captive whose return to Victorian society hinged on repeated renunciation of miscegenation, desires to return to Mohave society, and the indelible mark of a chin tattoo, María Amparo Ruiz de Burton grafts a tale of a Mexicana whose moral and class standards far surpass those of her adopted New England community, whose chastity is endangered by a former clergyman, and whose physical markings of captivity prove temporary. By drawing on Oatman's captivity, Ruiz de Burton weaves yet another critical connection between East and West. By narrating a story that deals with border crossings in the vein of a quintessential American trope — the captivity narrative — she gives us a critical story of the border that draws upon a different history from the one commonly told or known in the nineteenth century. One such story is the capture and return of Olive Oatman.

I was initially drawn to the history and narrative of Oatman's captivity (1851–56) because of its uncanny resemblance to the fictional account of Lola and Doña Theresa Medina in Ruiz de Burton's *Who Would Have Thought It?* (1872). The same location serves as the spot of rescue or abduction; both captives are trafficked between Apaches and Mohaves; and both retain the physical markings that reinforce their otherness even after their rescue. Ruiz de Burton was residing in San Francisco when accounts of the Oatman massacre and Olive's rescue appeared in local newspapers.

Oatman's story permitted Ruiz de Burton to address several issues regarding the status of Mexican residents in the newly annexed Southwest: religious difference, full cultural and political acceptance into the United States, and the problematic insistence on the whiteness of Californios.[1] In short, the terms negotiated for Olive's reabsorption into Anglo society (religion, guardianship, sexual purity, and loyalty to Anglo American culture) made her captivity, and all the attendant media attention thereafter, the ideal foundation for Ruiz de Burton to redress grievances after the U.S.–Mexican War.

In February 1856, the newspaper presses in the newly formed state of California were working at a feverish pace. Olive Oatman had been rescued after five years in captivity. The *San Francisco Herald* and *Golden Era*, among others, published sensational accounts of Oatman's abduction and rescue, including an interview with the former captive. The California public was familiar with Olive and her sister Mary Ann because of attempts by their brother, Lorenzo, to obtain state and federal aid in their rescue (Rice 98).[2]

The nine members of the Oatman family had broken from the Mormon Church (they belonged to a splinter sect that followed James Colin Brewster)[3] and were seeking their own "promised land of Bashan where the Colorado River neared the Gulf of Mexico" (Dillon 46). By the time they arrived at the mouth of the Colorado and Gila Rivers, eighty miles from Fort Yuma (the exact location where the fictional captives of *Who Would Have Thought It?* were rescued), their food was almost gone and their hopes were low. As Olive Oatman recalls in her lecture notes, some Apaches approached her father: "They asked for more [food] and this my father denied them. . . . They brought out [huge clubs] and brandished [them] in the air screaming and leaping like so many deamons [*sic*] began their cruel slaughter" (10). All but Olive and Mary were murdered; Lorenzo was left for dead.

Olive and Mary were forced to travel long distances to where the Yavapais lived. Pimas nursed Lorenzo back to health and later returned him to members of the emigrant party (Ira Thompson became his guardian). As Olive describes in her lecture notes, within a year, they were sold to a party sent by the Mohave chief (16). Extreme drought marked their residence among the Mohaves, and several tribe members died of starvation; Mary was among the dead. Mary's death was not the only event to mark Olive's time in captivity. Both sisters were tattooed with five vertical lines extending from their lower lips to their chins. Sketches and photographs of Olive accentuate these tell-tale marks of captivity, and speculation continues regarding their significance.[4] In the mid-nineteenth century, however, Olive's chin tattoo may have garnered as much interest from spectators who flocked to her lectures as her harrowing tale of five years among the Yavapais and Mohaves.[5] Olive's tattoo functions as an indelible reminder of her time in captivity and of her proximity to "savages." Wearing the mark of the savage in the form of a chin tattoo stands in for other forms of commingling with the Mohaves. Lola Medina's skin dye, however, proves temporary, as does her association with Native Americans.

Olive's five-year captivity, the famed massacre of her family, and her celebrated return to Anglo American society initially elicited reactions of pity. A correspondent from the *Daily Herald* in San Francisco called for "some of our philanthropic San Francisco ladies [to] offer their services to either provide a home for her, or [to] use their influence in procuring her admission to the Orphan Asylum" (Rice 98). Quite swiftly, however, the tide of public opinion shifted to tawdry speculation over Olive's chastity. Rumors began circulating that Olive mourned her Mohave children — two sons born to her and the chief's son. This rumor was supposedly corroborated and thickened with detail by Sarah Thompson, Olive's friend and fellow Mormon. One newspaper account published two months after her rescue discounted the rumor quite plainly: "She has not been made a wife" (*Golden Era*, April 27, 1856).

Similar disclaimers or retractions were printed regarding Olive's adherence to Victorian standards of chastity. Allusions to Olive's lost virginity hindered her return to Anglo society. Repeated themes of polite decorum and civility cautioned against a certain line of questioning and against treatment of Olive as an oddity on display: "The lady-like deportment of Miss Oatman, her pleasing manners and amiable disposition, are the wonder and remark of all who see her. She has more delicacy than many who, although they may pretend to the usual question of politeness and civility, rush to see her and stare at her, with about as much sense of feeling as they would in a show of wild animals" (*Golden Era*, April 27, 1856).

When Olive and Lorenzo were reunited, they traveled with their cousin Harvey Oatman[6] to Yreka, California, in 1856. There they met the Rev. Royal B. Stratton, a Methodist minister who became instrumental in the publication of Olive's sensational tale and the promotion of her lecture circuit. What readers in 1856 did not know were the circumstances of Olive's abduction, the death of her sister, and the other events that brought her into the hands of the Mohaves as a slave. Two editions of *The Captivity of the Oatman Girls* were published in San Francisco in 1857 and the third was published in New York in 1858 (Derounian-Stodola 37). During the years leading to and spanning the Civil War, Olive Oatman was on the lecture circuit, describing her harrowing adventures in eastern cities. The popularity of Oatman's lectures and captivity narrative and the setting of Ruiz de Burton's novel during the Civil War complicate nineteenth-century race relations, which graphed a black/white binary onto the Mason-Dixon line. The sensational and violent account of the attack and the spectacle of a tattooed Victorian lady seem to have captivated audiences.

Upon her arrival at Fort Yuma on February 29, 1856, Capt. Martin Burke interviewed Olive with a particular "personal curiosity of her treatment whilst among the Indians" (Kroeber and Kroeber 311). The interview itself, which appeared in the *Los Angeles Star* on April 19, 1856, before it was reprinted in other newspapers like the *San Francisco Bulletin*, seems truncated and limited by Olive's sketchy language skills.

The agenda behind these questions is clearly an attempt to realign her identity away from the Mohaves and back toward her nuclear family, her sisters Lucy and Mary and her brother Lorenzo. When asked if she would recognize Lorenzo, Olive "intimate[s] that he looked like herself" (reported in Kroeber and Kroeber 312). What is striking is the use of her own body, her own image, to indicate kinship and familiarity with Lorenzo, especially in light of her chin tattoo. The interview and its attendant detailed narrative frame work assiduously to return Olive to Anglo American society by excluding any mention of difference, such as her rusty English.

Further, Olive's response to a direct question of the Mohaves' treatment of her and her sister — "answered 'very well' (from her manner seemed perfectly pleased) they had never whipped her but always treated her well" — warrants no commentary (reported in Kroeber and Kroeber 312). Instead, the reporter's line of inquiry shifts to focus on Mary's death from starvation, as if to counter her assessment of the Mohaves' dealings with her. Kroeber and Kroeber read the interview against statements of heathenism and cruel psychological and physical mistreatment repeated in the captivity narrative, and they conclude that the "sensational narrative" is "written by Reverend Royal B. Stratton . . . its keynote being 'Olive's misery among the degraded savages' " (309–10).

Kathryn Derounian-Stodola agrees, charging that Stratton inflated and oversentimentalized the rhetoric and demonized the native peoples in his quest to promote Christianity and increase his church's coffers. The cloud of speculation regarding Rev. Stratton likewise hangs over the fictional Reverend Hackwell, who threatens not only to deplete Lola's inheritance but also to force her into marriage and thus threaten her virginity and her reputation. The silencing of Olive's voice appears in manifold form in *Who Would Have Thought It?* Lola's captivity narrative is first told by Dr. Norval. Repeated defenses of Lola's bloodlines are ignored by the New England community, and Lola's mother's *testimonio* is lost for years in the dead-letter office.

Olive's interview, widely reprinted after its initial appearance in the *Los Angeles Star*, bears comparison with the fictional interrogation and examination of Lola Medina, particularly with respect to parentage and an assessment of ethnic affiliation. *Who Would Have Thought It?* opens with the much anticipated arrival of Dr. Norval and his equipage from a trip to the West Coast where he has been gathering specimens for the past four years. Ruiz de Burton quickly shifts focus from Norval to the enigmatic figure in the red shawl accompanying him — Lola Medina. When Lola's shawl falls to the ground, the figure revealed is that of a "little girl very black indeed" (16).

Lola's red shawl, and the bizarre striptease regarding her racial identity that accompanies both its removal and the eventual fading of her skin dye, are sharply juxtaposed by accounts of Olive's scant clothing and humility when she is returned to Fort Yuma.[7] Lola's multiple layers, when stripped off, do not reveal a shameful, naked core; rather, they disclose an identity that is both class- and race-inflected as white. A sketch of Olive's return depicts her undressed not just for Victorian standards but even for current American prudery. Newspaper accounts relate how "she was dressed in the scanty costume of the Mohave females, and upon the approach of white men, with instinctive modesty, prostrated herself in the sand, and refused to rise until provided with more becoming wardrobe" (*Golden Era*, March 16, 1856). Olive belittles herself in the moments anticipating her return to Victorian dress and customs; Lola, who is imagined to be an Aztec, a Native American, or a "mixture of Indian and Negro," already wears the appropriate clothing and disdains to reply when treated roughly (20).

By the time Ruiz de Burton published her novel, travel narratives and early ethnographies set in the Southwest had already drawn conclusive associations between clothing, ethnic identity, and moral standing.[8] Against the Enlightenment model of the "noble savage," whose premise of people living in Edenic bliss was buttressed by the comparative degree of "undress," Mexican women were described as creatures eager to play Eve to their white male's Adam. The image of a bare-chested female, which Rebecca

Blevins Faery convincingly argues in *Cartographies of Desire* to be a complicated emblem of the Americas, appears in different form in captivity narratives: the nude Native American female's heaving breasts "[signify] the validating welcome the white colonists received from the Indians," and "the captive white woman's nakedness . . . signifies the violence of dark savagery against her person" (176–77).

Ruiz de Burton's heroine displays manners absent in members of the New England community, who take on "savage" characteristics such as Jemima Norval's infernal imps and Hackwell's "private menagerie" of "wild beasts." Lola's ethnic and class status are hyperbolically superior to those of her New England neighbors, so much so that the French waiting maid, Mina, prefers to serve Lola rather than Ruth Norval, and "the Indian paint" that occasions inquiry into Lola's ethnic identity is discovered by the novel's end to have "kept her white skin under cover, making it whiter by bleaching it" (232). And yet most of the work of proving Lola's status involves her class position because she remains in blackface for the bulk of the novel.

Ruiz de Burton suspends an account of Lola's skin dye until the felicitous completion of the marriage plot between her and Julian Norval; as a result, members of the Norval family and surrounding community engage in a farcical interrogation of Lola's ethnic identity. Close inspection of her phenotypic traits — especially her lips and hands — mimics the racist, pseudo-scientific discourse prominent in the nineteenth century as "scientists" sought to quantify racial distinctions and classes through an arithmetic of blood and a taxonomy of races. For the purposes of this essay, I wish to note how the Norval family's conjectures and attempts to corral and label Lola reflect national race-based preoccupations — the savagery of Native Americans and the enslavement of Africans and African Americans.[9]

Lola's racial ambiguity penetrates the linguistic realm as Mattie misinterprets Lola's silence as her ignorance of English during an interrogation by Mattie, Lavinia, and Hackwell, among others who bat around possible identities for her. When Hackwell hands Lola a buttered piece of bread, "presented with a smile," she politely thanks him "in very good English" (20). Alarmed, Mattie suddenly realizes that Lola has heard and understood their conversation carried on in front of her; Lola's silence is no longer attributed to her racial identity but is instead recast along class lines. Dr. Norval had already explained Lola's silence to Ruth, clarifying, "[Lola] not liking your manner . . . disdains to answer your question" (20).

The story of how Lola, a young Mexican lady, came into the Norval household is, Dr. Norval assures his wife, "more romantic than that of half of the heroines of [Mrs. Norval's] trashy novels" (17). An anonymous article published in the *Golden Era* regarding the Oatman captivity closely echoes the language and tenor of Dr. Norval's characterization of Lola's history to his wife: "Here is the foundation for as romantic a story as ever was fingered." In both instances, the story's appeal is connected to its romantic elements, the very means by which women enter into the national imaginary in book form. The male genre of adventure is reformulated in both narratives into romance, a more traditional genre in which to cast a female heroine.

In Ruiz de Burton's novel, Dr. Norval takes over the tragic story of Lola and her mother. Doña Theresa's own account, lost in the dead-letter office, only circulates among the circumscribed readership of her immediate family. And as for profit, Lola certainly gains financially from her captivity, her mother having parlayed her status as the chief's wife to gain gold and jewels for Lola's future. But it is Jemima Norval, her daughters, and Hackwell who attempt to squander Lola's fortune and claim it as their own. As Sánchez and Pita note in their introduction to the novel, "The wealth Doña Theresa hoards as her daughter's 'dowry' is entirely naturalized and masks the plunder of Indian lands and resources" (lxi).

For Ruiz de Burton, the mystery of Lola's ethnicity provides the vehicle for negotiating a Mexican identity within a New England community and readership who imagine ethnic identity along a black/white axis. Beth Fisher believes "Ruiz de Burton's interest in using the captivity theme to validate a hierarchical, caste-segregated social order becomes more clear as she connects the threats posed to Theresa (and Lola) by the Mohaves to threats posed to Lola within the Norval home" (61). Both Fisher and Anne E. Goldman consider Lola's captivity extended rather than terminated when she enters the Norval compound. Goldman views Lola's "second remove" as Ruiz de Burton's attempt to disrupt the centrality of the New England home as the site of civility and whiteness. Fisher sees Lola imprisoned by bourgeois greed (embodied in the figure of Jemima Norval, who uses Lola's inheritance to satisfy her class-climbing ambitions) as symbolic of the financial and territorial gains of the United States after the U.S.–Mexican War.

Fisher, like Sánchez and Pita, cites the historical account of two "light-skinned Mexican women" abducted during Indian raids on the Jamul Ranch in 1837 as the basis for Lola's captivity (61). Whiteness is shored up against the savagery of the Native American captors, and in this manner Ruiz de Burton's employment of the captivity narrative functions as Nina Baym has argued about fictional accounts of captivity — they whiten the heroine through stark contrast (21, 96, 121). Ruiz de Burton is not, however, merely defaulting to a well-entrenched and gendered plotline of racial encounter between Indians and Anglo Europeans. Her narrative of Lola and Theresa's captivity certainly does draw upon this well-known genre figuring women between ethnic and geographic borders, but Ruiz de Burton compels her audience to recognize and acknowledge Lola's identity and, in extrapolated form, that of all Mexicans who became de facto American citizens at the culmination of the U.S.–Mexican War. Her purpose was not only to claim whiteness for Mexicans of "pure Spanish blood" like Lola but also to rightfully and legally claim U.S. citizenship and its attendant rights and privileges. If the captive woman functions as a symbolic representation of the nation under attack and in need of protection, then the casting of a Californiana insists upon the Californios' national and ethnic identity as American and white.

The Norvals' adoption of Lola, like the pleas for members of San Francisco's elite to take in the orphaned Olive, return them to white, well-heeled society and thus confirm their gender and ethnic status. Historian William Rice reports that a "San Diego family offered [Olive] a home, where care and instruction, it was remarked, would enable her 'to resume that position in society which five years of savage bondage has deprived her' " (98). Lola's age in captivity effectively removes her from the threat of miscegenation and from the trope of the fallen woman. Her mother absorbs this role instead. Olive's status within the Mohave community remains a mystery. One rumor identified her as the wife of the chief's son and the mother of two sons. Part of this question over Olive's "honor" seems to revolve around her age.[10]

Not wishing to perpetuate the stereotype of Mexicanas as sexually licentious creatures, a myth propagated by travel narratives into the Southwest, Ruiz de Burton carefully separates Lola from her mother, writing the latter into the role of ravaged female martyr. Lola's chastity, when taken together with the timing of her birth and her young age when rescued by Dr. Norval, is further substantiated by what is read as her mother's ultimate sacrifice. The close ties between both captives and the chief function to raise the status of these women beyond anonymous slave to exceptional members of the Mohave tribe. Yet this status does not translate back into white society where the women are imagined as being defiled and degraded because of their carnal knowledge of "savage" men. Indeed, Lola's mother mysteriously dies before she can be carried off to freedom with her daughter. Dr. Norval interprets her sudden death in the following manner: "She did not wish to see her family now, after ten years of such life as had been forced upon her" (35).

When Doña Theresa's *testimonio* is finally recovered from the dead-letter office and delivered to her husband and father, the reader learns more explicitly of Doña Theresa's fate while among the Mohaves: "I forgive the horrible savages who inflicted upon me the most terrible torture that the human soul can know — the agony of living in degradation forever on earth" (202). Husband and father weep over Doña Theresa's final words and, gazing lovingly at her portrait, imagine her to say, "Do not weep for me. I was always pure, for my soul did not sin, although I was insulted by a savage" (202).

If Ruiz de Burton had read this account, perhaps what would have interested her in the Oatman captivity were Olive's tattoo, her capture outside the bounds of the United States, her questionable sexual status upon return, and the blending of Mexican and Native American languages and customs.[11] Combined, these elements provided sturdy material for building a case against the U.S. government, its policy of Manifest Destiny, and its failure to ratify and maintain the promise outlined in the peace treaty of Guadalupe Hidalgo. As mentioned in Article XI of the treaty, the United States was responsible for policing the newly defined border between Mexico and the United States against Indian raids and for outlawing the economy reliant upon ransoms paid for hostages. Both Lola and Olive are in Mexican territory when captured. As Washburn notes in his introduction to Oatman's text, "The Oatman party was in Mexican territory (the Gadsden Purchase had not yet occurred)" (ix). The first article of the Gadsden Purchase establishes the boundary between the United States and Mexico. As this treaty was not entered upon until 1853, five years after the fictional capture of Doña Theresa and two years after the historical capture of Olive and Mary Ann Oatman, both sets of captives were in Mexican territory at the time of their capture.

Regardless of the territorial ownership of the land in question — the confluence of the Gila and Colorado Rivers — which is the site of rescue for Ruiz de Burton's characters and that of attack and capture for the Oatmans, the government is severely chastised for not preventing the attack. The narrator of *Who Would Have Thought It?* conjectures: "If Mexico were well governed, if her frontiers were well protected, the fate of Doña Theresa would have been next to an impossibility. When it is a known fact that savages will devastate towns that are not well guarded, is there any excuse for a government that will neglect to provide sufficient protection?" (201). One recalls Lorenzo Oatman's failed petition to California governor J. Neely Johnson for assistance in recovering his sisters and the California newspapers' published admonishments to Johnson for not acting in a timely manner.

Lola's reunion with her father and maternal grandfather occasions Ruiz de Burton's redressing of grievances after 1848. The fate of Doña María and Lola is blamed on the U.S. government and its unprotected frontier (201). Here Ruiz de Burton alludes to Article XI of the Treaty of Guadalupe Hidalgo, which addressed the issue of captivity and the trafficking of human beings in the following manner: "It shall not be lawful, under any pretext whatever, for any inhabitant of the United States, to purchase or acquire any Mexican or any foreigner residing in Mexico, who may have been captured by Indians inhabiting the territory of either of the two Republics" (reported in Griswold del Castillo 191). The U.S. government established the first border patrol to prevent Indian raids and the trafficking of individuals across the newly erected border. This article, along with Ruiz de Burton's reframing of the captivity narrative, shifts the geographical and racial imaginings of the nation or, more specifically, the domestic. For Ruiz de Burton, both Native Americans and Anglo Americans are the invaders who enter Mexico's domestic space, capturing wives and marrying into Mexican families for profit and financial gain.

When I first began researching Olive Oatman's captivity, I came across an article by Richard Dillon stating that "a Mexican soldier told [Captain] García that the Oatman sisters were being held by Mohaves" (54). Dillon adds parenthetically: "Actually, Mary Ann was dead, but her place had been taken by a Mexican girl who was confused with her. The Mexicana was eventually released with Olive" (54). No other scholar mentions this Mexican woman accompanying Olive on her return; perhaps she is an amalgam of the Mexicana captive who was caught escaping and tortured to death and the chief's daughter, who was among the party appearing at Fort Yuma with Olive and Francisco, the Yuma Indian who rescued her. Thus far, I have been unable to locate any newspaper accounts that describe a Mexican woman in Olive's rescue party. Oatman briefly mentions a fellow captive with whom she became acquainted during her residence among the Mohaves. She describes in her lecture notes "a young woman of twenty-five years of age . . . who called herself Nowercha." No details regarding the circumstances of her abduction are provided except that Nowercha "had a husband and a child left behind" when "her tribe [the Cochoba] was put to flight" (20). It is possible that Dillon mistook the chief's daughter for this woman, who was recaptured, tortured, and killed before Olive's horrified eyes. It is also worth entertaining the possibility that Ruiz de Burton was drawn to another female captive briefly mentioned or on the fringes of the Oatman abduction.

Captivity narratives have functioned traditionally as the crucible through which "white" women have crossed cultural and racial borders, gained agency and notoriety through the publication of their harrowing tales of life among "savages," and critiqued patriarchal constraints. In their assessment of the racial dynamics of *Hobomok* and *Hope Leslie*, Nina Baym and Priscilla Wald have argued that a negative dialectic fuels the whitening of captive heroines. For Christopher Castiglia, the captivity, or more specifically its telling, affords white women a degree of agency otherwise unavailable.

Ultimately, Ruiz de Burton's revision of the captivity narrative operates under a different geographical and racial imaginary than the one commonly animating captivity narratives. It focuses attention on the Southwest Territory, on the broken promises of the Treaty of Guadalupe Hidalgo, on the co-optive actions of people like Hubert Howe Bancroft, on the primacy of the Southwest Territory in nation building, on U.S. imperialism, and on the U.S./Mexican border.

Notes

I wish to thank José Aranda, Amelia María de la Luz Montes, Anne E. Goldman, Jesse Alemán, Laurie Lambeth, and the FHE at Utah State University for suggestions with this essay. I also want to thank Walter Brem at the Bancroft Library. Finally, I want to dedicate this article to my father, who passed away before he could see it in print.

1. See Tomás Almaguer's *Racial Fault Lines* for more on the history of the social category "white Mexican."

2. See 34th Cong., 3rd sess., H. report 55, and 34th Cong., 1st sess., S. Exec. Doc. 66, pp. 67–68.

3. The Oatmans' religious beliefs were largely suppressed in newspaper accounts, Olive's lecture notes, and the Rev. Royal B. Stratton's introduction to the captivity narrative.

4. Taylor and Wallace write that Olive's chin tattoo guaranteed her entrance into Sil'aid (Land of the Dead)" (5).

5. Derounian-Stodola argues that "illustrations played a much more important role in the second and third editions of the Oatman publication . . . the number of engravings rose from twelve to sixteen, and the treatment of the subject generally became more sensational and sentimental" (38).

6. In what Rice describes as "acrimonious correspondence," Ira Thompson questioned the motives of Harvey Oatman's brother, Harrison, by asking what had prevented him from caring for Lorenzo from 1853 to 1855 (99). Lola Medina's reunion with her father and grandfather in Mexico privileges blood relations and condemns the pecuniary interests motivating her white adoptive family, the Norvals.

7. Lola first appears at the Norval household in blackface. Over time, the dye fades away, leaving Lola spotted. For Olive, however, this bodily mark of her association with "savages" proves indelible. Newspaper articles contain the anecdote about Fort Yuma soldiers contributing money to buy Olive new clothes.

8. "Stripping the captive woman or ripping off her clothing is as

much a stock trope in captivity tales . . . as is the habitual nakedness of Native women in representations of the nineteenth century and earlier" (Blevins Faery 177). Regarding moral standing, see Walter Colton, Richard Henry Dana, Susan Magoffin, and Charles Lummis, to name but a few.

9. See Horsman's *Race and Manifest Destiny* for a study of physiognomy and U.S. expansionist politics.

10. Kroeber and Kroeber speculate that Stratton may have tinkered with Olive's age to sensationalize her story and boost sales.

11. Olive's father, Royce Oatman, communicated with the Apaches (Yavapais) in Spanish; Olive's rescuer, Francisco, was fluent in both Spanish and his native tongue.

4

Discovering Ruiz de Burton's Theatrical Vision

Precarious Performances:
Ruiz de Burton's Theatrical Vision of the Gilded Age Female Consumer

BETH FISHER

Who Would Have Thought It? is a melodrama in narrative form, that does not ask the most implicit belief from the reader, but amuses by its broad contrasts, frank mess-room humor, and boldly-shaped diversities of character. ❦ (*Lippincott's Magazine*, Nov. 1872, 607)

Soon after the publication of *Who Would Have Thought It?* by J. B. Lippincott, a favorable review appeared in *Lippincott's Magazine*. Given their shared publisher, the magazine's endorsement of the novel is not in itself remarkable. Instead, the significance of this anonymous review lies in its classification of the novel as "a melodrama in narrative form." Citing an improbable yet entertaining plot and a heroine disguised in "blackface," the review suggests that the original readers of *Who Would Have Thought It?* may have seen something in the novel that is not immediately apparent to more recent readers — its affinity with contemporaneous theater.[1] In fact, María Amparo Ruiz de Burton drew directly on popular theatrical modes to tell the story of Lola Medina, a Mexican girl rescued from captivity among Indians in California, adopted by an aspiring middle-class family in New England, and robbed of her wealth and status before being restored to her own family in Mexico. Faced with the task of presenting to a predominantly Anglo American audience a vision of Yankees as hypocritical, self-serving, and eager to get their hands on Mexican property, Ruiz de Burton crafted a melodramatic satire whose plot twists and comic devices would have been familiar to readers well versed in the theatrical culture of the urban Northeast.

The author of two novels, Ruiz de Burton also pursued a sustained interest in the theater. During the 1850s, she was the likely writer of a series of plays performed at Mission San Diego by U.S. army soldiers under the command of her husband, Capt. Henry S. Burton. In 1876, her comic play *Don Quixote* was published in San Francisco. For a significant part of the intervening years, she lived in various cities and on military posts in the northeastern United States. Her husband's service in the Union army during and after the Civil War provided her with the opportunity to participate in, and to observe, elite society in the East, where she became acquainted with luminaries on both sides of the conflict, including President Lincoln and Mrs. Jefferson Davis. In the meantime, she gathered material for *Who Would Have Thought It?* which would be published anonymously in 1872, three years after the death of her husband and two years after she returned to her native California and took up a series of legal battles to maintain title to her property. [2]

The main plot of *Who Would Have Thought It?* unfolds against a historical backdrop that directly connects the economic boom of the post–Civil War era to a national project of westward expansion culminating in the war against Mexico, which began in 1846 and ended in 1848 with the annexation of a third of Mexican territory by the United States. The fantastic story of Lola Medina begins in 1846, when her pregnant mother, Doña Theresa Medina, is kidnapped by Apaches in Sonora, Mexico, and then sold to a group of Mohaves. Eleven years later, Dr. James Norval encounters the dying Theresa, rescues Lola, and returns with her to his home in New England. James's adoption of Lola subjects her to the wrath of his wife, Jemima, a xenophobic Presbyterian who despises Lola for her dark skin, her Catholicism, and her foreignness. What Jemima does not immediately realize, however, is that the darkness of Lola's skin is merely the result of a disguise applied by her Mohave captors.

Furthermore, Lola is astonishingly wealthy. Doña Theresa has turned over to James Norval not only her daughter but also the fortune in gold and gems she collected during her captivity. As soon as Jemima hears what later proves to be a false report of her husband's death, she begins to pilfer large sums of Lola's wealth. She is aided by her lover and former minister, John Hackwell, a slick confidence man who hopes to get closer to Lola and her money by encouraging Jemima's erupting passions. Soon Jemima buys a mansion in New York City. As much as Hackwell, Jemima is the villain of this melodramatic plot. The narrative of her rapid ascent from the rural middle class into the urban elite articulates Ruiz de Burton's contention that the acquisitive desires of northeastern women are the motivating force behind mid-nineteenth-century U.S. expansionism.

Ruiz de Burton portrays Jemima Norval as a woman engaged in a series of performances, first as a frugal middle-class housewife and then as a wealthy consumer who appropriates Mexican property. This strategy exposes ideological connections between the rhetorics of Manifest Destiny and domestic womanhood. More specifically, Ruiz de Burton rejects a common presumption in the nineteenth century that the Anglo American woman's capacity for economic and sexual self-denial would make her home a haven from the aggression, competitiveness, and acquisitiveness associated with male activity in the marketplace and on the frontier. Her novel thus anticipates the perspective of contemporary critics such as Amy Kaplan, who has recently located in nineteenth-century literature a discourse of womanly cultural dominance that she terms "Manifest Domesticity." Further, *Who Would Have Thought It?* both documents and promotes a cultural shift that was dismantling the ideal of the self-denying, or "passionless," woman in the Gilded Age.[3] As the novel makes clear, this shift was prompted, in part, by a proliferation of dry-goods emporia, theaters, and parks — urban sites that were integrating domesticity and commerce and creating new opportunities for women to appear in public. During this era of intense economic volatility, the rapid expansion of commerce and industry spurred the rise of a newly prosperous middle class and swelled the ranks of the elite, but also made downward mobility an ever-present threat. In this context, the consumerist activities of middle-class women, and their apparent capacity to spend too much, became subjects of widespread concern.[4]

Ruiz de Burton surveys the growing prosperity of northeastern Americans from the perspective of a Californiana who experienced firsthand the loss of property and political clout suffered by her class as rapid capitalist development came to California.[5] Invoking theatrical modes such as the melodrama and the social comedy, in *Who Would Have Thought It?* she portrays the northeastern elite as a group that consists entirely of nouveau riche, essentially middle-class Anglo Americans who have profited at the expense of Mexicanos and Californios. Her theatrical vision of the female consumer demonstrates that, rather than opposing the "dominant" literature of the Gilded Age (Sánchez and Pita, 1997 Introduction xxx), *Who Would Have Thought It?* contributed to a culture replete with anxieties about the burgeoning capitalist economy and the social instability it fostered, anxieties that were often focused on the desires of women consumers.

The story of Lola Medina's adoption into the Norval household may have seemed quite familiar to readers who attended the theater during the late 1860s, when Augustin Daly's *Under the Gaslight* became a hit. *Gaslight* opened in New York in 1867 and played there for thirteen weeks before enjoying successful runs in Boston and Philadelphia; it was revived many times during the following year and well into the 1880s (McConachie 206; Odell 301–4). According to theater historian Bruce McConachie, *Gaslight* was typical of the "sensation melodrama," a type of play most popular from the mid-1850s through the early 1870s. These plays commenced with chance events or misunderstandings that caused bourgeois heroes and heroines to lose their wealth and social status. At the start of *Under the Gaslight*, heroine Laura Courtland is mistakenly identified as an orphan of lower-class origins and cast out of polite society. However, her restrained behavior and standard English distinguish her from working-class and Irish characters, who speak in dialect (McConachie 214–15). Laura's restoration at the end of the play to an elite social position, McConachie has observed, confirms that her status is based on " 'natural' attributes resulting from birth and upbringing" (215). This plot, he contends, appealed to middle-class audiences who came to the theater "burdened" with feelings of illegitimacy provoked by economic volatility and by their own attempts to adhere to a contradictory code of etiquette demanding both sincerity and an outward show of "respectability" (210). *Gaslight* may have thus reassured these theater-goers that their claims to social status, like Laura's, were legitimate.[6]

Ruiz de Burton turns this plot on its head by representing Lola Medina as a Spanish Mexican aristocrat whose "natural" nobility and racial purity expose the false pretenses of middle-class and elite Yankees. When Lola arrives for the first time at the Norval home, the darkness of her skin leads Jemima and her daughter Ruth to denigrate her as a "black girl" and the child of "Indians or negroes, or both" (16–17). As Rosaura Sánchez and Beatrice Pita note, Lola's "blackface performance" functions as a plot device that reveals the racist hatred and thus the hypocrisy of the abolitionist, outwardly respectable Jemima (Introduction xx–xxi). Indeed, just as Lola's disguise wears off to uncover her true whiteness, Jemima's disguise of moral propriety fades, revealing the greed, sexual passion, and ambition that will transform her into a wealthy consumer. The dark disguise covering Lola's skin literalizes the degraded position into which she is placed in the Norval home; eventually, however, her gradually revealed whiteness will function with her "pure Spanish blood" and refined behavior as "natural" signs that she deserves wealth and status (28). Lola's proficiency in English differentiates her from the Irish servants and thus further confounds Mrs. Norval's perception of her as a lower-class black girl (30–31). Lola's story therefore follows the conventions of the "sensation melodrama" even as it locates social legitimacy not among bourgeois Anglo Americans but among aristocratic Mexicans.

Indeed, Ruiz de Burton's account of the upwardly mobile Norvals seems designed to confirm the concerns about class that *Gaslight* allayed. The story of Jemima Norval's transformation from a frugal middle-class housewife into a free-spending woman of the urban elite takes precedence over Lola's experience of social descent and restoration. A character who, at the beginning of the novel, exhibits an emotional self-control broken only by declarations of "hatred towards everything and everybody that [is] not Presbyterian," Jemima becomes an extravagant, passionate bourgeois matron (231). Once a strict Puritan who associates the theater with "foreigners" and "worldly" women who dress in "low necks and short sleeves," she learns to enjoy going to the theater and displaying herself in expensive clothing (87, 173). A woman of new wealth and few social graces, Jemima is a cultural descendant of Mrs. Tiffany in Anna Cora Mowatt's 1845 play, *Fashion*, and Mrs. Apex in Sidney Bateman's 1856 play, *Self*— social comedies that poked fun at the unrefined manners, ostentatious tastes, and snobbery of new arrivals in high society. *Fashion* was reprised in New York during the spring of 1868; it played at the Park Theatre less than two months before a production of *Under the Gaslight* was staged there (Odell 381–84). In the meantime, new comedies such as Irving Browne's *Our Best Society* (1868) and Bronson Howard's *Saratoga* (1870) kept this genre alive through the end of the decade.[7]

If, as McConachie argues, the "sensation melodrama" naturalized the wealth and social status of prosperous middle-class people, the social comedy represented class as the product of appearance, dress, and behavior — aspects of character that are performative. Theater historian Rosemarie Bank describes Bateman's *Self* as emblematic of the theater's function in the 1840s and 1850s as a cultural form that valorized the performance of class as a fluid category (103–10). The revival of the social comedy in the late 1860s suggests that after the Civil War, as economic and cultural divisions among classes became more apparent, representations of class as performative remained popular, perhaps due to the uncertainties

about social authenticity that McConachie identifies among theater audiences during this period. Northeasterners anxious about
their own claims to middle-class status may have appreciated the
melodrama's reassuring message of legitimacy while still enjoying
the social comedy's mockery of wealthy *arrivistes* — whose rapid
upward mobility and exaggerated pretensions may have seemed
both familiar and safely distinct from their own.

Ruiz de Burton capitalizes on this ambivalence by satirizing
Jemima Norval's rise from the rural middle class into the urban
elite, an ascent made possible by practices of material acquisition
and display. Soon after she begins to appropriate large sums of
Lola's money, Jemima moves into a New York mansion, where she
proves her elevated status by exhibiting expensive commodities;
her new home is a site of "conspicuous consumption." Jemima's
Puritan distrust of ostentation means that she initially finds herself
"uncomfortable" in this spectacular home. Looking around the
mansion, she is "frightened" to find herself reflected over and over
again in the "magnificent mirrors" that adorn every room (125).
Ruiz de Burton implies here that Jemima's consumerist activities
have transformed her into a woman whose image of herself depends
upon and is constituted by material objects. Jemima appears to
be caught in the position that Rachel Bowlby has described as
one result of women's participation in the late-nineteenth-century
capitalist economy: acquiring fashionable gowns and a luxurious
home in order to please her lover, she becomes both a consumer
and a commodity, a subject and an object.[8] It is at this point
in the narrative that Jemima seems most clearly a pawn of John
Hackwell, as Anne E. Goldman has represented her ("Who Ever
Heard" 64). Yet Jemima's vulnerability seems to refer less to a sexual
vulnerability shared by all women than to the compromised agency
of wealthy women consumers in a society where their purchases
make them passive symbols of male economic power.

Ruiz de Burton's critique of the commodification of women
fades quickly, however, as Jemima begins to revel in her new role

as a consumer and agent in the expanding economy. She learns to enjoy spending money, hosting lavish receptions, and wearing expensive gowns, thereby making public a "natural impulse" toward acquisition that she has previously displayed only in private (25). Late in the novel, the narrator notes that, for most of Jemima's life, her only "ambition" has been to save "more five- and ten-cent pieces than any of her neighbors" (231). The celebrated frugality of middle-class Anglo American women appears in this case to conceal greed: Jemima's self-restraint is a performance that hides her desire. When she establishes herself among the elite, she can put aside this role to take up another. Her new role as a wealthy consumer corresponds more closely to her desirous nature, but it also represents a pose that is no less artificial than her previous performance of self-denial. Ruiz de Burton thus rejects the idea that women like Jemima are innately free of material and sexual desires; she implies instead that in the northeastern United States, women perform roles defined by frugality or extravagance, sexual restraint or passion, depending on the class to which they wish to claim membership. Social status thus appears as the product of public performances in which women are the lead actors.

Ruiz de Burton was not alone in linking women's activities as consumers to upward mobility and the performativity of status during this period. In their 1873 novel, *The Gilded Age*, a satire that has much in common with *Who Would Have Thought It?* Mark Twain and Charles Dudley Warner identified the nouveau riche with acquisitiveness, ambition, and false pretensions. Proponents of domestic womanhood such as Harriet Beecher Stowe, moreover, expressed concern after the Civil War that women consumers were transforming their homes into commercial showplaces. In her 1872 novel, *Pink and White Tyranny*, for example, Stowe told the story of Lillie Seymour, an ambitious middle-class woman who uses her beauty to attract a husband who can afford the material goods she desires. After her marriage, Lillie's social world is not limited to the environs around her home in New England; rather, it extends to resorts such as Newport and the New York home of her friend Mrs. Follingsbee, which is decorated in a luxurious style that Stowe compares to the spectacular set of *The Black Crook* (261). This popular and controversial play also figures prominently in *Who Would Have Thought It?* For Stowe, the desires of aspiring women exemplified the threat posed to a New England domestic ideal by external, urban influences, including theater, fashion, and consumerism. For Ruiz de Burton, these materialist desires epitomized a northeastern, Protestant elite that had willfully traded New England domesticity for New York consumerism.

In their shared critique of women consumers, however, both Stowe and Ruiz de Burton commented upon economic and social changes that were making the urban home, the store, and the theater co-extensive spaces in the Gilded Age. Just as the emerging urban middle class was beginning to integrate material acquisition into women's domestic practices, retail stores and theaters were defining, and catering to, the desires of female patrons. McConachie observes that by the early 1870s, several theaters had been constructed in the Union Square area of New York, an area that constituted "a part of the 'Ladies Mile' of fashionable shops and restaurants along the city's main artery of business-class retail commerce" (251). Further, attending theatrical performances had itself become a "fashionable commodity" and a means for women and men to demonstrate their status among the middle class and the elite. Attending a play, McConachie notes, had become an activity akin to "purchasing the latest fashion in hat design" (244). These developments extended what Stuart Blumin calls an "axis of respectability" within which middle-class women could move from home to marketplace and back again (238). Yet, as *Pink and White Tyranny* and *Who Would Have Thought It?* suggest, the public presence of these women remained fraught with moral danger in this period, perhaps because this "axis" was associated with the spectacular displays of the theater.

Ruiz de Burton elaborates on this point in chapter 37, "Mrs.

Norval's Mental Debut," which recounts a night at the Italian opera as an occasion for Mrs. Norval and her daughter Ruth, as well as John Hackwell and his sister Emma, to advertise their new status as wealthy urbanites. Written during a period when the Italian opera was being transformed from a popular to an elite musical form, this account of Jemima's "debut" appearance in New York society implies that the consumption of opera by an uncultured nouveau riche elite undermines essential divisions between "high" and "low" art and between the middle and upper classes.[9] Upon arriving at the opera, Ruth Norval sizes up the situation immediately: She takes her seat in a conspicuous "proscenium box" and prepares "to stare and be stared at" (167). Before the drama begins, she raises her opera glass and makes a great show of scanning the audience. The narrator comments sardonically on Ruth's scorn for the assembled "fashionable wives and daughters of the railroad kings and princes of the gold room," noting that since Ruth has recently traveled abroad, she has "seen too many real princes of the blood and danced with too many *bona fide* dukes and counts of aristocratic foundation to care for these whom a tumble in the stocks might dethrone tomorrow" (167, emphasis in original). Although Ruiz de Burton ridicules Ruth's snobbery, she also confirms this character's assessment of the New York elite by assigning members of the opera audience comic names that undercut their claims to prestige: General Julius Caesar Cackle, the Misses McCods, the Misses Pinchinghams, the Misses Squeezephat, and Mrs. Von Kraut (166–67). This satirical scene links Ruiz de Burton to the many foreign visitors to the United States who had, since the late eighteenth century, expressed disdain for the unrefined manners and exaggerated pretensions of New York's elite (Jaher 245–46).

At the same time, she responds quite specifically to the rampant speculation and unregulated growth of industry that created a host of new millionaires in New York during and after the Civil War. Looking around the opera house, Ruth Norval "affect[s]" "a contempt for '*Shoddy*' " — or cheaply made fabric — in the dresses of her fellow spectators (167, emphasis in original). Ruth's scorn for the phony aristocrats in the audience is a performance that conceals this young woman's own recent arrival in high society. Her "affected" disdain for inferior dry-goods, moreover, alludes to wartime profiteering: "shoddy" was a term applied during the war to the wool fabric Brooks Brothers pieced together and sold at a great profit to the New York State Military Board (Burrows and Wallace 875).[10] In a contemporaneous essay published in London's *Cornhill Magazine*, Mary Mapes Dodge observes that "the American word 'shoddy'" means "pretense, vulgarity, assumption, the depth of folly, and the highest height of the ridiculous; also gilded ignorance, mock patriotism, wire-pulling, successful knavery, swindling, nay, treason itself" (44). In *Who Would Have Thought It?* fashion appears as both product and symbol of the dishonest practices by which opportunists are defrauding the government and appropriating Mexican property. Thus, Ruth Norval and Emma Hackwell appear at the opera wearing expensive dresses that were "bought with Lola's money" (167). By placing the Norvals within a social circle where "the wives and daughters of railroad kings" hold court, furthermore, Ruiz de Burton connects wealthy women consumers to the railroad monopolists whom she would identify in her second novel, *The Squatter and the Don* (1885), as the most corrupt of the capitalists who profit from westward U.S. expansion.

If Ruiz de Burton's account of the Norval women's performance at the opera draws attention to the ties between "conspicuous consumption" in the Northeast and territorial appropriation in the West, it also relies upon an image of sexualized female performance that became a focal point for anxieties about women's presence in urban, public spaces during the late 1860s. As she watches the opera, Jemima can understand neither the Italian in which it is sung nor the actions of the performers. Losing her ordinarily stern demeanor, she laughs boisterously, then finds her lover so amused by her outbursts that she is "tempted to leap upon the stage and begin to sing her own love." At this point, the narrator concedes in an aside to the reader that "it is very fortunate that the 'leg opera' [has] not yet blossomed on the New York stage," explaining that if Jemima, who "would never utter the word '*leg*,'" had the occasion to watch the "yellow-haired nymphs of the 'eighty-leg opera'" and to see that the "half-nude females tossing their legs so promiscuously [. . .] pleased her adored John," she would be "willing to pirouette too" (168). With this aside, Ruiz de Burton compares Jemima's appearance at the opera to productions of *The Black Crook* and — in her reference to "yellow-haired nymphs" — to performances by Lydia Thompson's "British Blondes" burlesque troupe, both of which featured scantily clad female performers. *The Black Crook*, a spectacular ballet, opened at Niblo's Garden Theater in New York during the 1866–67 season; Thompson's troupe, after a successful debut at George Wood's Broadway Theater in the autumn of 1868, moved on to Niblo's Garden in the winter and spring of 1869.[11]

Clearly aware of the controversies generated by performances of *The Black Crook* and Thompson's "British Blondes," Ruiz de Burton exploited in her novel the combination of fear and fascination with which contemporary commentators responded to these shows. In her description of the "leg opera," the performers appear as both objects of a male gaze and an unruly force that can victimize spectators: They are "five hundred bare [legs], in entangling evolutions, like so many polypi let loose to crawl upon the stage, cuttlefish dangling merrily their tentacula, with a sure instinct of fastening on poor, gaping oysters, which would be sucked dry" (168). Robert C. Allen has argued that for bourgeois male spectators, in particular, the performers of the "leg show" embodied a brazen sexuality that these men associated with lower-class women and with the fashionable women of their own class, women who appeared unescorted on city streets and attended urban amusements including the theater. The transgressive qualities that these spectators attributed to the "leg show" may therefore be understood as a product of its perceived potential to erase class boundaries among women.[12] Similarly, Ruiz de Burton's reference to the "leg opera" places Jemima Norval's consumerist practices in a familiar, provocative context of female sexual display, thus underscoring the idea that middle-class and elite women consumers of theater and fashion could no longer be held aloof as "passionless."[13]

Throughout the novel, Ruiz de Burton contrasts the vulgar performances of upwardly mobile Yankees with the refined manners of Lola Medina and her family. Lola's simple tastes, modesty, and moral incorruptibility stand in clear opposition to the extravagance, vanity, and moral hypocrisy of the Norval women and their peers; these qualities also mark Lola as an authentic aristocrat who will, according to the conventions of the "sensation melodrama," regain her rightful social position at the end of the narrative. When the Norval women appear at a reception "richly dressed" in fashionable gowns and expensive jewelry, for example, Lola appears wearing a dress made of white muslin (232). At another point, the narrator notes that Lola is on her way to "do some shopping"; however, she omits any direct mention of Lola's purchases (229). Lola's apparent freedom from the excessive acquisitiveness of the Norval women seems a result of her identity as an aristocrat who has no need to put on an outward show of her status. Ruiz de Burton correlates Lola's refined manners, moreover, with her whiteness and "pure Spanish blood." This strategy reflects the author's acculturation within a Mexican social system that conflated land ownership and elevated status with whiteness and European ancestry. Lola's cultural refinement appears to be a trait inherited from her father and grandfather, whose cultivated manners and fine tastes distinguish them from uncultured Anglo Americans.[14]

Although she is a minor character in the novel, Doña Theresa Medina plays a symbolically central role in Ruiz de Burton's vision of the aristocratic Mexican society that has been nearly destroyed by U.S. expansionism. Theresa embodies a nobility that is recognized even by her Mohave captors, who address her as "my lady" (34). Furthermore, her "accidental" acquisition of a fortune in gold and gems during her captivity implies that propertied Mexicans have a "natural" claim (over the competing claims of Indians) to the land and resources of California (29). It is precisely this claim, moreover, that the author represents as threatened by acquisitive Yankees like Jemima Norval. The narrative of the capture and death of Doña Theresa expresses Ruiz de Burton's pronounced nostalgia for a lost Spanish colonial past, thus complicating, as José F. Aranda and Goldman have each noted, her resistance to imperialistic fervor in the United States (Aranda, "Contradictory Impulses" 572–74; Goldman, "Who Ever Heard" 74–75). Indeed, each of her novels wages a protest against U.S. expansionism on behalf of a Mexican population that conspicuously excludes Indians, people of color, and manual laborers. Lola's birth into captivity and her adoption by a greedy Protestant mother signify the social and economic degradation suffered by the propertied Mexicans who became citizens of the United States in 1848. On the other hand, her marriage near the conclusion of the novel to Jemima's son Julian, who displays his honorable character by recognizing Lola's whiteness and Spanish heritage, suggests the author's hope that Mexican Americans would retain the wealth and status they deserved precisely by proving to sympathetic Yankees their "true" identity as white, Spanish aristocrats.[15]

In *Who Would Have Thought It?* however, the marriage of Lola and Julian occupies a secondary place in a plot that focuses primarily on satirizing middle-class Yankees' false pretensions to social prominence and racial purity. In one comic scene, Mattie, the more sympathetic of the two Norval daughters, comments that Lola "is the prettiest girl in these United States." "Talk of Spanish women being dark," she remarks, "can anything be whiter than Lola's neck and shoulders?" When her friend Emma Hackwell protests, Mattie jokes that Emma must be envious of Lola, since her own complexion is marred by freckles (232). This suggestion that Anglo American women are imperfectly white merits further consideration, especially in regard to Jemima Norval, whose first name may link her to "Old Aunt Jemima," a song that Robert C. Toll traces to blackface minstrel performances during the mid-nineteenth century.[16]

Jemima's final descent into madness symbolizes the more general state of social and moral disorder within which Ruiz de Burton leaves her Yankee characters at the end of the novel. While Jemima succumbs to a "brain fever" when her husband returns from Africa, very much alive (267), her daughter Ruth takes center-stage in New York high society. Unlike her mother, Ruth has no doubts about the delights of "conspicuous consumption"; she sees expensive dresses and luxurious interiors, as well as the wealth and status they signify, as her prerogative. Like Theodore Dreiser's protagonist in *Sister Carrie* (1900), Ruth is an acquisitive consumer who perfects the art of feminine performance. Yet *Who Would Have Thought It?* has more in common with the social comedies of the Gilded Age than with the naturalist fiction of the turn of the century. The narrator remarks, for example, that Ruth sees "her life dream realized" in marriage to a man who has risen rapidly into the urban elite: "She [sees] herself as the leader of American *bon-ton*, quoted and imitated by all the fashionable belles of New York and Washington, of Long Branch and Newport — all the well-dressed women who [. . .] have a perfect right to be spendthrifts, because their husbands have, by extortion and driving hard bargains, accumulated princely fortunes [. . .] all of this fortunate class Ruth wishe[s] to lead, and she [feels] equal to the task" (287–88). Envisioned through the perspective of Ruiz de Burton, terms such as "American *bon-ton*" seem both ridiculous and meaningless. Furthermore, the aspirations of Yankee women and men appear to be intertwined: Ruth's performances as a wealthy consumer will be financed by her husband's profiteering. With this account of Ruth's dubious ambitions, Ruiz de Burton warns her readers that the desires of female consumers are the driving force behind a capitalist economy that, if left unrestrained, will transform the entire United States into a place dominated by false pretense, self-interest, and poor taste —

a place that is inhospitable, as well as unattractive, to authentic Mexican and Mexican American aristocrats.

In *Who Would Have Though It?* Ruiz de Burton stages recent U.S. history to reveal the rise of an Anglo American elite in Gilded Age New York as an amusing, but ultimately disturbing, spectacle. Appealing to her audience through the language of theater, she reinforces prevailing anxieties about the insatiable appetites of middle-class and elite women. Jemima's unrestrained desires embody the destructive force of an expanding, nearly unregulated economy that persistently obscures class distinctions. With this character, Ruiz de Burton suggests that the influx of money is all it takes to transform the most frugal housewife into an extravagant consumer. From her vantage point, the upward mobility of Yankees like Jemima signifies social and moral disintegration rather than economic opportunity, particularly as it depends upon the outright theft of property rightfully belonging to Mexicans and Mexican Americans.

Ruiz de Burton thus contends that, in its relations with Mexico, the United States has taken on a new national mythology, one that has less to do with democracy than it does with the rise of a capitalist empire in the New World. In response to those who see the Gilded Age as a culmination of the Manifest Destiny of Anglo Americans, she characterizes the era instead as one of social disorder wrought by unbridled greed. The contrast she draws between unrefined Anglo American upstarts and an authentic Mexican aristocracy reflects her engagement with the "two colonial legacies" that shaped her life and work (Aranda, "Contradictory Impulses" 574). This contrast, however, also demonstrates her interest in merging the "sensation melodrama" and the social comedy, theatrical modes that represent elite status as, respectively, the inevitable result of "natural," inherited qualities and a product of social performance.

A novel in some senses at odds with itself, *Who Would Have Thought It?* clarifies Ruiz de Burton's contributions to a theatrical culture within which competing concepts of American identity were put on display, exposed to scrutiny, and performed for the consumption of spectators whose fears of social illegitimacy lingered amidst the bravado of Manifest Destiny and Union victory in the Civil War. Placing before the public a novel that couched political satire within a melodramatic plot, Ruiz de Burton enacted a precarious performance of her own. As the *Lippincott's* review implies, the comedic elements of her narrative may have overshadowed its critique of the presumed moral and cultural supremacy of a rising northeastern elite. Whether or not Ruiz de Burton succeeded in her bid to entertain as well as to enlighten her audience, she clearly found in the extravagant female consumer a provocative means of disturbing her readers' perceptions of what was real and what was merely a show.

Notes

I am grateful to Kim Marra for her insightful response to an earlier version of this essay.

1. In addition to the *Lippincott's* notice, contemporaneous commentary on *Who Would Have Thought It?* includes unfavorable reviews in *Godey's Lady's Book* (Sept. 1872) and *Literary World* (1 Aug. 1872) and a favorable piece in *Daily Alta California* (15 Sept. 1872; rpt. in Sánchez and Pita, *Conflicts* 569–72).

2. Sánchez and Pita report that Ruiz de Burton attended the theater in Washington DC on at least one occasion as the guest of Matías Romero, who became Mexico's ambassador to the United States in 1863 (*Conflicts* 191). Biographical information on the author comes from Montes's dissertation, 188–90; Sánchez and Pita, Introduction vii–ix and *Conflicts* 91, 230–31, 554–55; Haas 78–79; and Aranda, "Contradictory Impulses" 554–63.

3. I explore Ruiz de Burton's critique of the Anglo American ideology of domestic womanhood in greater detail in "The Captive Mexicana and the Desiring Bourgeois Woman." See also Sánchez and Pita, Introduction xxviii–xxxvi. For analyses of domesticity as a cultural discourse that countered the masculine values of the capitalist

marketplace, see, for example, Tompkins 141–46 and G. Brown 13–60. For discussions of self-restraint as a code of behavior central to an emergent middle-class identity, see Halttunen 92–123 and Ryan, *Cradle of the Middle Class* 155–65, 199–201. I employ the concept of "passionlessness" as it is defined in Cott's essay of the same name.

Ruiz de Burton's rejection of the "passionless" ideal may reflect her awareness of how this ideal informed the negative images of Mexican American women that appeared in mid- to late-nineteenth-century Anglo American accounts of California history. See Castañeda 8–10.

4. See Blumin 184–88, 238–39; Ryan, *Women in Public* 76–82; and G. Brown 182–84.

5. For historical accounts of the Californio ranchers in this era, see Pitt and Haas 32–38, 45–88.

6. In contrast to McConachie, Halttunen sees such concerns with social legitimacy as most prominent in the 1830s and 1840s and waning by the 1850s and 1860s. See *Confidence Men*, esp. 27–32, 186–90. The revival during the late 1860s of social comedies such as *Fashion* suggests that these anxieties endured after the Civil War.

7. On the popularity of social comedies between 1840 and 1870, see T. Miller 243–52.

8. See Bowlby 10–11, 18–34. The term "conspicuous consumption" comes from Thorstein Veblen's *Theory of the Leisure Class* (1899). See, in particular, 68–101, 178–82.

9. On opera's development into an elite entertainment during the second half of the nineteenth century, see Levine 93–104. My analysis of this chapter is indebted to Bank's discussion of the multiple and shifting meanings associated with the presence of women in the antebellum theater (122, 128–38).

10. Sánchez and Pita also note the historical significance of this allusion (Introduction xxvi–xxvii). On the wartime boom in New York, see Burrows and Wallace 872–78.

11. A frequent visitor to New York during this period, Ruiz de Burton moved to Staten Island shortly after the death of her husband, in April 1869 (Sánchez and Pita, *Conflicts* 227, 279–83). On *The Black*

Crook and performances of the "British Blondes" in 1868–69, see Allen 3–21, 108–17.

12. See Allen 137–48.

13. Goldman notes that *Who Would Have Thought It?* defies the conventions governing representations of mature women's sexuality in both Mexican American and Anglo American texts from this period ("Who Ever Heard" 64–67).

14. Goldman makes a similar point ("Who Ever Heard" 72–75). For analyses of the political and cultural logic behind the Californios' representations of themselves as white and Spanish, see Rosales and M. Sánchez. On this strategy in Ruiz de Burton's fiction, see, for example, Sánchez and Pita, Introduction xvi–xxi; M. Sánchez 79–87; and Luis-Brown 813–22, 829–31.

15. Ruiz de Burton would develop this idea further in the more prominent, and more complex, courtship plot of *The Squatter and the Don*. See Luis-Brown 820–22 and J. Saldívar, *Border Matters* 173–83.

16. See Toll, 254, 260–61, 268 n. 41. "Old Aunt Jemima" would become the alleged inspiration for the advertising icon first used nationally by the R. T. Davis Milling Company in the 1890s and sold to Quaker Oats in 1926. See Witt 26–33.

Toll notes that one verse of the song featured a comic reversal of power relations in the account of an "old missus" who promised to grant a slave freedom when she died, then lived "so long her head got bald" (qtd. in Toll 260); a similar reversal befalls Jemima at the end of the novel when she succumbs to apparent insanity and loses the authority she once exerted over Lola.

"Mine Is the Mission to Redress": The New Order of Knight-Errantry in *Don Quixote de la Mancha: A Comedy in Five Acts*

AMELIA MARÍA DE LA LUZ MONTES

Enter troop of black devils with lighted torches, carrying a large cage-like carriage on four wheels, drawn by twelve black imps—one at each wheel, four in front, and four behind. They take Don Quixote and put him into the cage. ♣ (Ruiz de Burton, DQ 5.6,63)

How unfortunate I am! Everyone I love sends me cruelty in return. I am a poor wretch. ♣ (Ruiz de Burton, 15 Jan. 1874)

One of María Amparo Ruiz de Burton's objectives in rewriting Miguel de Cervantes's novel into a play concerns a reclaiming of her cultural and literary heritage on California lands—an impossible task by 1876. As the epigraphs reveal, Ruiz de Burton's negotiation of land and livelihood on American soil (once Mexican) was fraught with frustration and disappointment in often conflicting and contradictory ways. She channeled these frustrations by writing letters to Mariano Guadalupe Vallejo from Senate Chamber meetings in Washington DC, urging Vallejo to take political actions she felt were necessary, and by writing two novels, using the genres of satire and romance.

In *The Squatter and the Don*, she breaks the narrative in the final chapter to personally acknowledge her grievances directly to the reader—a characteristic of the protest novel.[1] Although the characters in her play are not encouraged to speak directly to the audience, the characters and scenes Ruiz de Burton chooses from the Cervantes novel create a nostalgia for a hacienda community which Vincent Pérez also investigates in Ruiz de Burton's novels. In California, San Francisco specifically (where this play was published), Ruiz de Burton's stated nostalgia points to the Spanish administration or the Presidio construct of Alta California (late 1700s/early 1800s).

By first investigating the historical background surrounding this play, and then focusing upon the play itself, I offer another perspective of Ruiz de Burton's writings: her complex political and social alliances, which connect her to Alta California history. Like Vallejo, Ruiz de Burton would remain conflicted between Mexican and American alliances: disappointed by Mexico's lax support of Californios and angered by U.S. government colonization. Alta California's Presidio was once a *castillo*, which cannot be maintained from a distance (first Spain, then Mexico). In her play, Ruiz de Burton rides back to the Presidio to "redress" the wrongs of neglect, but finds that nothing can be done. The play, then, is a satirical critique of Alta California.

Ruiz de Burton's activity in the theater marks yet another avenue for her to speak. This play also emphasizes her rich California heritage in theater — something that has not been discussed in contemporary scholarship. This essay looks at the historical background surrounding Ruiz de Burton as a playwright, and also closely analyzes how she shapes the play to bring her Californiana political and social beliefs to the stage through the use of satire.

Historical Background

First, theater was quite popular up and down the coast of California during Ruiz de Burton's lifetime. Second, the popularity of the drama came from as far south as Mexico City. Plays performed in Mexico City's Gran Teatro Imperial and the Gran Teatro Nacional found their way north, and American drama and culture traveled south. Spanish-language plays from Mexico first arrived in Monterey in 1789.[2] By then, Mexico City's theater productions were well known to Californios. The kind of plays that were being produced reflected popular culture and taste also present in French, Italian, and Spanish literature and drama. In 1864 (roughly ten years before Ruiz de Burton's *Don Quixote* was published in San Francisco), novelist and playwright Don Juan A. Mateos wrote a one-act piece entitled *El Prólogo del Quijote*.[3] The short piece inspired by Cervantes's novel received much acclaim in Mexico and California. Even before the 1860s, Cervantes's name was known not only by the Mexican Californios on land but also by Americans on the waters of the Pacific. In 1836, the *Don Quixote* was an American ship that aided Don Juan Bautista Alvarado in his efforts to depose the Mexican governor, Nicolás Gutierrez, and pronounce California independent from Mexico. According to Robert Miller, "William Hinckley, the American captain of the *Don Quixote* . . . contributed arms and men to the rebel cause" (*Juan Alvarado* 49). The *Don Quixote* reappears in 1845 during an insurrection against Don Juan. Again the *Don Quixote* retrieves Don Juan's allies and sails to Monterey.

The 1836 incident is an important historical moment because California moved away from the earlier social construction of the presidio when it served as a military post under Spain (1776–1822). At that time, Alta California was divided into four fortified districts known as Presidios, which were constructed much like Spanish *castillos* — replete with fourteen-foot-high adobe walls, moats, and only one imposing gate from which one could enter or leave. Between 1769 and 1846, each presidio functioned as its own integral town with residential and military housing, church, stables, and trading post.[4] However, the Alta California Presidio decayed from poor funding, desertion, and neglect.[5] Today one can visit the Presidio of San Francisco, which became part of the Golden Gate National Recreation Area in October 1994. In place of adobe walls and moats, however, are remnants of U.S. brick barracks and military paraphernalia. It is the presidio culture that serves as a backdrop to Ruiz de Burton's play as well as Mateos's one-act piece.

Mateos's short play on Quixote received much acclaim. Mateos was also producing adaptations of novels such as a six-act drama (in verse) of Victor Hugo's *Les Misérables*. Mateos became one of the most important Mexican playwrights of the Maximilian era (1864–67). Mateos's plays varied widely: from original works to adaptations and works whose themes reflected contemporary events. In 1865, he presented *La Muerte de Lincoln* (*The Death of Lincoln*). He followed this play with an original play-in-verse entitled *Un Mexicano en Pekín* (*A Mexican in Peking*). Mateos was not the only playwright to present such diverse topics within his plays. In addition to producing their own original works, Bruno Flores, Ignacio Rodríguez Galván, and José María García adapted Italian and Spanish novels, opera, and plays for the Mexican stage (Reyes de la Maza 21, 162).[6]

In Los Angeles, theater houses were busily producing plays before and after the Mexican American War. Don Antonio F. Coronel (married to Mariana Williamson), who was mayor of Los Angeles in 1853–54, produced Spanish- and English-language productions in the theater he had built in his home, which had space for an audience of three hundred (Kanellos 2–3). Nicolás Kanellos points out the connection between Mexican and California theater:

> By the 1860s the professional stage in California had become so established and important to the Spanish-speaking community that companies that once toured the Mexican Republic and abroad began to settle down as resident companies in California. Such was the case of the Compañía Española de la Familia Estrella, which later came under the directorship of its leading man, renowned Mexican actor Gerardo López del Castillo. . . . At least two other professional companies were performing in

the San Francisco area at this time. . . . On July 19 [1874], *La Cabaña de Tom* (adaptation of *Uncle Tom's Cabin*), translated by Ramón Saavedra [was performed]. (Kanellos 4, 205)

The San Francisco performance of *La Cabaña de Tom* took place at Maguire's Opera House, only a few blocks from Washington Street, where the John Carmany publishing house would print Ruiz de Burton's play. Theaters like Maguire's were large, seating three to four hundred people at a time. Their opulence reveals the monetary support they received from the public.

Felicia Hardison Londré and Daniel J. Watermeier point out that San Francisco became the mecca of West Coast theater: "Between 1849 and 1869, San Francisco would become California's theatrical capital, offering a wide range of entertainments. In the decade 1850–1859 alone, there were 1,105 theater productions in San Francisco: 907 plays, 48 operas (in five different languages), 84 extravaganzas, ballets, or pantomimes, and 66 minstrel shows. . . . Audiences, moreover, were heterogeneous, enthusiastic, and catholic in their tastes. They enjoyed Shakespeare, farce, opera, burlesque, minstrelsy, circus" (133–34).

During the late 1850s and 1870s, Ruiz de Burton spent much of her time in San Francisco. In the late 1850s she was a young woman in her twenties, living with her husband in Monterey. They often came to San Francisco to see Vallejo and his family. It would not be unrealistic to imagine Ruiz de Burton in a San Francisco theater watching a Spanish-language play — especially since her husband was also bilingual.[7] During the 1860s, Ruiz de Burton left with her husband for the East Coast, where she would spend ten years negotiating Washington DC upper-class society, experiencing the Civil War, suffering through her husband's painful bout with and eventual death from malaria, adapting to New York as a widow, and determining how to manage the numerous debts her husband had left (as well as pending lawsuits and claims concerning California lands). She returned to California in the 1870s, dividing her time between San Diego and San Francisco.[8] The 1870s were her most prolific years of writing. *Don Quixote de la Mancha: A Comedy in Five Acts* was published by the John Carmany publishing house in San Francisco in 1876. The playwright was listed as Mrs. H. S. Burton.

The play has no known record of performance. However, because of the existing proliferation of theaters and theater performances, I conjecture that Ruiz de Burton had found a stage on which to direct her play and a willing audience to enjoy it. Other evidence points to Ruiz de Burton as an active playwright. In the introduction to this book, I offer the San Diego Mission Theater as a possible outlet for Ruiz de Burton's theatrical endeavors. Ruiz de Burton's husband was headquartered at the Mission, and he, his family, and troops lived on the premises. Ruiz de Burton's actors could have been members of her husband's regiment. This is not substantiated, but Londré and Watermeier describe American soldiers as actors: "The origins of English-language theater in California can be traced to March 1847, when soldiers of the Seventh Regiment of New York Volunteers arrived in San Francisco to occupy California at the end of the Mexican War. On their long voyage around Cape Horn, the soldiers had amused themselves with amateur theatricals and they continued their activities after landing with performances of melodramas and farces. As the soldiers were dispersed to other outposts at Sonoma, Monterey, Santa Barbara, and Los Angeles, they carried their theatrical enthusiasms with them" (133). How popular she was as a playwright is still unknown. However, the original manuscript copy reveals some information. In the frontispiece she has written: "Mr. Hubert H. Bancroft. A souvenir from the author. March 6, 1876." The powerful and well-known Bancroft knew she was a playwright. Perhaps he had helped furnish a theater for her dramatic directorial pursuits. Perhaps. What is more important, I believe, is the literary and historical significance this play presents to contemporary scholars. Ruiz de Burton's play falls in line with Mexican and American plays being performed in Mexico and California during the nineteenth century. San Francisco, a city that brings together a multitude of cultures, is a perfect backdrop for Ruiz de Burton to explore the Mexican/Spanish influences she brings to her adaptation of Don Quixote.

The Play

ACT I. SC. I. — Open country. View of an Inn.
Enter Don Quixote in full armor, on horseback.

DON QUI. [Soliloquizing.] Yes, the world shall ring with my name. My fame shall go forth, and like the rays of a rising sun spread over the earth. The glory of reviving the order of knight-errantry shall be mine, and mine shall be the mission to redress. Onward! to eclipse the Amadises and Orlandos! . . . There, there, in that castle yonder, must be knights who can dub me knight. . . . I see no dwarf on the ramparts, and no herald to announce my arrival. They have not seen me, perhaps. I shall go around by the front gate. I fear discipline is rather lax. Still, one must not be too severe a critic. I am glad I came to a castle where I can be made a knight so very soon. This is a good omen. Onward! to glory! to fame! (5–6)

In the voice of Quixote, Ruiz de Burton's mission does not need a higher authority. Ruiz de Burton's Quixote is ready to take on the world and become famous while redressing all the wrongs he sees. Even in this short soliloquy, Ruiz de Burton creates a Quixote who reveals a discriminating personality.

As Quixote approaches the castle, he notices no one minding it. "I fear discipline is rather lax," he says. It is a direct reference to Ruiz de Burton's frustrations with the Californios. In her personal letters, Ruiz de Burton often addressed Vallejo and the Californios as being "lax" in their struggles to retain their rights in California. In her play, Quixote is forgiving in the first scene and decides to ignore the inattentiveness of castle residents. After all, it is his first venture out into the open country and all looks bright. Yet it is clear to the reader/audience that his ill-fitted armor and his eagerness to correct what only he can see will eventually head him toward miscommunication, disaster, and tragedy.

The entire first act is drawn from the first part of Cervantes's novel. Don Quixote recruits Sancho, and they are off to fight windmills, struggle with a herd of sheep, battle with the innkeeper, and experience the innkeeper's daughter's trickery. Back home, the curate and Carrasco burn Don Quixote's books of chivalry. Through these initial adventures, the audience becomes familiar with Quixote's supporting cast: Sancho, Carrasco, curate, and Dulcinea. These scenes are the most familiar of the Cervantes novel and establish Quixote's character. They are also what Vladimir Nabokov describes as "samples of cheerful physical cruelty" (51) that can be compared to slapstick humor.

I note Nabokov here because he believes there are two types of cruelty that are played out in Cervantes's novel: the aforementioned "cheerful" type, and mental cruelties that occur in the second part. Ruiz de Burton uses both types of cruelty in similar ways. Her cruelties, however, are set within the Californio society. Nabokov writes: "The Spaniards of Don Quixote's day were not more cruel in their behavior toward madmen and animals, subordinates and non-conformers, than any other nation of that brutal and brilliant era. . . . That the rustler in the chain gang which Don Quixote meets on the road had been given the rack is mentioned as a matter of course, for torture was as generously — though more openly — applied in old Spain or old Italy as it is in our time in totalitarian states" (52). How fitting, then, if we follow Nabokov's line of thinking, to have these cruel scenes enacted in San Francisco: home of bull and bear fights, lynchings, brothels, gambling, drinking, and people (lawyers, squatters, immigrants) who are fighting for lands after the rush of war and discoveries of gold in the Sierras.[9] Moreover, the 1870s are the cruelest years for the Californios because by then they are bankrupt after years of litigation. Griswold del Castillo writes, "[M]ost Californio landholders lost their lands because of the tremendous expense of litigation and legal fees. To pay for the legal defense of their lands, the Californios were forced to mortgage their ranchos. Falling cattle prices and usurious rates of interest conspired to wipe them out as a landholding class" (73–74). Coupled with the prejudice against the Mexican Americans and the print propaganda that belittled and stereotyped them, the cruelties incurred upon the "new" subaltern minorities during the rapidly changing and tumultuous settling of California lands match Nabokov's claims of cruelty in Spain, Italy, and England. Ruiz de Burton sought to uncover these cruelties by exploiting the genre of satire. The cruelest scenes involve two judges who bray, Sancho as governor, and the trickery of Carrasco, the Duke, and the Duchess. These scenes well serve Ruiz de Burton's intentions to laugh at her real-life persecutors in a clandestine way. She depicts the lawyers, judges, and high government officials as lowbred people.

The Cervantes and Ruiz de Burton versions of the braying judges are interesting to compare. Ruiz de Burton clearly wants to portray them as simple-minded and coarse. In contrast, the judges in Cervantes's version do not initially appear in person. In Ruiz de Burton's play, at the end of the first scene in the second act, two judges enter on opposite sides of the stage without introduction. The backdrop for this scene is a road through a wood. The view of Sierra Morena is behind them. The backdrop of the Sierra is a symbol of Californio Sierra lands. The exchange that occurs is the longest encounter not involving Quixote or Sancho. One of the judges has lost his donkey, and the other volunteers to help find it. They agree to bray at opposite ends of the wood in order to coax its return. The judges first discuss their abilities in braying:

2D JUDGE. Can you bray?

1ST JUDGE. Yes, very finely indeed; that is, I think I can, but I don't like to be vain and praise myself.

2D JUDGE. Of course, because you are a modest man, as a good Judge always is; but I am sure you bray finely, and so do I. So, then, hear my plan: I go this way, and you go that way, around the wood. . . .

1ST JUDGE. [Shaking hands again.] You are a genius; you are the most talented Judge I know. (18)

The fact that Ruiz de Burton devotes so much time to this encounter (almost a full scene) only underlines her intent to focus her satirical criticism upon the political/legal profession.

In contrast, Cervantes recounts the braying story through a man Quixote meets at an inn. In this story, the lost donkey has already been devoured by wolves while they are braying. When they meet, they are surprised at how well they brayed. " 'Well then, I can tell you, friend,' said the ass's owner, 'that between you and an ass there's no difference as far as braying goes for I never in all my life heard anything more natural' " (Cervantes 564). The men go home and tell their story. The story spreads to the point that other villagers bray at the sight of anyone from the judges' town. It causes violent fights, and Quixote is asked to come and put a stop to the violence. When they reach the town, Quixote begins to win people over with his eloquence, but then Sancho steps in and ruins it by braying, which only causes violence against the two main characters.

It is the conversation between the judges in the Ruiz de Burton version, however, that makes the story become realistic rather than romantic. Cervantes's device is a frame-story. Ruiz de Burton's intent is direct satire, as in the following exchange between the judges:

2D JUDGE. I know I can bray well, but your bray is superior to mine. Your tones are rich, your time correct, your notes well sustained, and the cadences abrupt, well measured, expressive, and beautiful. It is a pity that rare abilities are lost to the world, and often bestowed upon those who do not employ them to advantage.

1ST JUDGE. That is true, but we can not justly complain, for our merit is certainly appreciated. Do we not get re-elected all the time? We are the most popular judges, let alone our braying, which goes to prove the sagacity of the people.

2D JUDGE. That is the point, that though we are so popular, our brightest gift is unknown.

1ST JUDGE. I don't catch your meaning. You are too deep at times, but this I do know, that no two judges or two real asses could have brayed better than we have to day.

2D JUDGE. Of course not. We deserve our popularity. (19)

In 1876, when this play was published, Ruiz de Burton had experienced roughly six years of standing in front of California Land Commission judges (and a number of them squatters cloaked in judicial robes), defending her land grants and working with an army of lawyers.[10] The judges' pumped-up egos and eventual violence when they return to town is a scene that Ruiz de Burton duplicates in other writings. For example, in *Who Would Have Thought It?* when the Honorable Le Grand Gunn thinks he's being laughed at, he picks a fight with Isaac Sprig.[11] She also uses Sancho's short tenure as governor to make fun of the American system. Sancho experiences life as governor of his own island in act 4. He presides over ludicrous court cases that prevent him from eating his usual hearty meals, and he is called at all hours of the night to physically defend his lands. It only takes a day for Sancho to return to the Duchess and abdicate his rule.

In the second half of the play, the satire becomes lugubrious. The scenes cease to be light slapstick. Ruiz de Burton's dialogue also takes on a more serious literary tone, mixing classic literature within the overall romance adventure story. The cruelty Quixote experiences becomes internal, as it does in the Cervantes novel. In acts 3 and 4, the Duke and Duchess chapters (from the Cervantes novel) are the focus. They unleash a series of cruel tricks upon Sancho and Don Quixote, toying with their sincere beliefs in knight-errantry. In act 3, the Duke convinces Quixote and Sancho to break Malambruno's spell, which has transformed Princess Antonomasia into a brass monkey and Don Clavijo into a metal crocodile. The spell has also caused the duennas to have bearded faces. When Quixote agrees to break the spell, the Duke wheels a wooden horse to the middle of the stage. Quixote and Sancho must mount the horse and fly to where Quixote will battle Malambruno. The scene is grand folly at the expense of our main hero, who is rapidly becoming a continual object of ridicule. It also makes for exciting dramatic spectacle. When they "supposedly" lift off, the crowd of jokesters spurs them on:

ALL. They soar like an eagle . . . and astonish the world below them! They will soon reach the clouds!
SANCHO. . . . this thing of flying through the clouds is unnatural, sir; very unnatural, unpleasant. . . .
DON QUIXOTE. Doubtless we are in the region where hail and snow are formed, and we will soon reach the third region, where thunder and lightning are engendered, and we will pass to that of fire. But how to turn this peg, so as to avoid mounting to where we might melt, I know not. (Ruiz de Burton, DQ 3.4, 41)

This scene especially illustrates Ruiz de Burton's personal writing style, which distinguishes her from Cervantes. In the scene, Sancho focuses upon the unnaturalness of flying, and Quixote's answer is a classical one: He first describes what he is seeing as if he were being led by Virgil through the second circle of hell. [12] The comparison fits here because the second circle concerns lust, which is the theme within the Malambruno story.[13] Quixote is also hoping he does not turn into Icarus, whose wings melted when he flew too close to the sun. Ruiz de Burton's allusions to classical works and mythology in her drama are not unusual for nineteenth-century American literature and drama.

At the end of this scene, the horse explodes, throwing Quixote and Sancho across the stage. The Duke and Duchess then tell Quixote he has been successful in his quest to break the spell. Special effects were popular in nineteenth-century drama. Louisa Medina's play *The Last Days of Pompeii* was the longest running production in New York in 1835.[14] Amelia Howe Kritzer explains that Medina, a resident playwright for the famous Bowery Theater, "specialized in effective dramatic adaptations of popular novels of the day, especially those that offered opportunities for impressive spectacle" (22–23). At the end of *Don Quixote*, the stage is filled with explosions, fountains, statuary, lightning and thunder, and an army of actors dressed in red-spangled devil costumes brandishing lighted torches.

The fifth and final act emphasizes Quixote's transformation into a conquered Californio Hidalgo. Quixote becomes much like Ruiz de Burton's character Gabriel in *The Squatter and the Don*. Gabriel is transformed from a proud Californio son who will someday inherit his father's ranch and lands to a lowly hod carrier — an impoverished, broken man in lower-class American society. In the Quixote play, this transformation occurs when Carrasco, the Duke, and the Duchess trick Don Quixote one last time so that he will return to La Mancha and give up knight-errantry. The joke is ultimately on Quixote because everyone around him now is using enchantment at his expense and for their own self-interest.

Disguised as the Knight of the White Moon, Carrasco triumphs over Quixote and places him in an oxcart. In the Cervantes version, the cart scene happens at the end of part 1. In the novel, Quixote is brought home, sitting on a bale of hay in an oxen-led cart. He has suffered a severe blow from a Penitente while trying to "save" what was really a statue of the Virgin Mary in the Penitente procession. The canon, priest, and barber direct the driver of the cart to bring him home.

In contrast, Ruiz de Burton transforms Cervantes's scene into a dark, foreboding spectacle. Carrasco challenges Quixote to a duel and wins. He brings Quixote a sedan (symbol of royalty) on which to sit. When Carrasco disappears, red devils appear and take the sedan from Don Quixote. The play ends in a strange dance of duennas and a duel of devils. In Ruiz de Burton's hands, the cart becomes a hearse, and the last scene is a funeral on its way to hell. Consider the following stage directions that end the play:

> Enter troop of black devils with lighted torches, carrying a large cage-like carriage on four wheels, drawn by twelve black imps — one at each wheel, four in front, and four behind. They take Don Quixote and put him into the cage. Immediately enter a troop of red devils in red and spangles, brandishing lighted torches. The thunder becomes louder, and lightning more vivid. Flashes and flames shoot into the stage. More red-spangled imps come in; then more black — all with torches. They dance and fight around the cage, and draw it about around the stage. Sancho crouches and hides, frightened. The stage has been illumined with a red light ever since the dancers came in. A bell tolls. A white light succeeds the red. "The Knight of the White Moon" enters; he fights the black and red imps with his sword alone. They fight him with lighted torches. During the fight the curtain falls. (5.6, 63)

The last act departs most from the Cervantes novel and culminates in wild pyrotechnics and dance. Carrasco, who was behind the trickeries played upon Quixote, is exultant. Ruiz de Burton's play follows forms and manners of Mexican and American nineteenth-century drama. She also inserts her political beliefs through the use of satire.

In Ruiz de Burton's play, Quixote is a Californio Hidalgo who has been tricked and conquered by jokesters (squatters) who pretend aristocratic lineage. I turn to Nabokov once more to point out the significance of Quixote as Californio Hidalgo and how the cart at the end of the play contributes to this symbol. Nabokov writes:

> If we go back from Malory of the fifteenth century to the thirteenth century we find the earliest text dealing with Lancelot of the Lake and Guinevere, a French prose romance, the Roman de la Charrete by Chrétien de Troyes. (The theme under different names had been current in Ireland centuries earlier.) In this thirteenth-century romance a cart passes driven by a dwarf who tells Lancelot that if he climbs into the cart he will be driven to Queen Guinevere. He accepts and braves disgrace. (The disgrace element depends on the fact that carts were used to parade criminals.) Don Quixote submitting to the disgrace of the oxcart because he is told by enchanters that he will be driven to Dulcinea is exactly in the same boat, in the same cart. (46)

Note Nabokov's comparison of Chrétien de Troyes's cart and Cervantes's cart. The objective of Quixote and Lancelot is to reach their intended loves. They will risk public dishonor for the sake of a higher state: agape love. Without this lofty objective in the Ruiz de Burton play, the cart solely becomes the element of 'disgrace that Nabokov describes. In Ruiz de Burton's play, then, Quixote is transformed into a criminal, a displaced Californio who ends up a disgraced, lower-class indigent with no one to defend him — not even Sancho, who crouches in fear.

After the bell tolls, a white light guides Carrasco (as Knight of the White Moon) to center stage. Could this be a comment upon the "white" Anglo Americans who have invaded the Californio lands? In 1869, seven years before the publication of this play, Ruiz de Burton wrote to Vallejo, decrying Anglo American colonization:

I feel . . . a strong hatred and contempt (like a good Mexican) for that "Manifest Destiny." . . . Of all the evil phrases ever invented . . . there is not one phrase more detestable for me than that one, the most offensive, the most insulting; my blood rises to the top of my head when I hear it, and I see as if in a photographic instance, all that the Yankies have done to make Mexicans suffer — the robbery of Texas; war; the robbery of California; the death of Maximilian. . . . [S]ince the death of the Emperor, I also do not know what to hope for. With him went the hope to break the evil spell, the influence this country has over my own, an influence like the shadow of a vine tree that kills everything not of its own species. (February 15, 1869)

In symbolic and direct ways, Ruiz de Burton produces a play that reenacts how the Alta California Presidio was mismanaged and then easily taken. When the Quixote in her play is caged in her black carriage, it is a symbolic death to her aristocratic heritage and her land rights.

Is Quixote, then, a symbol of Ruiz de Burton? Don Quixote, a Californio Hidalgo living in a post–Mexican American war, is transformed into a Mexican American who rides through stolen lands and believes she/he is truly a Spanish savior who must redress the wrongs of her/his people and end this enchantment. There may be some evidence that would point to my completely subjective claim here. The manuscript copy I have of the play contains (as I have earlier pointed out) an inscription written in Ruiz de Burton's hand dedicated to the book collector Hubert H. Bancroft. I point this out once again to emphasize another aspect of this dedication. In the first two lines, Ruiz de Burton writes: "Mr. Hubert H. Bancroft. A souvenir from." Below the word "from" is the title of the play *Don Quixote* in large letters. Below the title, her lettering again appears: "The Author, March 6, 1876." Altogether, then, the dedication reads: "A souvenir from Don Quixote the Author." Because of Ruiz de Burton's sharp wit and her use of satire in her personal letters and novels, I would argue that she is making a statement here as well. The Don Quixote in the play may be male, but he is certainly an aspect of Ruiz de Burton's own self—a woman who began her life as an aristocrat but spent most of her adult life defending her aristocratic heritage despite her destitute and second-class citizenry on lands that have become American and appropriated by rogue squatters. The enchantment is that she is no longer an aristocrat but a poor woman who is slowly appropriated personally and publicly. The cruelty of her fate pervades her rendering of the play.

Ruiz de Burton's dramatic rendering of *Don Quixote* relies upon the genre of satire to create a play that is Californian in flavor rather than Spanish. Her drama reveals the Mexican American cultural and political issues prevalent in nineteenth-century California. Ruiz de Burton's play is about the loss of her lands and those of her people at the hands of Anglo Americans who fervently believe they have the divine right to colonize. In her play, Ruiz de Burton seeks to re-dress as Quixote as well as redress the wrongs she continually sees happening upon the Californio.

Notes

1. See "Strategies for the Classroom" (this volume) where Pérez says, "I also use [Juan Rulfo's *Pedro Paramo*] to historicize Californio representations of nineteenth-century Mexican hacienda society and particularly Ruiz de Burton's *The Squatter and the Don*, which I refer to as a sentimental 'protest' novel." However, it can also be seen as a protest novel within the genre of Upton Sinclair. Both Sinclair's *The Jungle* and *The Squatter and the Don* end with direct appeals: "Chicago will be ours!" and "Emancipate the White Slaves of California!"

2. Theater historian Nicolás Kanellos writes, "The documentary evidence comes first from Monterey, California. A play manuscript dated in that year, *Astucias por heredar un sobrino a su tío*, written

by Fernando de Reygados and copied by Mariano Guadalupe Vallejo (1807–1890), exists today in the Bancroft Collection of the University of California" (1). The play had been performed under numerous titles, and there is evidence that it was performed by Spanish soldiers, which would date the play before 1821, when Mexico won independence from Spain.

3. This short piece was resurrected in 1905 when playwright Manuel José Othón combined it with his own piece, *El Último Capítulo*, in honor of the third centennial of Cervantes's novel.

4. See Zoeth Skinner Eldredge on San Francisco history.

5. Eldredge's portrait of the Presidio is certainly romantic. John Phillip Langellier and Daniel B. Rosen give a well documented and realistic portrayal of the difficulties Californios suffered during the presidio era.

6. See the works of theater historian Luis Reyes de la Maza, who published a number of volumes tracing the plays and operas that were performed in Mexico from 1862 to 1872. This information was taken from *El Teatro en Mexico durante el Segundo Imperio* (1862–67).

7. This was true of the majority of Anglo Americans living in California, especially San Francisco. The gold rush, immigration, and homesteading all contributed to Anglo Americans learning the Spanish language. Spanish-language tutors crowded the advertising pages of California newspapers.

8. In San Francisco she stayed at the Grand Hotel and the Lick House, both well appointed establishments. In San Diego she stayed at the Horton House, the newest and most fashionable hotel. Her Jamul ranch, east of San Diego, was sometimes not available to her due to legal problems with squatter claims. I add this information to give a better picture of Ruiz de Burton's whereabouts and to reveal how, as a single mother, she traveled quite freely.

9. In Cervantes's novel, Quixote roams the Sierra Morena. In California, the Sierra Mountains are magical because of their promise of gold. The Sierras bring people from all over the world to dig for

riches. In many cases, this adventure also brings violence, destitution, and death. See Susan Lee Johnson, "Bulls, Bears, and Dancing Boys: Race, Gender, and Leisure in the California Gold Rush."

10. In letters between Ruiz de Burton's friend Don Pablo de la Guerra and his lawyer, H. W. Halleck, it is clear that the Land Commission was corrupt in its dealings with the Californios. In one letter, dated January 29, 1852, Halleck writes, "The squatters are making a tremendous effort to prevent the confirmation of titles. They have even gone so far as to direct threatening letters to the commissioners" (Santa Barbara Mission Archive Library).

11. See chap. 13 of *Who Would Have Thought It?*

12. In the second circle, they fly through a cold harsh area. By the end of Ruiz de Burton's play, Quixote will be without hope. Dante writes:

> As the wings of wintering starlings bear them on
> in their great wheeling flights . . .
> Here, there, up, down, they whirl, and, whirling, strain
> with never a hope of hope to comfort them, not of
> release, but even of less pain. (59)

13. The countess Trifaldi was entrusted with the princess Antonomasia, who was betrothed to a prince equal to her social standing. But the princess fell in love with Don Clavijo, who was far from a nobleman. The queen had entrusted the countess with her princess, and she died when she discovered the secret marriage. At her burial site appears her cousin, the "German, the giant magician Malambruno," who then curses the lovers by transforming them into objects (3.4,39).

14. Kritzer points out that Medina wrote thirty-four plays. "Of these, eleven — all produced during the period of about five years during which she was associated with the Bowery — have been documented as her work. Only three of Medina's plays were published. [Among them were] *The Last Days of Pompeii*, a love story set amid the banquets, entertainments, and ceremonies of ancient Pompeii and replete with seduction and betrayals" (23).

❧ 5 ❧

Teaching Ruiz de Burton

Strategies for the Classroom

How do you teach Ruiz de Burton?

JOHN GONZÁLEZ: One task is to encourage students to think about the linkages between race, gender, and class for the Californios, as a former colonial elite, within the new context of post-Reconstruction white supremacy. Additionally, there is the metacritical aspect of teaching this novel: How does this text challenge the methodological assumptions we bring to the reading of "Chicana/Chicano" narratives, and how does this challenge in turn change our methodology? What might this mean for literary recovery projects? Ultimately, the issue is how the way we interpret cultural productions intervenes in the knowledge-making processes of higher education.

BETH FISHER: Ruiz de Burton's work provides a fascinating entrée into an exploration of changing constructs of gender, race, and class in the nineteenth century. My aim is to lead students to an understanding of Ruiz de Burton's keen awareness of an ideological discord between Californio and Yankee culture, a discord that she would have needed to continually negotiate in her personal life. Thus, students should consider questions such as these: How does Ruiz de Burton construct the central conflict in *The Squatter and the Don* as a conflict between two gender ideologies? How does she challenge representations of Mexican racial identity in each of her novels? How are whiteness and status defined by her Mexican and Mexican American characters, as opposed to how her Anglo American characters see these aspects of identity?

JENNIFER TUTTLE: I have found that *The Squatter and the Don* raises fascinating issues about Ruiz de Burton's class position, particularly as it is under debate in Chicana/Chicano studies. Her simultaneous claims of victim status, appropriation of "native" status, and assertions of whiteness (which not only deny the mestizo status of most Californios but also are enabled by the erased labor of indigenous peoples) present complicated and crucial questions for students. I situate the book on my syllabus so that it falls after we have had a detailed discussion of Native Americans in the region, which we accomplish through reading John Rollin Ridge's *Life and Adventures of Joaquin Murieta* (1854) and Helen Hunt Jackson's *Ramona* (1884), along with relevant readings and lectures about historical context. Once students are made aware of these issues, they are better able to understand the complexity of her defense of the Californios and they can articulate the multiple, often contradictory, positions Ruiz de Burton assumes as she represents Californios, mestizos, and Native Americans in her novel.

AMELIA MARÍA DE LA LUZ MONTES: I teach Ruiz de Burton within an American Studies context. Therefore, I begin with a close analysis of the Treaty of Guadalupe Hidalgo before reading Ruiz de Burton. Here is a concrete example in guiding students to an understanding of the Treaty of Guadalupe Hidalgo, what it meant to Californios, and how it was dishonored. I place students in pairs and ask them to pretend they are Californianas and Californios. To play the part, we answer the question, "What does it mean to be a Californio?" In answering this question, we discuss historical facts about land ownership and identity using articles such as Antonia I. Castañeda's "The Political Economy of Nineteenth-Century Stereotypes of Californianas." Then I distribute Article VIII of the Treaty of Guadalupe Hidalgo. I ask students to discuss, with their "Californio" partner, the salient points of Article VIII. Most students choose the sentence that reads, "In the said territories, property of every kind, now belonging to Mexicans, not established there, shall be inviolably respected." After discussion, I divide the class in half: Californios and Anglo American settlers. The settlers fall into two categories: squatters, and those willing to buy land if the land they choose is owned. I ask the Anglo American squatters to place their desks in close proximity to Californios. I point out that suddenly these Californios have squatters on their land. How will Californios explain to squatters that they cannot settle there — that their lands "must be inviolably respected"? We discuss language problems — the need for a Californio to hire a translator if she/he does not speak English. I explain how some Californios may have legal papers regarding their land, but that their papers are in Spanish. Some Californios could have acquired their land simply with a handshake from a Mexican official generations ago. How will they convince the squatter not to settle on their lands?

The next step is to introduce the formation of the California Land Commission to the students. They begin to understand the frustration Californios experienced when they realize Californios had to hire lawyers and translators to redraw and write the original papers in English in order to present them to the commission. They also begin to understand how, while the Californios had to wait five, ten, and sometimes twenty years to have their papers legally confirmed by the commission, the squatters would be building homes and cultivating on Californio lands. They learn that Californios had to pay taxes on the squatter settlements, and they had to pay taxes on any profits squatters made on the cultivation of land. Californios soon were facing bankruptcy before facing the commission. After reading and discussing these historical issues, I distribute copies of a letter written on November 22, 1853, by the lawyer Henry Wagner Halleck, who was representing the Californio Pablo de la Guerra from Santa Barbara. Halleck expresses frustration with the commission. He tells de la Guerra that the commission is rejecting and confirming lands on very faulty premises: "I have no further confidence in this Board, & I am fully satisfied that they are — or at least 2 of them are — Squatters, and were appointed by squatters. I should now not be surprised if all your father's titles were rejected." After reading this letter, the students are amazed — in a concrete way — how colonization works in subtle ways, how easily a treaty can be dishonored, and how Manifest Destiny is enacted. With this background, students understand the passion with which Ruiz de Burton writes, and they are better able to discuss the novels within historical, cultural, social, and gender contexts. I say gender because the Antonia Castañeda article helps students understand how, under Mexican law, Californianas could inherit land and litigate in court. U.S. law did not recognize women within the context of land and litigation. This was all the more frustrating for Ruiz de Burton, who could draw up her own legal papers and yet was not recognized under U.S. law.

What narrative contexts do you provide for the novels?

JOHN GONZÁLEZ: Insofar as Chicana and Chicano Studies and (more recently) American Studies have focused upon struggles against U.S. imperialism, I consider both fields as crucial to contextualizing Ruiz de Burton's texts. I pair *The Squatter and the Don* with *Ramona*, since the contrast throws the ideological concerns of each into sharp relief. They draw upon the tradition of the domestic romance for quite different purposes. Jackson focuses upon the landless "Mission" Indians of California as part of her interest in the Indian Reform Movement, with the novel's Californios as the exotic criollo and mestizo intermediaries between white and Native communities. Ruiz de Burton writes against the state dispossession of Californio land, with little concern for the fate of Indian laborers whom the Californios helped subjugate. In essence, one can see the clash of two narrative projects with these two novels as the elites of the Spanish/Mexican colonial *frontera* encounter the elite culture of U.S. imperialism. Another useful text is the 1859 Petition of

Californio landowners to the U.S. Congress, which outlines the problems with the 1851 Land Act some twenty-six years before *The Squatter and the Don*.

AMELIA MARÍA DE LA LUZ MONTES: When I began teaching *The Squatter and the Don* and *Who Would Have Thought It?* I would connect this work with Helen Hunt Jackson's *Ramona* or Lydia Maria Child's critical writings concerning the Indian. While I teach these texts, I also feel it is important to represent Native American voices. Possible texts or excerpts of texts by indigenous writers are Sarah Winnemucca Hopkins's *Life among the Piutes: Their Wrongs and Claims* and Susan Bordeaux Bettelyoun's *With My Own Eyes: A Lakota Woman Tells Her People's History*. These nineteenth-century writings are by women who, like Ruiz de Burton, are complex and contradictory in their perspectives. Nevertheless, they had the means to write their stories. My interest is always to connect works from the same era, but also to connect these works with later or contemporary works that offer students a way to think about how history directly affects contemporary events. I have found that Craig S. Womack's book *Red on Red: Native American Literary Separatism* is critical reading to a discussion concerning education, language, land, culture, and how the events impacting Native Americans in the nineteenth and early twentieth centuries connect to contemporary Chicana/Chicano considerations of Mestizaje. Contemporary Native American perspectives on land rights are imperative to a discussion of nineteenth-century Manifest Destiny. Therefore, I include essays from Leslie Marmon Silko's *Yellow Woman and a Beauty of the Spirit* to connect migration, language, land rights, U.S. Indian policy, and contemporary confrontations with the U.S. Border Patrol. I also show a PBS POV (point of view) documentary concerning contemporary issues about land rights. Manifest Destiny is at the heart of the discussion in this film. The documentary, *In the Light of Reverence*, documents the Wintu, Lakota, and Hopi tribes, who are struggling to preserve and maintain their sacred lands in California, Wyoming, and New Mexico. I have also used Ana Castillo's *So Far from God* (1993), Helena María Viramontes's *Under the Feet of Jesus* (1995), and Norma Cantu's *Canícula* (1995) with these texts and narratives. Sandra Cisneros's novel *Caramelo* (2002) and an American Studies text by Martha Menchaca, *Recovering History, Constructing Race: The Indian, Black, and White Roots of Mexican Americans*, are also excellent to use.

JENNIFER TUTTLE: To contextualize *The Squatter and the Don*, I have students read the Treaty of Guadalupe Hidalgo and Helen Hunt Jackson's *Report on the Condition and Needs of the Mission Indians of California*. I have found that Tomás Almaguer's introduction to *Racial Fault Lines* works very well to help students understand some of the historical and theoretical issues Ruiz de Burton addresses in her novel.

JULIE RUIZ: Some of the primary texts I teach alongside Ruiz de Burton's letters and novels include the California testimonios, "An Old Woman and Her Recollections" (1877) by Eulalia Pérez; "Occurrences in Hispanic California" (1870) by Augustias de la Guerra Ord; selections from "Historical and Personal Memories Relating to Alta California" (1874) by Mariano Guadalupe Vallejo; and autobiographies such as *The History of Alta California* (1851) by Antonio María Osio. Examining differences in genres — testimonio, autobiography, letters, and novels — helps to provide connections between the historical background and literary contexts. How is historical experience affected by the collective, public, and mediated histories of the testimonio; the individual, private "I" of autobiographies; and the fictionalized histories of the novel?

I narrow or expand narrative and historical contexts depending on the emphasis of my course. For my class "Chicana Repossessions," I examine the dynamics of dispossession resulting from sites of conflict such as war — both literal and metaphorical. We begin looking at this theme in the works of nineteenth-century

Californianas such as María Amparo Ruiz de Burton, Eulalia Pérez, and Angustias de la Guerra Ord and works by twentieth-century Chicanas such as *So Far from God* (1993) by Ana Castillo, *Emplumada* (1981) by Lorna Dee Cervantes, *The Last of the Menu Girls* (1986) by Denise Chávez, *Woman Hollering Creek* (1991) by Sandra Cisneros, *Cactus Blood* (1995) by Lucha Corpi, and *Loving in the War Years/Lo que nunca pasó por sus labios* (1983) by Cherríe Moraga.

In "Chicano/a Transnationalisms," I use the Mexican War of 1846 and the Mexican Revolution of 1910 to trace the formation of a Chicano and Chicana identity based on different theories of the transnational. I pair both of Ruiz de Burton's novels with writings by Californianas and Californios and compare these texts to those by Chicanas and Chicanos such as Oscar Zeta Acosta's *The Revolt of the Cockroach People* (1973), Arturo Islas's *The Rain God* (1984), Cherríe Moraga's *The Last Generation* (1993), and Ana Castillo's *Sapagonia* (1990).

In "Hybrid Narratives," I teach Ruiz de Burton's work in conjunction with other nineteenth-century narratives that explore the mid- through late-nineteenth-century authorial concern with the split, divided, or hybrid self. This course might include a comparison between Ruiz de Burton's *Who Would Have Thought It?* and Henry James's "The Beast in the Jungle" (1903), William Wells Brown's *Clotel* (1853), Charles Chesnutt's *The Marrow of Tradition* (1901), selections from Walt Whitman's "Song of Myself" (1855), and Charlotte Perkins Gilman's "The Yellow Wallpaper" (1892). For this course, I also provide historical background on abolitionism, the Civil War, transcendentalism, racial science, slavery, Reconstruction, and the Fugitive Slave Law.

BETH FISHER: As Lisbeth Haas notes in her book *Conquests and Historical Identities in California, 1769–1936*, *The Squatter and the Don* recounts the decline of the Californios in fairly accurate detail, but one of the most interesting aspects of this novel from a literary standpoint is its recasting of recent history as the tragic story of a ranchero family under threat from outside antagonists. Reading this novel alongside contemporaneous Californio *testimonios* as well as Anglo American accounts of westward expansion (diaries as well as earlier fiction such as Caroline Kirkland's *A New Home, Who'll Follow?* [1839]) highlights the contradictory terms through which the family figured as a trope for the nation in the nineteenth century, a contradiction that Ruiz de Burton refers to explicitly in the story of the confrontation between the Darrells and the Alamars. Alternately, this novel may be taught as part of the genre of reform fiction, much of which was written by women, including Harriet Beecher Stowe (*Uncle Tom's Cabin*, 1852), Rebecca Harding Davis (*Life in the Iron Mills*, 1861), and Elizabeth Stuart Phelps (*The Silent Partner*, 1871).

I see *Who Would Have Thought It?* as fully engaged in a Gilded Age American culture in which commentators from across the social spectrum were responding to a rapidly expanding capitalist economy. This approach places the novel in dialogue with other fiction from the 1870s, such as *The Gilded Age* (1873) by Mark Twain and Charles Dudley Warner and *Pink and White Tyranny* (1872) by Harriet Beecher Stowe, a strategy that clarifies Ruiz de Burton's contributions to this larger set of critiques while highlighting the distinctness of her point of view as an aristocratic Californiana. In addition, reading the novel in the context of contemporaneous theater brings to light Ruiz de Burton's interest in couching a pointed political satire in a form that her readers would find simultaneously familiar and unsettling. Rather than seeing Ruiz de Burton as occupying a marginal position in relation to an established culturally uniform literary canon, then, students see her as a central figure within an evolving literary culture that was shaped by internal contention.

VINCENT PÉREZ: I teach *The Squatter and the Don* with Mariano Guadalupe Vallejo's "Historical and Personal Memoirs Relating to Alta California" (1875). We compare the Californio vision of history to Hubert Howe Bancroft's romantic depiction of California history in *California Inter Pocula* (1888) from which we read excerpts. I sometimes teach Alvar Nuñez Cabeza de Vaca's *Adventures in the Unknown Interior of America* (1542) the week prior to covering Ruiz de Burton and Vallejo. I do this to discuss Spanish colonialism and the social status of the Indians. When this question comes up in the context of ranch and hacienda society as depicted in Californio texts, I find it easier to teach because students already know something about the Spanish colonial project. Just after the Californio narratives, I always teach excerpts from Reginald Horsman's *Race and Manifest Destiny* (1981). I also spend one session on writings about the California "bandidos," usually a chapter from John Rollin Ridge's *The Life and Adventures of Joaquin Murieta* (1854). Early in the semester I spend a week on Juan Rulfo's novel *Pedro Paramo* (1955). I include this work to discuss the historical roots of Mexican immigrants who came to the United States during the Mexican Revolution. I also use it to historicize Californio representations of nineteenth-century Mexican hacienda society and particularly Ruiz de Burton's *The Squatter and the Don*, which I refer to as a sentimental "protest" novel.

How do you place Ruiz de Burton within the context of Chicana/Chicano literature and Chicana/Chicano studies?

VINCENT PÉREZ: I encourage students to engage Californio texts critically, but I also explain why the Californio and Mexican view of history is so different from Bancroft's and that of other hegemonic U.S. authors. I emphasize that Californio works are counterdiscursive in that they question the dominant U.S. nationalist ideology of the era. I don't teach Californio authors as "proto-Chicanos"; rather, I teach them as historical figures very much of their nineteenth-century epoch and late colonial era "hacienda" culture. I see them as ideologically conservative writers who were

235

opposed to the sociocultural forces which they associated with modernization and capitalism (i.e., individualism and materialism). Their anti-Yankee and/or "ethnic" perspective is deeply influenced by their broader engagement with capitalist modernity. This is especially true of Ruiz de Burton, despite her recently published letters, which portray her as an astute businesswoman. Their imagined identities as genteel "Spanish" aristocrats capture this traditional perspective. These identities embrace a "hacienda" cultural ethos which Ruiz de Burton and Vallejo view as fundamentally superior to a modern (capitalist) outlook. I use the following discussion questions for *The Squatter and the Don* and Vallejo's "Memoirs": How and where in the texts do Vallejo and Ruiz de Burton voice the grievances of the Mexican American community? How do Mexicans view Anglo Americans, and vice versa, in the narratives? How do Vallejo and Ruiz de Burton portray pre-1848 Mexican California? Why? How was this era different from the one in which they wrote or narrated their works? Account for the differences between Vallejo's work and Ruiz de Burton's? Why is Vallejo more circumspect in his criticism of the United States? How do the Californios view the Indians? Why the Californio recourse to their imagined Hispanic/Creole heritage? Where in the texts does the concept of Manifest Destiny appear in the works? How do the Californio works respond to cultural racism against Mexicans? What do the narratives posit as a response to the status and condition of Mexican Americans under U.S. rule?

BETH FISHER: The Californio *testimonios* collected by Hubert Howe Bancroft and his assistant provide a contemporaneous context for understanding Ruiz de Burton's accounts of the aftermath of the Mexican War, and for investigating why she may have preferred not to contribute her own story to Bancroft's archives. In addition, Ruiz de Burton's fiction may be read instructively as a prelude to the work of contemporary Chicana writers, such as Cherríe Moraga, who have critiqued the use of the Malinche myth to represent Chicanas as traitors to their race. *The Squatter and the Don* speaks to this issue most directly in its representation of the Alamar women as fiercely loyal to the patriarch. Given the way that Ruiz de Burton herself was represented by Bancroft and others in the popular stories of her marriage to Henry Burton, she had reason to underscore her own loyalty to Californio men, even as she is often critical of the secondary status that she was afforded as a woman in a patriarchal culture. Again, the work of historian Antonia Castañeda helps to elucidate this strategy. As many critics have pointed out, placing Ruiz de Burton within a Chicano literary tradition requires attention to the author's marked elitism and insistence on the pure Spanish heritage of Californios, a stance that is historically and politically distinct from that of contemporary Chicano writers.

JULIE RUIZ: Ruiz de Burton voices a nineteenth-century nascent ethnic consciousness through her novels, which challenges the scope and definitions of Chicano cultural studies and Chicano literature while providing a genealogical link between Californianas/os and Chicanas/os. One way in which Ruiz de Burton's work promises to redefine the Chicano canon is by clarifying the role of the border in writings by Californianas and Chicanas. In her novels, Ruiz de Burton, like other Californianas, relocates the border from the periphery of the nation (represented by the Río Grande and the division between Alta and Baja California) to the interior of the nation through the intertwining of the domestic and national. This same movement within occurs in works by Chicanas as well.

Ruiz de Burton also rewrites the formation of the border as a moment in time that redeems a criollo or Spanish/Mexican national identity even as she traces the cost of that border for Mexican Americans. She, like most other Californianas, lays claim to a mythical Spanish heritage in her work in order to claim the rights of citizenship for Mexican Americans. In this way, Ruiz de Burton's use of the Mexican War to privilege a fantasy Spanish heritage provides much needed background for Chicano works that use the Mexican War to project a Chicano national spirit based on indigenous roots.

How do you place Ruiz de Burton within the context of American Studies?

VINCENT PÉREZ: Because I include a number of U.S. Southern texts in my American literature survey course, I inevitably discuss *The Squatter and the Don*'s conservative "hacienda" outlook, which I compare to the anti-industrialist political perspective of nineteenth-century Southern plantation and domestic fiction. For Ruiz de Burton and Vallejo, the "hacienda" constitutes a traditional "organic" community in the same sense that the plantation did for white Southern authors of roughly the same era. When we read *Huckleberry Finn* two weeks later, a novel published the same year as *The Squatter and the Don*, we talk about how Twain satirized the romantic plantation narratives of his era, works which uniformly embraced the myth of the "lost cause." Despite Ruiz de Burton's elitist politics and traditional "hacienda" cultural outlook, she seeks to debunk the romantic narrative of official U.S. historical knowledge in much the same way that Twain overturns the romance of traditional plantation narrative. Yet Twain is carrying out his critique from a "liberal" viewpoint, whereas I believe Ruiz de Burton is doing so from a "conservative" ideological perspective developed out of her "hacienda" (class, caste, race-based) identities.

In my "Historical Novel of the Americas" graduate seminar, I teach Ruiz de Burton and Vallejo alongside such authors as Herman Melville, Harriet Jacobs, William Faulkner, Toni Morrison, José Martí, Juan Rulfo, W. E. B. Du Bois, and Gabriel García Marquez. *The Squatter and the Don*'s project to erase the boundary between history and fiction/romance illustrates the course's thematic focus on the "literary" as a valid form of historical knowledge. As the above list suggests, the course examines a selection of historical and literary narratives spanning 1850–1970 by North American and Latin American (that is, Latino/a) authors. Through discussion and analysis of these narratives, the course charts the common sociohistorical condition shared by different societies and cultures of the Americas (i.e., United States Southern, African American, Caribbean, and Mexican American), allowing this condition to be measured against the North American social experience. By foregrounding questions about historical knowledge, nationhood, and identity, the course links as well as contrasts the discursive traditions that emerged out of nineteenth-century U.S. and Latino/a literature. These traditions include (1) debates about slavery and the construction of U.S. Southern history, (2) U.S. expansionism and the history of the Hispanic Southwest, (3) nineteenth- and twentieth-century constructions of "race" and "ethnicity," and (4) colonialism/neocolonialism and the literary imagination. The course traces the convergences and divergences of North American and Latin American (Latino/a) narratives to consider how historical and ideological issues are linked to a set of literary projects to recover and narrate the past. The course is concerned primarily with novelistic representation that is historical, though it includes works from other genres such as autobiography, nonfiction, legend, and popular culture.

JULIE RUIZ: Ruiz de Burton's work not only fills the gap between Californiana/o and Chicana/o writings but also makes an important contribution to American Studies by helping to elucidate the role of race, citizenship, and property rights in the nineteenth century and the failure of the Reconstruction Amendments and the Treaty of Guadalupe Hidalgo to protect these rights for Mexican Americans. Her work forces us to consider what it means to look at nationhood in the nineteenth century in terms beyond black and white binaries and to ask how analyzing the Civil War through the Mexican War might change these binaries. Finally, Ruiz de Burton's writing adds a new dimension to American Studies. The trend in

Chicana/o theory has been to move away from conceptualizing the border as a frontier zone of conflict toward reconfiguring it as a borderlands space. Ruiz de Burton adds a missing step in this evolution of frontier-to twentieth-century border by focusing on the rise of a collective subjectivity in the nineteenth-century borderlands.

What particular chapters and portions of Ruiz de Burton's novels do you ask students to read closely?

VINCENT PÉREZ: When I cannot assign all of *The Squatter and the Don*, I give a synopsis of the story and select various chapters that best summarize the Californios' central political grievance:

> Chapter 2. The Don's View of the Treaty of Guadalupe Hidalgo
> Chapter 16. Spanish Land Grants Viewed Retrospectively
> Chapter 20. At the Capitol
> Chapter 25. The Squatter and the Don
> Chapter 32. A False Friend Sent to Deceive the Southerners
> Chapter 33. San Diego's Sentence Is Irrevocable
> Chapter 34. The Sins of Our Legislators

JENNIFER TUTTLE: I always end our discussion of *The Squatter and the Don* by doing a close reading of pages 363–64 and the novel's last chapter. In these sections, Ruiz de Burton offers glimpses into her own stakes in this fictional tale; we look at the ways in which she self-consciously seeks to intervene in legal discourses outside the text. This is particularly evident in the last chapter, in which she makes no pretense of plot at all, and links the character of Doña Josefa with her own biographical self, revealing the novel's explicitly political purpose and the cultural work she hopes it will accomplish.

JULIE RUIZ: In *Who Would Have Thought It?* I ask students to read closely the beginning chapters, "The Arrival" and "The

Little Black Girl," in conjunction with one of the ending chapters such as chapter 60, "Only the Dead Do Not Return." What role do the border and crossing geographical boundaries play in terms of Lola's racial and national unmasking? I also ask students to compare and contrast passages where Ruiz de Burton uses animals and satire (such as the canaries and Lavvy on page 85, Julius Caesar and his horse on page 75, and Jack Sprig and Mrs. Cackle on page 12), scenes where male characters fall ill (Julian and Hackwell, or Don Luis's "weeping like a weak woman" [200]), and passages where Ruiz de Burton contrasts Spanish and Anglo whiteness (for example, Lola compared with Emma on page 232).

In *The Squatter and the Don*, I ask students to read chapter 37, "Reunited at Last," and the last chapter, "Out with the Invader." Do the narrator's and Doña Josefa's voices seem to merge in these last chapters? What is the role of legal procedure and narrative in the final chapters? Is there really resolution through the marriage plot or a lack thereof in these last chapters? Other passages I ask students to contrast include portions of the novel that differentiate squatter from Californio parents, the Alamar rancho compared with the Darrell "colony" room, and Don Alamar's descriptions of the Treaty of Guadalupe Hidalgo (65) compared with his description of sixteenth-century Spanish/Mexican colonialism and nineteenth-century U.S. imperialism (163).

BETH FISHER: In *The Squatter and the Don*, close readings of the first two chapters establish the gendered terms through which Ruiz de Burton constructs the confrontation between Anglo Americans and Californios. Numerous subsequent chapters develop this particular theme in detail, including chapter 25, which features a mock battle between William Darrell and the Alamar men, and chapter 37, in which Doña Josefa castigates Yankee men for their blind allegiance to commerce. In *Who Would Have*

Thought It? students should read closely the first few chapters re-counting Lola Medina's interactions with the Norval family and with the Irish servants employed by the Norvals. These chapters highlight the constructs of Anglo American racial and religious superiority that Ruiz de Burton will critique throughout the novel. In addition, these chapters demonstrate the author's interest in interweaving various literary and theatrical forms that would have been familiar to her readers, including melodrama, social comedy, and the Indian captivity tale. Other important chapters include chapter 37 ("Mrs. Norval's Mental Debut"), for its satire of the showy performances of women consumers, chapter 43 ("Isaac in the Land of the Aztecs"), and the conclusion.

How do you assess student responses to Ruiz de Burton?

JULIE RUIZ: Students typically find the contradictions of Ruiz de Burton's work interesting and important; that is, her position as both colonizer and colonized, as well as the cross-comparisons they are able to make between her work and that of other authors across genres and centuries. They find the ambiguity of her narrative fascinating as well, because it allows them to view issues from multiple perspectives. For example, in *Who Would Have Thought It?* students are always intrigued, perplexed, and divided by Mrs. Norval's fall into insanity — was it caused by her own failings or by external circumstances beyond her control? They also like to talk about filial rebellion and the gap between generations in both of Ruiz de Burton's novels. They tend to miss how characters function as foils or mediators, so I have them do comparisons between two or three characters with specific themes in mind. They also tend to overlook the difference between Spanish and Puritan colonialisms as well as Mexico's history (Mexican Independence, the French invasion, etc.). I encourage my students to take notice of these issues through the historical background I provide.

ANDREA TINNEMEYER: Students tend to conflate all Latinas/Latinos into one category and treat the ethnic groups as if they were monolithic. I find that explaining the racial arithmetic inherited from Spanish colonialism aids them tremendously. They also seem to understand the hacendado system best when it is compared with the plantation system from the U.S. South.

VINCENT PÉREZ: Depending on background and preparation, unless students have read the "official" historical narrative, they may be confused by the critique of dominant history by Californio authors. But most students learn to appreciate the "counterhistory" offered by Californio writers. All of my students are surprised to learn that Mexican Americans were writing and publishing books in the nineteenth century and particularly that a Mexican American woman could achieve the status of author during that period. Although students have some difficulty with the rather staid genre of historical romance, once we have discussed the symbolic meaning of romantic unions in *The Squatter and the Don*, they tend to respond more positively.

Ruiz de Burton's portrayal of aristocratic Mexican American society in *The Squatter and the Don* raises a number of questions from students. While not dismissing the tide of anti-Mexican racism in the nineteenth century, one student asserted that by making the Mexican aristocrats the protagonists and the Anglo American squatters the antagonists, the novel simply inverted cultural stereotypes. Students, sometimes with my encouragement, also raise the question of the conspicuously invisible Indian "other." The novel's biases against Indians and lower-class mestizos problematize its criticism of dominant history. Some students said that they could not trust a narrator who depicted the usurpation of Mexican land while excluding the plight of Indian and mestizo campesinos under the Mexican hacienda system. A few students rejected what they characterized as the novel's elitist — as opposed to nationalist or "ethnic" — land entitlement argument. How could a novel drawn from the cultural memory of the conquered Mexican American community erase the presence of the Indians as it "humanized" Mexican Californio ranchers by portraying them as equals to members of the white upper class?

Responding to this line of criticism, one student offered an analogy that captured the Californio political perspective in *The Squatter and the Don*. As she put it, "If a person enters your home and with the support of the law unjustly dispossesses you of your house and property, and you decide to write a book about your family's mistreatment, the perpetrator of the crime can hardly be expected to be depicted sympathetically." Though I endorsed the student's argument, I silently took a different view of the manner in which Ruiz de Burton's novel is sometimes judged by students. Would the predominantly middle-class white students in my American literature survey courses make the same case against nineteenth-century canonical works by white authors in which blacks, Indians, and Mexicans were either objectified or erased from history altogether? After one patronizing comment regarding Ruiz de Burton's work that suggested her work was propagandistic, I was reminded of a discussion in another of my ethnic literature classes several years earlier. Upset about claims by a black student that her view of the O. J. Simpson case was racist, a white student argued that her belief in Simpson's guilt had nothing to do with race but rather with the compelling evidence presented against him. When I asked her if she thought race had influenced the mostly black jury who acquitted Simpson, she was speechless. Although she was on the verge of saying what she felt — that race had everything to do with their judgment (and therefore with her own) — upon recognizing the double standard, she stopped in midsentence. Particularly in American literature survey courses and other classes that do not include large numbers of minority students, these interpretive questions inevitably arise in discussions of Ruiz de Burton.

Chronology of Events in the Life of María Amparo Ruiz de Burton

1832 Born July 3 in Loreto, Baja Mexico (sixteen years before the Treaty of Guadalupe Hidalgo was signed). Aristocratic family; maternal grandfather, Don José Manuel Ruiz, commander of the Mexican northern frontier in Baja and later governor (1822–25) of Baja California. Related by blood and marriage to most prominent families in Alta California: Vallejo, Carillo, Noriega, Alvarado, Pacheco, Castro, Pico, etc.

1847 Meets Captain Henry S. Burton of Norwich, Vermont, when he is stationed in Loreto as occupied territory.

1848 Treaty of Guadalupe Hidalgo. Baja to remain Mexican; Alta California becomes part of the United States.

1848 Ruiz goes to San Francisco Bay Area (along with five hundred or so Baja Californians who took up offer of U.S. officials to move up to San Francisco Bay in Alta California).

1849 Marries Burton on July 9, six days after seventeenth birthday.

1850 First child, Nellie, born July 4.

1852 Burton assigned to San Diego. Second child, Henry, born November 24.

1853 Burtons purchase land from Pío Pico's Jamul land grant.

1855 While living at Mission San Diego, writes popular productions for the Mission Theater.

1859 Henry Burton is ordered east; stays in Rhode Island, New York, Washington, Delaware, and Virginia for the next ten years; María becomes intimate of Mary Lincoln and has audience with President Lincoln to increase her husband's pension.

1865 Becomes good friends with Verena Davis while Jefferson Davis is prisoner of war at Fortress Monroe, where Burton becomes commander.

1870 Returns to San Diego after husband's death (of malaria) in 1869.

1870s Litigates suits against Jamul land grant and begins writing career in earnest.

1895 Dies in Chicago; body taken to San Diego for burial.

Published Works

NOVELS

Who Would Have Thought It? (Philadelphia: Lippincott, 1872).
The Squatter and the Don (San Francisco: Carson, 1885).

PLAYS

Don Quixote de la Mancha: A Comedy, in Five Acts, Taken from Cervantes' Novel of That Name (San Francisco: Carmany, 1876).

Ruiz de Burton's Litigation Correspondence and Letters

The following three letters — dated 15 February 1869, 12 August 1869, and 21 July 1871 — all correlate to one or more of the essays in this volume. They were originally written in Spanish and have been translated below. The translation seeks to be true to the original letter; therefore, spellings or phrasing may appear different from contemporary English writing. For further study of her letters, see *Conflicts of Interest: The Letters of María Amparo Ruiz de Burton*.

Staten Island
12 of August 1869

My, as always, dear friend
Here are two very short letters from July 30 and August 1st. I received them day before yesterday, and the one from the 4th of August (even shorter) yesterday. Thank you, a million (not feigned) thanks, for your sympathy. All the expressions of affections from my friends are for me doubly pleasing. Yes, you speak well, telling me that "I should not let the pain overwhelm me." I know. Well now I am both *father* and *mother* of my children; I am surrounded by difficulties, with *God* knows what for support, and even though God is good and powerful, the *human* heart always searches and yearns for some *other* support here on earth. I do not have it, nor do I hope for it, and still however, it is right that we *keep living*. To let myself be overwhelmed by this torrent would be cowardly and would embarrass me and my friends as well. And so I think I will

accept my destiny with all the resolve that I can when it appears to me at times that a horrible cataclysm will overwhelm in my heart.

If my strength fails me . . . then I ask you not to judge me with severity. Remember that I am a woman . . . and mexican . . . with my soul enclosed in an iron cage. In this manner *Society* confines us as soon as we are born, like the Chinese and the feet of their women.

Write me often, but don't send me such laconic little letters. You are mistaken to think that because I am sad that long letters would annoy me. On the contrary. They amuse me and those from you, you know, I prefer and am very grateful. Write me and tell me everything that comes to your head. What of Mr. Vega? What of the railroad to Vallejo? Are you interested in it? What news from Lower Cal.a and of the border? Concerning my papers, I have written you that you should send them express and address them "in care of Don Federico R. Prieto No 70 1/2 Pine Street N. York."

I will not write more today because my eyes prevent me. When I just use them a little they begin to ache as if they are going to burst and for this reason I must use them with caution. When they recover, I will write more. I have much to tell you. If only I could see you, that you would come now that we are in Staten Island. What plans do you have for now? What are you doing that prevents you from coming on the Pacific railroad? Or are you waiting for that famous Aviator so you can come through the clouds? . . . Do you think that will have success? How magnificent would it be to travel in that Olympian way, no? . . .

Do you see how I manage to take interest in everything? . . . This is how I walk the path of life. Like the prisoners who go and do their work with a ball and chain fastened to their foot — this is how my soul carries my pain bound to its wings. . . . Goodbye, my good and faithful friend who I love very much. Much love to my cousin and to the rest of the family from my two little ones and from this heart of your sad cousin and friend,

M. A. Burton

New York Feb. 15 1869
No. 435 W. 23 St.

My esteemed friend

I do not know why I have not received a letter from you in a very long time. Have you been sick? Your last letter (which I quickly answered) had a 6 of Oct. '68 date! And you have sent one since then. In this one you tell me that you hope to receive my papers that Mr. Geo. C. Johnson has but I have not seen them. I also spoke to Mr. Johnson's son, who was here in October. I spoke with him in respect to the papers, and he promised me his cooperation to recover them. Maybe it might be good that you see him about this matter.

How your enthusiastic talk about the progress of California enthused me! . . . But later I relapse into a loss of heart and I say, ah, if I were a man! . . . What a miserable thing to be a woman! . . . and ugly . . . and poor! . . . oh! As if being a woman were not sufficient calamity without adding others. No, it is necessary that I do not become enthusiastic over the progress of the Continent. why? Neither my race nor my sex will benefit. And so I will not look any more at *N.o one* [?]. I mean at the endowed advantages that may come my way. And so, apropos, where are my twelve acres of land? Do you think that I am going to be content with telling me that you gave it to your son because he married? No, my friend, you took away my twelve acres (a lo indio) and it is necessary for you to pay me. Pay me with lots in Vallejo City, or if you like help me to buy a few at a very cheap price. Make me that good deal and I will also repay you when we begin our enterprise in Ensenada.

When are you coming here? Or are you only giving me small handfuls of pleasure when you tell me that you are coming? And what are those indirect comments you tell with respect to Baja Cal.a, Vega and "Manifest Destiny"? These are three very incongruent things because I love California dearly. I feel much sympathy and interest for Mr. Vega and his strong hatred and contempt (like a good mexican) for that "Manifest Destiny." . . . Of all the evil phrases ever invented in order to create buffoons, there is not one phrase more detestable for me than that one, the most offensive, the most insulting; my blood rises to the top of my head when I hear it, and I see as if in a photographic instance, all that the Yankies have done to make Mexicans suffer — the robbery of Texas; war; the robbery of California; the death of Maximilian! . . . If I could believe in "Manifest Destiny," I would stop believing in justice or divine wisdom. No, my friend, Manifest Destiny is none other than "Manifest Yankie Trick," like their "wooden hams and wooden nutmegs" from Connecticut. Unfortunately, Mexicans are blind and stupid. I do not know what is the matter with them. And to tell you the truth, since the death of the Emperor, I also do not know what to hope for. With him went the hope to break the evil spell, the influence this country has over my own, an influence like the shadow of the Repas [?] tree, which kills everything that is not of its own species. . . . However, even though the truth is clearly evident, the Mexicans are easily led like little butterflies to the candle, to die, to perish. . . . Ah! the liberals, the liberals! like the dazzling shepherd who killed his most beloved little lamb. That is the way they are: crazy and blind.

Posterity will judge them and they will receive what they deserve and they will give thanks while the foot of the Saxon is on their neck . . . just as "Manifest Destiny" directs it to be.

But it is necessary that I do not speak of this because then I never know when to stop. You do not have the same sentiment about Mexico as I do. What a shame that I was not made a man in order to . . . No more foolishness . . . Goodbye . . . Write me, do not be ungrateful to such a faithful friend. Of all your friends there is none that better appreciates and loves you like I do. Tell my cousin I send her my affections. I send my cousin the photographs of my little chicks [children]. I shall send the one of me later.

The general greets you with much love. He is much better since we arrived north. My love to my cousin and also to you.

M. A. Burton

No 78 — Grand Hotel — San Francisco
July 21 of 1871

Dear Don Guadalupe

I suppose that you believe me to be in San Diego. We did not go due to my having fallen gravely ill. Today is the first day I have gone out since falling ill. I still do not feel very well, but at least I am recovering, and as in your last letter you complain that I did not respond to all that you had told me in yours, I hurry to tell you that I did not for two reasons: Because I was in bed and could hardly write, and because I believed that you would come and I could respond in person. You see that you do not have reason to complain. I have the letter here, and in this way you can come and I will respond. I think that perhaps we will not go to San Diego until September unless something happens that beckons me to go beforehand. And you, when do you plan to come? *It is necessary* that you come and take part in the election and work *for Pacheco.* The way I see things, it is the sacred obligation of all the sons of the country to have an interest that Romualdo achieve success. Political preferences should not be of importance. The matter here is of a much higher level; it touches upon Nationality and it is to sustain with all one's heart the poor race that spirals, weighed down by difficulties, overwhelmed by disdain, affronts, and humiliations. If the Californios had been more unified and from the beginning had supported those countrymen best able to be representatives, the government would not have boldly charged us with the weight of that odious legislation which is leaving us day by day begging for bread. Today the Californios, as they are, do not have a voice against the government, and they suffer everything silently, and why? because of their idleness in not supporting their own who are capable of representing them and defending our rights. Now, before descending the final rung, it is essential to make the effort, if not, there will be no other alternative than to kiss the ground. And so, you who are a well known man do not sleep within that fatal apathy which has been that of the Californio. Awaken and make it so that others awaken. Help Pacheco who, in addition to his great personal merit, has the blessing of belonging to our race, our contemptuous nationality. He will be a loyal defender of the Californios always when possible, and when he cannot help his compatriots directly, he will help with his influence.

As soon as you receive this one, come if you can. I have been and am sick, but I hope to recover. I am quite pleased at what you said about forgetfulness, concerning yourself — and nothing more —

Goodbye — Love to the family — and best wishes that you may prosper. Your affectionate as always,

M. A. Burton

The Treaty of Guadalupe Hidalgo

Article VIII

Mexicans now established in territories previously belonging to Mexico, and which remain for the future within the limits of the United States, as defined by the present Treaty, shall be free to continue where they now reside, or to remove at any time to the Mexican Republic, retaining the property which they possess in the said territories, or disposing thereof and removing the proceeds wherever they please; without their being subjected, on this account, to any contribution, tax or charge whatever.

Those who shall prefer to remain in the said territories, may either retain the title and rights of Mexican citizens, or acquire those of citizens of the United States. But, they shall be under the obligation to make their election within one year from the date of the exchange of ratifications of this treaty: and those who shall remain in the said territories, after the expiration of that year, without having declared their intention to retain the character of Mexicans, shall be considered to have elected to become citizens of the United States.

In the said territories, property of every kind, now belonging to Mexicans not established there, shall be inviolably respected. The present owners, the heirs of these, and all Mexicans who may hereafter acquire said property by contract, shall enjoy with respect to it, guaranties equally ample as if the same belonged to citizens of the United States.

Text from Charles I. Bevans, ed., *Treaties and Other International Agreements of the United States of America, 1776–1949*, vol. 9 (Washington DC: Department of State, 1972), 791–806.

Letter from Henry Wagner Halleck to Pablo de la Guerra on California Land Commissioners' Decisions to Confirm Lands

Santa Barbara Mission Archive Library

No. 487 — Halleck, Henry Wagner (H. W. H.) to Pablo de la Guerra

San Francisco Nov. 22, 1853
Don Pablo de la Guerra
Santa Barbara [California]

Dear Sir:

The commissioners to-day gave some more decisions confirming several claims and rejecting a number of others. Among these confirmed is the claim of Marin Antonia to "Corral de Cerote." This I hardly expected, for under the former decisions I really expected that this would be rejected. But what is still more astonishing, the claim of Teadoro Arrellanes to "El Rincon" was rejected. This had all the requisites. It was approved by the deputation, had juridical possession, and we proved occupation by the claimant for over 19 years. Nevertheless, it was rejected on the ground that the title did not sufficiently define the boundaries — a most flimsy excuse. One of the commissioners dissented and refused to sign the decree of rejection. Tell Arrellanes that there is every hope that the United States Court will confirm it on appeal.

After this decision I have no further confidence in this Board, & I am fully satisfied that they are — or at least 2 of them are — *Squatters*, and were appointed by squatters. I should now not be surprised if all your father's titles were rejected on the plea that the "boundaries described in the title are indefinite." And yet they may confirm them all. We have argued them as strongly as we could; and yet we can have no confidence in the result. The decisions are so variable that no one can calculate with any certainty whether the decision will be favorable or unfavorable. It is evident, however, that they will reject at least nineteen-twentieths of all the titles.

I will write you by every steamer and keep you advised of the result.

I think I told you in my last letter that Covarrubias, although frequently spoken to, neglected to do anything in his cases, or to furnish any money to get back papers from the Archives. In "Jonata" I paid out of my own pocket for the documents from the Archives. But in "Santa Ynez" I told him . . . that I could not pay out any more for him. The law Agent consented after a good deal of trouble that the case might be delayed for copies of these papers a few weeks. Some 4 or 5 weeks have not elapsed and he has paid no money for this purpose, and should not be at all surprised if the claim was taken up and rejected for want of these papers.

Yours truly,
H. W. Halleck

Teaching Resource Bibliography

Ruiz de Burton Publications

Ruiz de Burton, María Amparo. *Don Quixote de la Mancha: A Comedy, in Five Acts, Taken from Cervantes' Novel of That Name.* San Francisco: Carmany, 1876.

———. *The Squatter and the Don.* 1885. Ed. Rosaura Sánchez and Beatrice Pita. Houston: Arte Público Press, 1992, 1997.

———. *Who Would Have Thought It?* 1872. Ed. Rosaura Sánchez and Beatrice Pita. Houston: Arte Público Press, 1995.

Sánchez, Rosaura, and Beatrice Pita, eds. *Conflicts of Interest: The Letters of María Amparo Ruiz de Burton.* Houston: Arte Público Press, 2001.

Critical Assessments of Ruiz de Burton's Work

Alemán, Jesse. "Historical Amnesia and the Vanishing Mestiza: The Problem of Race in *The Squatter and the Don* and *Ramona*." *Aztlán* 27.1 (2002): 59–93.

Aranda, José F., Jr. "Breaking All the Rules: María Amparo Ruiz de Burton Writes a Civil War Novel." *Recovering the U.S. Hispanic Literary Heritage.* Vol. 3. Ed. María Herrera-Sobek and Virginia Sánchez-Korrol. Houston: Arte Público Press, 2000.

———. "Contradictory Impulses: María Amparo Ruiz de Burton, Resistance Theory, and the Politics of Chicano/a Studies." *American Literature* 70.3 (1998): 551–79.

———. "María Amparo Ruiz de Burton." *Dictionary of Literary*

Biography. Ed. Sharon Harris. New York: Gale Publications, 1999.

Chvany, Peter A. " 'Those Indians Are Great Thieves, I Suppose?' Historicizing the White Woman in *The Squatter and the Don*." *White Women in Racialized Spaces: Imaginative Transformation and Ethical Action in Literature*. Ed. Samina Najmi and Rajini Srikanth. Albany: State University of New York Press, 2002.

Fisher, Beth. "The Captive Mexicana and the Desiring Bourgeois Woman: Domesticity and Expansionism in Ruiz de Burton's *Who Would Have Thought It?*" *Legacy* 16 (1999): 59–69.

Goldman, Anne E. " 'I Think Our Romance Is Spoiled,' or, Crossing Genres: California History in Helen Hunt Jackson's *Ramona* and María Amparo Ruiz de Burton's *The Squatter and the Don*." *Over the Edge: Remapping the American West*. Ed. Valerie J. Matsumoto and Blake Allmendinger. Berkeley: University of California Press, 1999.

———. " 'Who Ever Heard of a Blue-Eyed Mexican?' Satire and Sentimentality in María Amparo Ruiz de Burton's *Who Would Have Thought It?*" *Recovering the U.S. Hispanic Literary Heritage*. Ed. Erlinda Gonzales-Berry and Chuck Tatum. Vol. 2. Houston: Arte Público Press, 1996.

González, John M. "Romancing Hegemony: Constructing Racialized Citizenship in María Amparo Ruiz de Burton's *The Squatter and the Don*." *Recovering the U.S. Hispanic Literary Heritage*. Vol. 2. Ed. Erlinda Gonzales-Berry and Chuck Tatum. Houston: Arte Público Press, 1996.

Jacobs, Margaret D. "Mixed-Bloods, Mestizas, and Pintos: Race, Gender, and Claims to Whiteness in Helen Hunt Jackson's *Ramona* and María Amparo Ruiz de Burton's *Who Would Have Thought It?*" *Western American Literature* 36.3 (2001): 212–313.

Luis-Brown, David. " 'White Slaves' and the 'Arrogant Mestiza': Reconfiguring Whiteness in *The Squatter and the Don* and *Ramona*." *American Literature* 69.4 (1997): 813–39.

Montes, Amelia María de la Luz. " 'Es Necesario Mirar Bien': Letter

Making, Fiction Writing, and American Nationhood in the Nineteenth Century." Diss. University of Denver, 1999.

———. "Es Necesario Mirar Bien: Nineteenth-Century Letter Making and Novel Writing in the Life of María Amparo Ruiz de Burton." *Recovering the U.S. Hispanic Literary Heritage.* Vol. 3. Ed. María Herrera-Sobek and Virginia Sánchez-Korrol. Houston: Arte Público Press, 2000.

———. "María Amparo Ruiz de Burton Negotiates American Literary Politics and Culture." *Challenging Boundaries: Gender and Periodization.* Ed. Joyce W. Warren and Margaret Dickie. Athens: University of Georgia Press, 2000.

———. " 'See How I Am Received': Nationalism, Race, and Gender in *Who Would Have Thought It? Decolonial Voices: Chicana and Chicano Cultural Studies in the Twenty-first Century.* Ed. Arturo J. Aldama and Naomi H. Quiñonez. Bloomington: Indiana University Press, 2002.

Oden, Frederick Bryant. "The Maid of Monterey, The Life of María Amparo Ruiz de Burton, 1832–1895." Thesis. University of San Diego, 1992.

Pérez, Vincent. "South by Southwest: Land and Community in María Amparo Ruiz de Burton's *The Squatter and the Don* and Mariano Guadalupe Vallejo's *Historical and Personal Memoirs Relating to Alta California.*" *Recovering the U.S. Hispanic Literary Heritage.* Vol. 4. Ed. José F. Aranda Jr. and Silvio Torres-V. Saillant. Houston: Arte Público Press, 2002.

Rev. of *Who Would Have Thought It? Godley's Lady's Book.* Sept. 1872: 273.

Rev. of *Who Would Have Thought It? Lippincott's Magazine of Popular Literature and Science.* Nov. 1872: 607.

Rev. of *Who Would Have Thought It? Literary World.* 1 Aug. 1872: 33–34.

Sánchez, Rosaura, and Beatrice Pita, eds. Introduction. *The Squatter and the Don.* By María Amparo Ruiz de Burton. Houston: Arte Público Press, 1992, 1997.

———. Introduction. *Who Would Have Thought It?* By María Amparo Ruiz de Burton. Houston: Arte Público Press, 1995.

Early California and Californio History

Almaguer, Tomás. *Racial Fault Lines: The Historical Origins of White Supremacy in California* Berkeley: University of California Press, 1994.

Anderson, M. Kat, Michael G. Barbour, and Valerie Whitworth. "A World of Balance and Plenty: Land, Plants, Animals, and Humans in a Pre-European California." *Contested Eden: California before the Gold Rush.* Ed. Ramón A. Gutiérrez and Richard J. Orsi. Berkeley: University of California Press, 1998.

Bancroft, Hubert Howe. *California Pastoral, 1769–1848.* San Francisco: History Company, 1888.

———. *History of California.* 7 vols. San Francisco: History Company, 1884–89.

Castañeda, Antonia I. "Gender, Race, and Culture: Spanish-Mexican Women in the Historiography of Frontier California." *Frontiers* 11 (1990): 8–20.

Conlogue, William. "Farmers' Rhetoric of Defense: California Settlers versus the Southern Pacific Railroad." *California History* 78.1 (1999): 40–55.

Griswold del Castillo, Richard. *The Treaty of Guadalupe Hidalgo: A Legacy of Conflict.* Norman: University of Oklahoma Press, 1990.

Haas, Lisbeth. *Conquests and Historical Identities in California, 1769–1936.* Berkeley: University of California Press, 1995.

Henderson, George L. *California and the Fictions of Capital.* New York: Oxford University Press, 1999.

Johnson, Susan Lee. "Bulls, Bears, and Dancing Boys: Race, Gender, and Leisure in the California Gold Rush." *Radical History Review* 60 (Fall 1994): 4–37.

Lapp, Rudolph M. *Blacks in Gold Rush California.* New Haven: Yale University Press, 1977.

Monroy, Douglas. *Thrown among Strangers: The Making of Mexican Culture in Frontier California.* Berkeley: University of California Press, 1990.

Perry, Claire. *Pacific Arcadia: Images of California, 1600–1915.* New York: Oxford University Press, 1999.

Pitt, Leonard. *The Decline of the Californios: A Social History of the Spanish-Speaking Californians, 1846–1890.* Berkeley: University of California Press, 1966.

Rosales, F. Arturo. " 'Fantasy Heritage' Reexamined: Race and Class in the Writings of the Bandini Family Authors and Other Californios, 1828–1965." *Recovering the U.S. Hispanic Literary Heritage.* Vol. 2. Ed. Erlinda Gonzales-Berry and Chuck Tatum. Houston: Arte Público Press, 1996. 81–104.

Simmons, William S. "Indian Peoples of California." In *Contested Eden: California before the Gold Rush.* Ed. Ramón A. Gutiérrez and Richard J. Orsi. Berkeley: University of California Press, 1998.

Vallejo, Mariano Guadalupe. "Recuerdos históricos y personales tocante a la alta California." 1874. Trans. Earl R. Hewitt. 1875. An unpublished testimonial from the collection of the Bancroft Library, University of California at Berkeley (BANC MSS C-D 17, 18, 19, 20, 21).

Mexican American and Chicano Studies

Gonzales-Berry, Erlinda, and Chuck Tatum, eds. *Recovering the U.S. Hispanic Literary Heritage.* Vol. 2. Houston: Arte Público Press, 1996.

Limón, José E. *American Encounters: Greater Mexico, the United States, and the Erotics of Culture.* Boston: Beacon Press, 1998.

McWilliams, Carey. *North from Mexico: The Spanish-Speaking People of the United States.* 1968. New York: Greenwood Press, 1990.

Menchaca, Martha. "Chicano Indianism: A Historical Account of Racial Repression in the United States." *American Ethnologist* 23 (1993): 583–603.

Moquin, Wayne, and Charles Van Doren. "The Treaty of Guadalupe Hidalgo." *A Documentary History of Mexican Americans.* Ed. Wayne Moquin and Charles Van Doren. New York: Praeger, 1971. 181–87.

Padilla, Genaro. *My History, Not Yours: The Formation of Mexican American Autobiography.* Madison: University of Wisconsin Press, 1993.

Paredes, Raymund. "The Evolution of Chicano Literature." *Three American Literatures: Essays in Chicano, Native American, and Asian American Literature for Teachers of American Literature.* Ed. Houston A. Baker Jr. New York: MLA, 1982.

Pérez, Vincent. "Teaching the Hacienda: Juan Rulfo and Mexican American Cultural Memory." *Western American Literature* 35.1 (Spring 2000): 33–44.

Rebolledo, Tey Diana. "Narrative Strategies of Resistance in Hispana Writing." *Journal of Narrative Technique* 20 (1990): 134–46.

Rodríguez, Manuel M. Martín. "Textual and Land Reclamations: The Critical Reception of Early Chicana/o Literature." *Recovering the U.S. Hispanic Literary Heritage.* Vol. 2. Ed. Erlinda Gonzales-Berry and Chuck Tatum. Houston: Arte Público Press, 1996.

Saldívar, José David. *Border Matters: Remapping American Cultural Studies.* Berkeley: University of California Press, 1997.

———. *The Dialectics of Our America: Genealogy, Cultural Critique, and Literary History.* Durham: Duke University Press, 1991.

Saldívar, Ramón. *Chicano Narrative: The Dialectics of Difference.* Madison: University of Wisconsin Press, 1990.

Sánchez, María Carla. "Whiteness Invisible: Early Mexican American Writing and the Color of Literary History." *Passing: Identity and Interpretation in Sexuality, Race, and Religion.* Ed. María

Carla Sánchez and Linda Schlossberg. New York: New York University Press, 2001.

Sánchez, Rosaura. *Telling Identities:* The Californio Testimonios. Minneapolis: University of Minnesota Press, 1995.

Weber, David J. *The Mexican Frontier, 1821–1846: The American Southwest under Mexico.* Albuquerque: University of New Mexico Press, 1982.

Studies of Nineteenth-Century American Cultures

Allen, Robert C. *Horrible Prettiness: Burlesque and American Culture.* Chapel Hill: University of North Carolina Press, 1991.

Bank, Rosemarie K. *Theater Culture in America, 1825–1860.* New York: Cambridge University Press, 1997.

Beard, George M. *American Nervousness: Its Causes and Consequences.* 1881. New York: Arno Press, 1972.

Blevins Faery, Rebecca. *Cartographies of Desire: Captivity, Race, and Sex in the Shaping of an American Nation.* Norman: University of Oklahoma Press, 1999.

Blumin, Stuart. *The Emergence of the Middle Class: Social Experience in the American City, 1760–1900.* New York: Cambridge University Press, 1989.

Bowlby, Rachel. *Just Looking: Consumer Culture in Dreiser, Gissing, and Zola.* New York: Methuen, 1985.

Briggs, Laura. "The Race of Hysteria: 'Overcivilization' and the 'Savage' Woman in Late-Nineteenth-Century Obstetrics and Gynecology." *American Quarterly* 52.2 (June 2000): 246–73.

Brown, Bill. "Science Fiction, the World's Fair, and the Prosthetics of Empire, 1910–1915." *Cultures of United States Imperialism.* Ed. Amy Kaplan and Donald E. Pease. Durham: Duke University Press, 1993.

Brown, Gillian. *Domestic Individualism: Imagining Self in Nineteenth-Century America.* Berkeley: University of California Press, 1990.

Brown, Richard Maxwell. "Part III, Vigilantism: the Conservative Mob." *The Strain of Violence: Historical Studies of American Violence and Vigilantism*. New York: Oxford University Press, 1975.

Buell, Lawrence. "Circling the Spheres: A Dialogue." *American Literature* 70.3 (1998): 465–90.

Burkholder, Mark A., and Lyman L. Johnson. *Colonial Latin America*. New York: Oxford University Press, 1990.

Burrows, Edwin G. and Mike Wallace. *Gotham: A History of New York City to 1898*. New York: Oxford University Press, 1999.

Castiglia, Christopher. *Bound and Determined: Captivity, Culture-Crossing, and White Womanhood from Mary Rowlandson to Patty Hearst*. Chicago: University of Chicago Press, 1996.

Chevigny, Bell Gale, and Gari Laguardia, eds. *Reinventing the Americas: Comparative Studies of the Literature of the United States and Spanish America*. Cambridge: Cambridge University Press, 1986.

Cheyfitz, Eric. "What Work Is There to Do?" *American Literature* 67 (1995): 843–53.

Cott, Nancy F. "Passionlessness: An Interpretation of Victorian Sexual Ideology, 1790–1850." *Signs* 4 (1978): 219–36.

Derounian-Stodola, Kathryn Zabelle. "The Indian Captivity Narratives of Mary Rowlandson and Olive Oatman: Case Studies in the Continuity, Evolution, and Exploitation of Literary Discourse." *Studies in Literary Imagination* 27.1 (1994): 33–46.

Dillon, Richard. "Tragedy at Oatman Flat: Massacre, Captivity, Mystery." *American West* 18 (1981): 46–59.

Dodge, Mary Mapes. "The Shoddy Aristocracy of America." *Cornhill Magazine* July 1865: 43–50.

Everitt, Lancelot. *Arguments in Favor of the Enforcement of the Monroe Doctrine*. New Orleans: Era Book and Job Office, 1864.

Franchot, Jenny. *Roads to Rome: The Antebellum Protestant En-*

counter with Catholicism. Berkeley: University of California Press, 1994.

Gruesz, Kirsten Silva. *Ambassadors of Culture*. Princeton: Princeton University Press, 2002.

Halttunen, Karen. *Confidence Men and Painted Women: A Study of Middle-Class Culture in America, 1830–1870*. New Haven: Yale University Press, 1982.

Harvey, David. "Cosmopolitanism and the Banalities of Geographic Evils." *Public Culture* 12.2 (2000): 529–64.

Herndl, Diane Price. *Invalid Women: Figuring Feminine Illness in American Fiction and Culture, 1840–1940*. Chapel Hill: University of North Carolina Press, 1993.

Ignatiev, Noel. *How the Irish Became White*. New York: Routledge, 1995.

Jaher, Frederic Cople. *The Urban Establishment: Upper Strata in Boston, New York, Charleston, Chicago, and Los Angeles*. Urbana: University of Illinois Press, 1982.

Jones, Anne Goodwyn. *Tomorrow Is Another Day: The Woman Writer in the South, 1859–1936*. Baton Rouge: Louisiana State University Press, 1981.

Kaplan, Amy. "Manifest Domesticity." *American Literature* 70 (Sept. 1998): 581–606.

———. "Nation, Region, and Empire." *Columbia History of the American Novel*. Ed. Emory Elliot. New York: Columbia University Press, 1991.

Kritzer, Amelia Howe. *Plays by Early American Women, 1775–1850*. 1851. Ann Arbor: University of Michigan Press, 1995.

Kroeber, A. L. "Olive Oatman's Return." Bancroft: University of California Press, Berkeley, 1951.

Kroeber, A. L. and Clifton B. Kroeber. "Olive Oatman's First Account of Her Captivity among the Mohave." *California Historical Society Quarterly* 41 (1962): 309–17.

Leavitt, Joshua. *The Monroe Doctrine.* New York: Sinclair Tousey, 1863.

Levine, Lawrence. *Highbrow/Lowbrow: The Emergence of Cultural Hierarchy in America.* Cambridge: Harvard University Press, 1988.

Londré, Felicia Hardison, and Daniel J. Watermeier. *The History of North American Theater: From Pre-Columbian Times to the Present.* New York: Continuum, 1998.

Lott, Eric. *Love and Theft: Blackface Minstrelsy and the American Working Class.* New York: Oxford University Press, 1993.

Luria, Susan. "The Architecture of Manners: Henry James, Edith Wharton, and the Mount." *American Quarterly* 49.2 (June 1997): 298–327.

Malcolmson, Scott L. "The Varieties of Cosmopolitan Experience." *Cosmopolitics: Thinking and Feeling beyond the Nation.* Ed. Pheng Cheah and Bruce Robbins. Minneapolis: University of Minnesota Press, 1998.

May, Ernest. *The Making of the Monroe Doctrine.* Cambridge: Belknap Press, 1975.

McConachie, Bruce. *Melodramatic Formations: American Theater and Society, 1820–1870.* Iowa City: University of Iowa Press, 1992.

Miller, Robert Ryan. "Arms across the Border: United States Aid to Juárez during the French Intervention in Mexico." *Transactions of the American Philosophic Society* 63.6 (1973): 3–65.

Miller, Tice L. "The Image of Fashionable Society in American Comedy, 1840–1870." *When They Weren't Doing Shakespeare: Essays on Nineteenth-Century British and American Theater.* Ed. Judith L. Fisher and Stephen Watt. Athens: Georgia University Press, 1989.

Monroe, James. "7th Annual Message, Dec. 1, 1823." *Writings of James Monroe.* Vol. 2. New York: G. P. Putnam, 1902.

Moss, Elizabeth. *Domestic Novelists in the Old South: Defenders of Southern Culture.* Baton Rouge: Louisiana State University Press, 1992.

O'Farrell, Mary Ann. *Telling Complexions: The Nineteenth-Century English Novel and the Blush*. Durham: Duke University Press, 1997.

Porter, Carolyn. "What We Know We Don't Know: Remapping American Literary Studies." *American Literary History* 6 (1994): 467–526.

Radway, Janice. "What's in a Name?" *American Quarterly* 51.5 (1999): 1–32.

Rice, William. "The Captivity of Olive Oatman: A Newspaper Account." *California Historical Society Quarterly* 21 (1942): 97–106.

Romine, Scott. *The Narrative Forms of Southern Community*. Baton Rouge: Louisiana State University Press, 1999.

Ryan, Mary. *Cradle of the Middle Class: The Family in Oneida County, New York, 1790–1865*. New York: Cambridge University Press, 1991.

———. *Women in Public: Between Banners and Ballots, 1825–1880*. Baltimore: Johns Hopkins University Press, 1990.

Streeter, H. W. "Some Deductions from Gynecological Experience." *Medical Press of Western New York* 1 (Jan. 1886): 104–17.

Taylor, Edith S., and William J. Wallace. "Mohave Tattooing and Face-Painting." *Southwest Museum Leaflets* 20 (1947): 1–13.

Toll, Robert C. *Blacking Up: The Minstrel Show in Nineteenth-Century America*. New York: Oxford University Press, 1974.

Tompkins, Jane. *Sensational Designs: The Cultural Work of American Fiction, 1790–1860*. New York: Oxford University Press, 1985.

Twain, Mark, and Charles Dudley Warner. *The Gilded Age: A Tale of Today*. 1873. New York: Penguin, 1980.

Tyler, Royall. "The Contrast." *Early American Drama*. Ed. Jeffrey Richards. New York: Penguin, 1997.

Wertheimer, Eric. *Imagined Empires: Incas, Aztecs, and the New World of American Literature, 1776–1876*. Cambridge: Harvard University Press, 1999.

Additional Primary and Secondary Works

Bevans, Charles I., ed. *Treaties and Other International Agreements of the United States of America, 1776–1949.* Vol. 9. Washington DC: Department of State, 1972.

Cervantes, Lorna Dee. *Emplumada.* Pittsburgh: University of Pittsburgh Press, 1981.

Cervantes, Miguel. *Don Quixote.* Trans. John Ormsby. Ed. Joseph R. Jones and Kenneth Douglas. New York: W. W. Norton, 1981.

Cooper, James Fenimore. *The Prairie.* 1827. Ed. James P. Elliott. Albany: State University of New York Press, 1985.

Dana, Richard Henry. *Two Years before the Mast.* 1840. Boston: Houghton Mifflin, 1911.

Hawthorne, Nathaniel. *The Scarlet Letter.* 1850. 3d ed. Ed. Seymour Gross, Sculley Bradley, Richmond Croom Beatty, and E. Hudson Long. New York: W. W. Norton, 1988.

Holman, C. Hugh and William Harmon. *A Handbook to Literature.* 6th ed. New York: Macmillan, 1992.

Islas, Arturo. *Migrant Souls.* New York: William Morrow, 1990.

Jackson, Helen Hunt. *Ramona.* Boston: Robert Brothers, 1884.

James, Henry. *The American Scene.* 1907. Middlesex, Eng.: Penguin Modern Classics, 1994.

———. *The Bostonians.* 1886. Middlesex, Eng.: Penguin Modern Classics, 1978.

Jefferson, Thomas. *The Portable Thomas Jefferson.* Ed. Merrill D. Peterson. New York: Viking Press, 1975.

Morrow, William Chambers. *Blood Money.* San Francisco: F. J. Walker, 1882.

Morsberger, Robert, and Katherine M. Morsberger. *Lew Wallace: Militant Romantic.* New York: McGraw-Hill, 1980.

Nabokov, Vladimir. *Lectures on Don Quixote.* Ed. Fredson Bowers. New York: Harcourt Brace Jovanovich, 1983.

Nordhoff, Charles. *California for Health, Pleasure, and Residence: A*

Book for Travellers and Settlers. Rev. ed. New York: Harper and Brothers, 1882.

Norris, Frank. *The Octopus: A Story of California*. New York: Doubleday, Page, 1901.

Oatman, Olive. *Olive Ann Oatman's Lecture Notes and Oatman Bibliography*. Ed. Edward J. Pettid. Bloomington CA: San Bernardino County Museum Association, 1968.

Odell, George C. D. *Annals of the New York Stage*. Vol. 8 (1865–70). New York: Columbia University Press, 1936.

Ord, Angustias María. *Occurrences in Hispanic California*. Trans. and ed. Francis Price and William H. Ellison. Richmond: William Byrd Press, 1956.

Polk, James. *Message from the President to the Two Houses of Congress*. Washington: Ritchie and Heiss, 1845.

Prescott, William Hickling. *The History of the Conquest of Mexico with a Preliminary View of the Ancient Mexican Civilization and the Life of the Conqueror Hernando Cortés*. 1843. New York: Modern Library, 1936.

Royce, Josiah. *The Feud of Oakfield Creek: A Novel of California Life*. Boston: Houghton Mifflin, 1887.

Schoonover, Thomas. *A Mexican View of America in the 1860s*. London: Associated University Presses, 1991.

Shew, A. M. *California as a Health Resort*. Boston: James S. Adams, 1885.

Stowe, Harriet Beecher. *Pink and White Tyranny: A Society Novel*. 1872. New York: New American Library, 1988.

———. *Uncle Tom's Cabin*. London: J. Cassell, 1852.

Stratton, Royal B. *Captivity of the Oatman Girls*. Lincoln: University of Nebraska Press, 1983.

Veblen, Thorstein. *The Theory of the Leisure Class*. 1899. New York: Penguin, 1994.

Viramontes, María Helena. *Under the Feet of Jesus*. New York: Plume Press, 1996.

Wallace, Lew. *An Autobiography*. Vol. 1. New York: Harper, 1906.

Washburn, Wilcomb E. Foreword. *Captivity of the Oatman Girls*. By Royal B. Stratton. Lincoln: University of Nebraska Press, 1983. v–xv.

Witt, Doris. *Black Hunger: Food and the Politics of U.S. Identity*. New York: Oxford University Press, 1999.

Works Cited

Alemán, Jesse. "Historical Amnesia and the Vanishing Mestiza: The Problem of Race in *The Squatter and the Don* and *Ramona.*" *Aztlán* 27.1 (2002): 59–93.

Allen, Robert C. *Horrible Prettiness: Burlesque and American Culture.* Chapel Hill: University of North Carolina Press, 1991.

Almaguer, Tomás. *Racial Fault Lines: The Historical Origins of White Supremacy in California.* Berkeley: University of California Press, 1994.

Anderson, M. Kat, Michael G. Barbour, and Valerie Whitworth. "A World of Balance and Plenty: Land, Plants, Animals, and Humans in a Pre-European California." *Contested Eden: California before the Gold Rush.* Ed. Ramón A. Gutiérrez and Richard J. Orsi. Berkeley: University of California Press, 1998. 12–47.

Aranda, José F., Jr. "Breaking All the Rules: María Amparo Ruiz de Burton Writes a Civil War Novel." *Recovering the U.S. Hispanic Literary Heritage.* Vol. 3. Ed. María Herrera-Sobek and Virginia Sánchez-Korrol. Houston: Arte Público Press, 2000.

———. "Contradictory Impulses: María Amparo Ruiz de Burton, Resistance Theory, and the Politics of Chicano/a Studies." *American Literature* 70.3 (1998): 551–79.

———. "María Amparo Ruiz de Burton." *Dictionary of Literary Biography.* Ed. Sharon Harris. New York: Gale Publications, 1999.

———. *When We Arrive: A New Literary History of Mexican America.* Tucson: University of Arizona Press, 2003.

Works Cited

Bancroft, Hubert Howe. "California Inter Pocula." 1888. *Gold Rush: A Literary Exploration*. Ed. Michael Kowalewski. Berkeley: Heyday Books, 1997. 375–77.

———. *California Pastoral, 1769–1848*. San Francisco: History Company, 1888.

———. *History of California*. 7 vols. San Francisco: History Company, 1884–89.

Bank, Rosemarie K. *Theatre Culture in America, 1825–1860*. New York: Cambridge University Press, 1997.

Baym, Nina. *Woman's Fiction: A Guide to Novels by and about Women in America, 1820–1870*. Urbana: University of Illinois Press, 1993.

Beard, George Miller. *American Nervousness: Its Causes and Consequences*. 1881. New York: Arno Press, 1972.

Bevans, Charles I., ed. *Treaties and Other International Agreements of the United States of America, 1776–1949*. Vol. 9. Washington DC: Department of State, 1972.

Blevins Faery, Rebecca. *Cartographies of Desire: Captivity, Race, and Sex in the Shaping of an American Nation*. Norman: University of Oklahoma Press, 1999.

Blumin, Stuart. *The Emergence of the Middle Class: Social Experience in the American City, 1760–1900*. New York: Cambridge University Press, 1989.

Bowlby, Rachel. *Just Looking: Consumer Culture in Dreiser, Gissing, and Zola*. New York: Methuen, 1985.

Briggs, Laura. "The Race of Hysteria: 'Overcivilization' and the 'Savage' Woman in Late-Nineteenth-Century Obstetrics and Gynecology." *American Quarterly* 52.2 (June 2000): 246–73.

Brown, Bill. "Science Fiction, the World's Fair, and the Prosthetics of Empire, 1910–1915." *Cultures of United States Imperialism*. Ed. Amy Kaplan and Donald E. Pease. Durham: Duke University Press, 1993.

Brown, Gillian. *Domestic Individualism: Imagining Self in Nine-*

teenth-Century America. Berkeley: University of California Press, 1990.

Brown, Richard Maxwell. "Part III, Vigilantism: The Conservative Mob." *The Strain of Violence: Historical Studies of American Violence and Vigilantism*. New York: Oxford University Press, 1975.

Buell, Lawrence. "Circling the Spheres: A Dialogue." *American Literature* 70.3 (1998): 465–90.

Burkholder, Mark A., and Lyman L. Johnson. *Colonial Latin America*. New York: Oxford University Press, 1990.

Burrows, Edwin G., and Mike Wallace. *Gotham: A History of New York City to 1898*. New York: Oxford University Press, 1999.

Castañeda, Antonia I. "Gender, Race, and Culture: Spanish-Mexican Women in the Historiography of Frontier California." *Frontiers* 11 (1990): 8–20.

———. "The Political Economy of Nineteenth-Century Stereotypes of Californianas." *Between Borders: Essays on Mexican/Chicana History*. Ed. Adelaida R. Castillo. Encino: Floricanto Press, 1990.

Castiglia, Christopher. *Bound and Determined: Captivity, Culture-Crossing, and White Womanhood from Mary Rowlandson to Patty Hearst*. Chicago: University of Chicago Press, 1996.

Cervantes, Lorna Dee. *Emplumada*. Pittsburgh: University of Pittsburgh Press, 1981.

Cervantes, Miguel. *Don Quixote*. Trans. John Ormsby. Ed. Joseph R. Jones and Kenneth Douglas. New York: Norton, 1981.

Chevigny, Bell Gale, and Gari Laguardia, eds. *Reinventing the Americas: Comparative Studies of the Literature of the United States and Spanish America*. Cambridge: Cambridge University Press, 1986.

Cheyfitz, Eric. "What Work Is There to Do?" *American Literature* 67 (1995): 843–53.

Chvany, Peter A. " 'Those Indians Are Great Thieves, I Suppose?'

Historicizing the White Woman in *The Squatter and the Don*." *White Women in Racialized Spaces: Imaginative Transformation and Ethical Action in Literature*. Ed. Samina Najmi and Rajini Srikanth. Albany: State University of New York Press, 2002. 105–18.

Cleland, Robert Glass. *The Cattle on a Thousand Hills: Southern California, 1850–1880*. San Marino: Huntington Library, 1951.

Conlogue, William. "Farmers' Rhetoric of Defense: California Settlers versus the Southern Pacific Railroad." *California History* 78.1 (1999): 40–55.

Cooper, James Fenimore. *The Prairie*. 1827. Ed. James P. Elliott. Albany: State University of New York Press, 1985.

Cott, Nancy F. "Passionlessness: An Interpretation of Victorian Sexual Ideology, 1790–1850." *Signs* 4 (1978): 219–36.

Dana, Richard Henry. *Two Years before the Mast*. 1840. Boston: Houghton Mifflin, 1911.

Dante Alighieri. *The Inferno*. Trans. John Ciardi. New York: New American Library, 1954.

Darwin, Charles. *The Expression of the Emotions in Man and Animals*. 1872. Chicago: University of Chicago Press, 1965.

Derounian-Stodola, Kathryn Zabelle. "The Indian Captivity Narratives of Mary Rowlandson and Olive Oatman: Case Studies in the Continuity, Evolution, and Exploitation of Literary Discourse." *Studies in Literary Imagination* 27.1 (1994): 33–46.

Dillon, Richard. "Tragedy at Oatman Flat: Massacre, Captivity, Mystery." *American West* 18 (1981): 46–59.

Dodge, Mary Mapes. "The Shoddy Aristocracy of America." *Cornhill Magazine* July 1865: 43–50.

Dreiser, Theodore. *Sister Carrie*. 1900. New York: Bantam, 1982.

Eldredge, Zoeth Skinner. *The Beginnings of San Francisco from the Expedition of Anza, 1774, to the City Charter of April 15, 1850*. New York: John C. Rankin, 1912.

Everitt, Lancelot. *Arguments in Favor of the Enforcement of the Monroe Doctrine*. New Orleans: Era Book and Job Office, 1864.

Fisher, Beth. "The Captive Mexicana and the Desiring Bourgeois Woman: Domesticity and Expansionism in Ruiz de Burton's *Who Would Have Thought It?*" *Legacy* 16 (1999): 59–69.

Fitzhugh, George. *Cannibals All! or, Slaves without Masters.* 1857. Ed. C. Vann Woodward. Cambridge: Belknap Press, 1960.

Franchot, Jenny. *Roads to Rome: The Antebellum Protestant Encounter with Catholicism.* Berkeley: University of California Press, 1994.

Goldman, Anne E. " 'I Think Our Romance Is Spoiled,' or, Crossing Genres: California History in Helen Hunt Jackson's *Ramona* and María Amparo Ruiz de Burton's *The Squatter and the Don.*" *Over the Edge: Remapping the American West.* Ed. Valerie J. Matsumoto and Blake Allmendinger. Berkeley: University of California Press, 1999. 65–84.

———. " 'Who Ever Heard of a Blue-Eyed Mexican?' Satire and Sentimentality in María Amparo Ruiz de Burton's *Who Would Have Thought It?*" *Recovering the U.S. Hispanic Literary Heritage.* Gonzales-Berry and Tatum 59–78.

Gonzales-Berry, Erlinda, and Chuck Tatum, eds. *Recovering the U.S. Hispanic Literary Heritage.* Vol. 2. Houston: Arte Público Press, 1996.

González, John M. "Romancing Hegemony: Constructing Racialized Citizenship in María Amparo Ruiz de Burton's *The Squatter and the Don.*" *Recovering the U.S. Hispanic Literary Heritage.* Vol. 2. Ed. Erlinda Gonzales-Berry and Chuck Tatum. Houston: Arte Público Press, 1996. 23–39.

Griswold del Castillo, Richard. *The Treaty of Guadalupe Hidalgo: A Legacy of Conflict.* Norman: University of Oklahoma Press, 1990.

Gruesz, Kirsten Silva. *Ambassadors of Culture.* Princeton: Princeton University Press, 2002.

Gutíerrez-Jones, Carl. *Rethinking the Borderlands: Between Chicano Culture and Legal Discourse.* Berkeley: University of California Press, 1995.

Haas, Lisbeth. *Conquests and Historical Identities in California, 1769–1936*. Berkeley: University of California Press, 1995.

Halttunen, Karen. *Confidence Men and Painted Women: A Study of Middle-Class Culture in America, 1830–1870*. New Haven: Yale University Press, 1982.

Harvey, David. "Cosmopolitanism and the Banalities of Geographic Evils." *Public Culture* 12.2 (2000): 529–64.

Hawthorne, Nathaniel. *The Scarlet Letter*. 1850. 3d ed. Ed. Seymour Gross, Sculley Bradley, Richmond Croom Beatty, and E. Hudson Long. New York: Norton, 1988.

Heizer, Robert F., and Alan F. Almquist. *The Other Californians: Prejudice and Discrimination under Spain, Mexico, and the United States to 1920*. Berkeley: University of California Press, 1971.

Henderson, George L. *California and the Fictions of Capital*. New York: Oxford University Press, 1999.

Herndl, Diane Price. *Invalid Women: Figuring Feminine Illness in American Fiction and Culture, 1840–1940*. Chapel Hill: University of North Carolina Press, 1993.

Holman, C. Hugh, and William Harmon. *A Handbook to Literature*. 6th ed. New York: Macmillan, 1992.

Horsman, Reginald. *Race and Manifest Destiny: The Origins of American Racial Anglo-Saxonism*. Cambridge: Harvard University Press, 1981.

Hurtado, Albert L. *Indian Survival on the California Frontier*. New Haven: Yale University Press, 1988.

Ignatiev, Noel. *How the Irish Became White*. New York: Routledge, 1995.

Islas, Arturo. *Migrant Souls*. New York: William Morrow, 1990.

Jacobs, Margaret D. "Mixed-Bloods, Mestizas, and Pintos: Race, Gender, and Claims to Whiteness in Helen Hunt Jackson's *Ramona* and María Amparo Ruiz de Burton's *Who Would Have Thought It?*" *Western American Literature* 36.3 (2001): 212–231.

Jackson, Helen Hunt. *Ramona*. Boston: Roberts Brothers, 1884.

Jaher, Frederic Cople. *The Urban Establishment: Upper Strata in Boston, New York, Charleston, Chicago, and Los Angeles*. Urbana: University of Illinois Press, 1982.

James, Henry. *The American Scene*. 1907. Middlesex, Eng.: Penguin Modern Classics, 1994.

———. *The Bostonians*. 1886. Middlesex, Eng.: Penguin Modern Classics, 1978.

Jefferson, Thomas. *Notes on the States of Virginia. The Portable Thomas Jefferson*. 1784. Ed. Merrill D. Peterson. New York: Viking Press, 1975.

Johnson, Susan Lee. "Bulls, Bears, and Dancing Boys: Race, Gender, and Leisure in the California Gold Rush." *Radical History Review* 60 (Fall 1994): 4–37.

Jones, Anne Goodwyn. *Tomorrow Is Another Day: The Woman Writer in the South, 1859–1936*. Baton Rouge: Louisiana State University Press, 1981.

Kanellos, Nicolás. *A History of Hispanic Theater in the United States: Origins to 1940*. Austin: University of Texas Press, 1990.

Kaplan, Amy. "Manifest Domesticity." *American Literature* 70 (Sept. 1998): 581–606.

———. "Nation, Region, and Empire." *Columbia History of the American Novel*. Ed. Emory Elliot. New York: Columbia University Press, 1991.

Kritzer, Amelia Howe. *Plays by Early American Women, 1775–1850*. 1851. Ann Arbor: University of Michigan Press, 1995.

Kroeber, A. L. "Olive Oatman's Return." Bancroft: University of California, Berkeley, 1951.

Kroeber, A. L., and Clifton B. Kroeber. "Olive Oatman's First Account of Her Captivity among the Mohave." *California Historical Society Quarterly* 41 (1962): 309–17.

Langellier, John Phillip, and Daniel B. Rosen. *El Presidio de San Francisco: A History under Spain and Mexico, 1776–1846*. Frontier Military Series XIX. Washington: Arthur H. Clark, 1996.

Works Cited

Leavitt, Joshua. *The Monroe Doctrine*. New York: Sinclair Tousey, 1863.

Lapp, Rudolph, M. *Blacks in Gold Rush California*. New Haven: Yale University Press, 1977.

Levine, Lawrence. *Highbrow/Lowbrow: The Emergence of Cultural Hierarchy in America*. Cambridge: Harvard University Press, 1988.

Limón, José E. *American Encounters: Greater Mexico, the United States, and the Erotics of Culture*. Boston: Beacon Press, 1998.

Lipsitz, George. *The Possessive Investment in Whiteness: How White People Profit from Identity Politics*. Philadelphia: Temple University Press, 1998.

Londré, Felicia Hardison, and Daniel J. Watermeier. *The History of North American Theater—The United States, Canada, and Mexico: From Pre-Columbian Times to the Present*. New York: Continuum, 1998.

Lott, Eric. *Love and Theft: Blackface Minstrelsy and the American Working Class*. New York: Oxford University Press, 1993.

Luis-Brown, David. " 'White Slaves' and the 'Arrogant Mestiza': Reconfiguring Whiteness in *The Squatter and the Don* and *Ramona*." *American Literature* 69.4 (1997): 813–39.

Luria, Susan. "The Architecture of Manners: Henry James, Edith Wharton, and the Mount." *American Quarterly* 49.2 (June 1997): 298–327.

Lutz, Tom. *American Nervousness, 1903: An Anecdotal History*. Ithaca: Cornell University Press, 1991.

Malcolmson, Scott L. "The Varieties of Cosmopolitan Experience." *Cosmopolitics: Thinking and Feeling beyond the Nation*. Ed. Pheng Cheah and Bruce Robbins. Minneapolis: University of Minnesota Press, 1998.

May, Ernest. *The Making of the Monroe Doctrine*. Cambridge: Belknap Press, 1975.

McConachie, Bruce. *Melodramatic Formations: American Theatre and Society, 1820–1870*. Iowa City: University of Iowa Press, 1992.

McWilliams, Carey. *North from Mexico: The Spanish-Speaking People of the United States.* 1968. New York: Greenwood, 1990.

Menchaca, Martha. "Chicano Indianism: A Historical Account of Racial Repression in the United States." *American Ethnologist* 23 (1993): 583–603.

Miller, Robert Ryan. "Arms across the Border: United States Aid to Juárez during the French Intervention in Mexico." *Transactions of the American Philosophic Society* 63.6 (1973): 3–65.

———. *Juan Alvarado, Governor of California, 1836–1842.* Norman: University of Oklahoma Press, 1998.

Miller, Tice L. "The Image of Fashionable Society in American Comedy, 1840–1870." *When They Weren't Doing Shakespeare: Essays on Nineteenth-Century British and American Theatre.* Ed. Judith L. Fisher and Stephen Watt. Athens: University of Georgia Press, 1989. 243–52.

Monroe, James. "7th Annual Message, Dec. 1, 1823." *Writings of James Monroe.* Vol. 2. New York: G. P. Putnam, 1902.

Monroy, Douglas. *Thrown among Strangers: The Making of Mexican Culture in Frontier California.* Berkeley: University of California Press, 1990.

Montes, Amelia María de la Luz. " 'Es Necesario Mirar Bien': Letter Making, Fiction Writing, and American Nationhood in the Nineteenth Century." Diss. University of Denver, 1999.

Montes, Amelia María de la Luz. "Es Necesario Mirar Bien: Nineteenth-Century Letter Making and Novel Writing in the Life of María Amparo Ruiz de Burton." *Recovering the U.S. Hispanic Literary Heritage.* Vol. 3. Ed. María Herrera-Sobek and Virginia Sánchez-Korrol. Houston: Arte Público Press, 2000.

———. "María Amparo Ruiz de Burton Negotiates American Literary Politics and Culture." *Challenging Boundaries: Gender and Periodization.* Ed. Joyce W. Warren and Margaret Dickie. Athens: University of Georgia Press, 2000.

———. "Reading the Nation in Nineteenth-Century American

Literature: The Life and Works of María Amparo Ruiz de Burton." Modern Language Association Conference, San Francisco, 1997.

Moquin, Wayne, and Charles Van Doren. "The Treaty of Guadalupe Hidalgo." *A Documentary History of Mexican Americans.* Ed. Wayne Moquin and Charles Van Doren. New York: Praeger, 1971. 181–87.

Morrow, William Chambers. *Blood Money.* San Francisco: F. J. Walker, 1882.

Morsberger, Robert, and Katherine M. Morsberger. *Lew Wallace: Militant Romantic.* New York: McGraw-Hill, 1980.

Moss, Elizabeth. *Domestic Novelists in the Old South: Defenders of Southern Culture.* Baton Rouge: Louisiana State University Press, 1992.

Mowatt, Anna Cora. *Fashion. Early American Drama.* Ed. Jeffrey Richards. New York: Penguin, 1997. 304–67.

Nabokov, Vladimir. *Lectures on Don Quixote.* Ed. Fredson Bowers. New York: Harcourt Brace Jovanovich, 1983.

Nordhoff, Charles. *California for Health, Pleasure, and Residence: A Book for Travellers and Settlers.* Rev. ed. New York: Harper and Brothers, 1882.

Norris, Frank. *The Octopus: A Story of California.* New York: Doubleday, Page, 1901.

Oatman, Olive. *Olive Ann Oatman's Lecture Notes and Oatman Bibliography.* Ed. Edward J. Pettid. Bloomington CA: San Bernardino County Museum Association, 1968.

Odell, George C. D. *Annals of the New York Stage.* Vol. 8 (1865–1870). New York: Columbia University Press, 1936.

Oden, Frederick Bryant. "The Maid of Monterey: The Life of María Amparo Ruiz de Burton, 1832–1895." Thesis. University of San Diego, 1992.

O'Farrell, Mary Ann. *Telling Complexions: The Nineteenth-Century English Novel and the Blush.* Durham: Duke University Press, 1997.

Ord, Angustias María. *Occurrences in Hispanic California*. Trans. and ed. Francis Price and William H. Ellison. Washington DC: Academy of American Franciscan History, 1956.

Padilla, Genaro. *My History, Not Yours: The Formation of Mexican American Autobiography*. Madison: University of Wisconsin Press, 1993.

Paredes, Raymund. "The Evolution of Chicano Literature." *Three American Literatures: Essays in Chicano, Native American, and Asian American Literature for Teachers of American Literature*. Ed. Houston A. Baker Jr. New York: MLA, 1982. 33–79.

Pérez, Vincent. "South by Southwest: Land and Community in María Amparo Ruiz de Burton's *The Squatter and the Don* and Mariano Guadalupe Vallejo's *Historical and Personal Memoirs Relating to Alta California*." *Recovering the U.S. Hispanic Literary Heritage*. Vol. 4. Ed. José F. Aranda Jr. and Silvio Torres-Saillant. Houston: Arte Público Press, 2002. 96–132.

———. "Teaching the Hacienda: Juan Rulfo and Mexican American Cultural Memory." *Western American Literature* 35.1 (Spring 2000): 33–44.

Perkins, Dexter. *The Monroe Doctrine, 1826–1867*. Cambridge: Harvard University Press, 1933.

Perry, Claire. *Pacific Arcadia: Images of California, 1600–1915*. New York: Oxford University Press, 1999.

Phillips, Irene. *Women of Distinction*. National City: South Bay Press, n.d.

Pitt, Leonard. *The Decline of the Californios: A Social History of the Spanish-Speaking Californians, 1846–1890*. Berkeley: University of California Press, 1966.

Polk, James. *Message from the President to the Two Houses of Congress*. Washington: Ritchie and Heiss, 1845.

Pomeroy, Earl. *In Search of the Golden West: The Tourist in Western America*. New York: Alfred A. Knopf, 1957.

Porter, Carolyn. "What We Know We Don't Know: Remapping

American Literary Studies." *American Literary History* 6 (1994): 467–526.

Prescott, William Hickling. *The History of the Conquest of Mexico with a Preliminary View of the Ancient Mexican Civilization and the Life of the Conqueror Hernando Cortés.* 1843. New York: Modern Library, 1936.

Radway, Janice. "What's in a Name?" *American Quarterly* 51.5 (1999): 1–32.

Rebolledo, Tey Diana. "Narrative Strategies of Resistance in Hispana Writing." *Journal of Narrative Technique* 20 (1990): 134–46.

Reyes de la Maza, Luis. *El Teatro en Mexico durante el Segundo Imperio (1862–1867).* Mexico: Imprenta Universitaria, 1959.

Rice, William. "The Captivity of Olive Oatman: A Newspaper Account." *California Historical Society Quarterly* 21 (1942): 97–106.

Rodríguez, Manuel M. Martín. "Textual and Land Reclamations: The Critical Reception of Early Chicana/o Literature." *Recovering the U.S. Hispanic Literary Heritage.* Vol. 2. Ed. Erlinda Gonzales-Berry and Chuck Tatum. Houston: Arte Público Press, 1996. 40–58.

Roediger, David. *The Wages of Whiteness: Race and the Making of the American Working Class.* New York: Verso, 1991.

Romine, Scott. *The Narrative Forms of Southern Community.* Baton Rouge: Louisiana State University Press, 1999.

Rosales, F. Arturo. " 'Fantasy Heritage' Reexamined: Race and Class in the Writings of the Bandini Family Authors and Other Californios, 1828–1965." *Recovering the U.S. Hispanic Literary Heritage.* Vol. 2. Ed. Erlinda Gonzales-Berry and Chuck Tatum. Houston: Arte Público Press, 1996. 81–104.

Royce, Josiah. *The Feud of Oakfield Creek: A Novel of California Life.* Boston: Houghton Mifflin, 1887.

Ruiz de Burton, María Amparo. *Don Quixote de la Mancha: A Comedy, in Five Acts, Taken from Cervantes' Novel of That Name.* San Francisco: Carmany, 1876.

———. Letters to George Davidson. George Davidson Papers, box 4, Bancroft Library, University of California, Berkeley.

———. Letters to Mariano Guadalupe Vallejo. De la Guerra Papers, Huntington Library, San Marino.

———. *The Squatter and the Don.* 1885. Ed. Rosaura Sánchez and Beatrice Pita. Houston: Arte Público Press, 1992, 1997.

———. *Who Would Have Thought It?* 1872. Ed. Rosaura Sánchez and Beatrice Pita. 1872. Houston: Arte Público Press, 1995.

Rev. of *Who Would Have Thought It? Godey's Lady's Book* Sept. 1872: 273.

Rev. of *Who Would Have Thought It? Lippincott's Magazine of Popular Literature and Science* Nov. 1872: 607.

Rev. of *Who Would Have Thought It? Literary World* 1 Aug. 1872: 33–34.

Ryan, Mary. *Cradle of the Middle Class: The Family in Oneida County, New York, 1790–1865.* New York: Cambridge University Press, 1991.

———. *Women in Public: Between Banners and Ballots, 1825–1880.* Baltimore: Johns Hopkins University Press, 1990.

Saldívar, José David. *Border Matters: Remapping American Cultural Studies.* Berkeley: University of California Press, 1997.

———. *The Dialectics of Our America: Genealogy, Cultural Critique, and Literary History.* Durham: Duke University Press, 1991.

Saldívar, Ramón. *Chicano Narrative: The Dialectics of Difference.* Madison: University of Wisconsin Press, 1990.

Sánchez, María Carla. "Whiteness Invisible: Early Mexican American Writing and the Color of Literary History." *Passing: Identity and Interpretation in Sexuality, Race, and Religion.* Ed. María Carla Sánchez and Linda Schlossberg. New York: New York University Press, 2001. 64–91.

Sánchez, Rosaura. *Telling Identities:* The Californio Testimonios. Minneapolis: University of Minnesota Press, 1995.

Sánchez, Rosaura, and Beatrice Pita, eds. *Conflicts of Interest: The Letters of María Amparo Ruiz de Burton*. Houston: Arte Público Press, 2001.

———. Introduction. *The Squatter and the Don*. By María Amparo Ruiz de Burton. 1885. Ed. Rosaura Sánchez and Beatrice Pita. 2d ed. Houston: Arte Público Press, 1997. 7–49.

———. Introduction. *Who Would Have Thought It?* Houston: Arte Público Press, 1995.

Schoonover, Thomas. *A Mexican View of America in the 1860s: A Foreign Diplomat Describes the Civil War and Reconstruction*. Cranbury NJ: Fairleigh Dickinson University Press, 1991.

Shew, A. M. *California as a Health Resort*. Boston: James S. Adams, 1885.

Sicherman, Barbara. "The Uses of a Diagnosis: Doctors, Patients, and Neurasthenia." *Sickness and Health in America: Readings in the History of Medicine and Public Health*. Ed. Judith Waltzer Leavitt and Ronald L. Numbers. Madison: University of Wisconsin Press, 1978. 25–38.

Simmons, William S. "Indian Peoples of California." *Contested Eden: California before the Gold Rush*. Ed. Ramón A. Gutiérrez and Richard J. Orsi. Berkeley: University of California Press, 1998. 48–77.

Slotkin, Richard. *Regeneration through Violence: The Mythology of the American Frontier, 1600–1860*. Norman: University of Oklahoma Press, 1973.

Starr, Kevin. *Americans and the California Dream, 1850–1915*. New York: Oxford University Press, 1973.

Stowe, Harriet Beecher. *Pink and White Tyranny: A Society Novel*. 1872. New York: New American Library, 1988.

———. *Uncle Tom's Cabin*. London: J. Cassell, 1852.

Stratton, Royal B. *Captivity of the Oatman Girls*. Lincoln: University of Nebraska Press, 1983.

Streeter, H. W. "Some Deductions from Gynecological Experience." *Medical Press of Western New York* 1 (Jan. 1886): 104–17.

Taylor, Edith S., and William J. Wallace. "Mohave Tattooing and Face-Painting." *Southwest Museum Leaflets* 20 (1947): 1–13.

Toll, Robert C. *Blacking Up: The Minstrel Show in Nineteenth-Century America.* New York: Oxford University Press, 1974.

Tompkins, Jane. *Sensational Designs: The Cultural Work of American Fiction, 1790–1860.* New York: Oxford University Press, 1985.

Twain, Mark, and Charles Dudley Warner. *The Gilded Age: A Tale of Today.* 1873. New York: Penguin, 1980.

Tyler, Royall. *The Contrast. Early American Drama.* Ed. Jeffrey Richards. New York: Penguin, 1997.

Vallejo, Mariano Guadalupe. "Recuerdos históricos y personales tocante a la alta California." 1874. Trans. Earl R. Hewitt. 1875. An unpublished testimonial from the collection of the Bancroft Library, University of California at Berkeley. (BANC MSS C-D 17, 18, 19, 20, 21).

Veblen, Thorstein. *The Theory of the Leisure Class.* 1899. New York: Penguin, 1994.

Viramontes, María Helena. *Under the Feet of Jesus.* New York: Plume Press, 1996.

Wald, Priscilla. "Terms of Assimilation: Legislating Subjectivity in the Emerging Nation." *Cultures of United States Imperialism.* Ed. Amy Kaplan and Donald E. Pease. Durham: Duke University Press, 1993.

Wallace, Lew. *An Autobiography.* Vol. 1. New York: Harper, 1906.

Washburn, Wilcomb E. Foreword. *Captivity of the Oatman Girls.* By Royal B. Stratton. Lincoln: University of Nebraska Press, 1983. v–xv.

Weber, David J. *The Mexican Frontier, 1821–1846: The American Southwest under Mexico.* Albuquerque: University of New Mexico Press, 1982.

Wertheimer, Eric. *Imagined Empires: Incas, Aztecs, and the New World of American Literature, 1776–1876.* Cambridge: Harvard University Press, 1999.

Whittier, John Greenleaf. "What the Voice Said." *The Poetical*

Works of John Greenleaf Whittier. Vol. 2. Boston: Houghton Mifflin, 1894. 213–16.

Wister, Owen. *The Virginian*. 1902. New York: Oxford University Press, 1988.

Witt, Doris. *Black Hunger: Food and the Politics of U.S. Identity*. New York: Oxford University Press, 1999.

Contributors

JESSE ALEMÁN is assistant professor of English at the University of New Mexico, where he teaches nineteenth-century American and Chicano/a literatures. His articles appear in *MELUS*, *Recovering the U.S. Hispanic Literary Heritage Project*, vol. 3 (Arte Público Press), *Aztlán*, and several edited book collections. He republished with an introduction and glossary Loreta Janeta Velazquez's 1874 *The Woman in Battle*, an autobiographical narrative of a Cuban woman who cross-dressed as a Confederate soldier (University of Wisconsin Press), and his current book project, *Pulp Nation*, examines the popular literature of the war between the United States and Mexico.

JOSÉ F. ARANDA JR. is associate professor of Chicano/a and American literature at Rice University. He has written articles on early U.S. criticism, nineteenth-century Mexican American literature, and the future of Chicano/a studies. His first book, *When We Arrive: A New Literary History of Mexican America*, was published by the University of Arizona Press. He sits on the board of the Recovering the U.S. Hispanic Literary Heritage Project.

BETH FISHER teaches in the Women and Gender Studies Program at Washington University in St. Louis. Her work on Ruiz de Burton, which has also appeared in *Legacy*, is part of a larger project investigating intersecting discourses of gender, class, and material consumption in nineteenth- and early-twentieth-century U.S. literature and culture.

Contributors

ANNE E. GOLDMAN teaches in the English Department at Sonoma State University, where she is an associate professor. She is the author of *Take My Word: Autobiographical Innovations of Ethnic American Working Women* (University of California Press) and *Continental Divides: Revisioning American Literature* (Palgrave/St. Martin's Press). Her current project considers Jewish American cultural studies from 1990 to the present.

JOHN M. GONZÁLEZ teaches Latina/o literature in the English Department and the Center for Mexican American Studies at the University of Texas at Austin, specializing in the nexus of national canons and subaltern traditions. He has published articles on late-nineteenth-century and early-twentieth-century Mexican American narratives. He is completing a study of the historical romance's role in refiguring U.S. national identity in the post-Reconstruction period.

AMELIA MARÍA DE LA LUZ MONTES is assistant professor of English and Ethnic Studies at the University of Nebraska–Lincoln. Among her publications are: "'Es Necesario Mirar Bien': The Letters of María Amparo Ruiz de Burton" in *Recovering the U.S. Hispanic Literary Heritage*, vol. 3 (Arte Público Press), and "María Amparo Ruiz de Burton Negotiates American Literary Politics and Culture" in *Challenging Boundaries: Gender and Periodization* (University of Georgia Press). In addition to critical publications, her fiction has appeared in *Saguaro* and in the anthologies *Chicana Literary and Artistic Expressions: Culture and Society in Dialogue* and *Circa 2000: Lesbian Fiction at the Millennium*. She is working on a critical book on Chicana and Latina narratives that focus on Midwestern borders, and she continues to publish fiction.

GRETCHEN MURPHY teaches U.S. literature at the University of Minnesota, Morris. She is currently at work on a book entitled "Hemispheric Imaginings: The Monroe Doctrine and Narratives of U.S. Empire."

Contributors

VINCENT PÉREZ teaches American literature at the University of Nevada, Las Vegas and has published articles on Chicano and African American literature in such journals as *Texas Studies in Literature and Language* and *MELUS*. His book *Remembering the Hacienda: History and Memory in the Mexican American Southwest* was published by Texas A&M University Press.

JULIE RUIZ is assistant professor of English and Latin American Studies at Wesleyan University, where she specializes in Chicana/o and Latina/o literatures and Cultural Studies. She is currently working on a book that explores how literary representations of the U.S.–Mexican War by Mexican American, Mexican, and Euro American authors contribute to the formation of an American identity across national borders. In theorizing national character, her work highlights the importance of understanding twentieth-century Chicana/o literature through its nineteenth-century origins.

ANDREA TINNEMEYER is assistant professor of English at Utah State University. She teaches Chicano/a Studies, American Studies, and nineteenth-century U.S. literature and culture. She has published a book on Sandra Cisneros's *House on Mango Street* (Greenwood Press), and she is researching the cross-border feminist movement during the Mexican Revolution of 1910.

JENNIFER S. TUTTLE is assistant professor of English at the University of New England in Maine, where she serves as the Dorothy M. Healy Chair in Literature and Health and is the faculty director of the Maine Women Writers Collection. She earned her Ph.D. from the University of California, San Diego in 1996. Her work has appeared in *Legacy: A Journal of American Women Writers* and *Popular Culture Review*, as well as in several edited collections; she also has published a scholarly edition of Charlotte Perkins Gilman's novel *The Crux* (1911).

Index

Index

To order or obtain more information on these or other University
of Nebraska Press titles, visit nebraskapress.unl.edu.

OTHER WORKS BY VICTORIA LAMONT

Judith Merril: A Critical Study (McFarland, 2012)